Square Rigger Days

Square Rigger Days

Autobiographies of Sail

EDITED BY Charles W Domville-Fife

INTRODUCTION BY Robert D Foulke

Naval Institute Press
ANNAPOLIS, MARYLAND

Title page: The American three-masted barque *Kaiulani* becalmed in the Pacific, 1941, after she had carried the last load of lumber under sail out of Grays Harbor, Washington State, bound for Durban. She was at sea when the Japanese attacked Pearl Harbor and, engineless, unarmed and with no ship's radio, sailed far south of Cape Horn to minimise the risk of encountering Japanese shipping. From Durban she loaded cordite explosive and sailed to Sydney. She was the last commercial square-rigged sailing ship to fly the Stars and Stripes.

Publishers' Note & Acknowledgements

This new edition of Charles Domville-Fife's book, first published in 1938, includes an introduction by Robert Foulke which originally appeared in the *Journal of British Studies*, published by the University of Chicago Press. Some photographs from the original edition have been reproduced but the majority have been specially chosen for this edition. Most of these have been lent from the collection of David Clement whom the publishers would like to thank for his generous help and support. Photographs not from that collection have been credited accordingly. Despite extensive inquiries it has not been possible to trace the copyright holder of *Square-Rigger Days*. The publishers would be pleased to hear from anyone with further information.

This edition © Seaforth Publishing 2007
Text copyright © Charles Domville-Fife 1938
Introduction copyright © The North American Conference on British Studies 1963

This edition first published in Great Britain in 2007 by

Seaforth Publishing
An imprint of Pen & Sword Books Ltd
47 Church Street
Barnsley
S Yorkshire S70 2AS

Published and distributed in the
United States of America and Canada by the
Naval Institute Press,
291 Wood Road, Annapolis,
Maryland 21402-5034

Library of Congress Control Number: 2007930119

ISBN 978-1-59114-848-7

This edition authorized for sale only in the United States of America, its territories and possessions, and Canada

Printed and bound in Singapore

Contents

Author's Introduction to 1938 Edition

IF this book were only the personal reminiscences of the Editor it would have consisted of one story of youthful misery – the answering of a call. It is, however, something far wider; and, moreover, it is intended to fill a very wide gap in the available literature of the sea.

There have been exhaustive works of great scholarship published during recent years describing and illustrating both the history of the sailing ship, that most beautiful creation of man throughout the ages, and of the great deeds of the men of sail, whose bravery, suffering, and endurance laid the foundations of commerce, Empire, and sea-power.

There has not been, so far as I know, any recent collection of personal stories by living seamen of their square-rigger days which combine to present a complete picture, in all its lights and shadows, and in all parts of the world, of the real life at sea as it was lived in those great days of sail, extending from the 'sixties of the nineteenth to the early years of the present century.

The illustrations have been collected over a period of many years, from all parts of the world, and themselves form a most complete collection of photographic studies of the ships and of life on board the old square-rigger in the days of sail.

It is a pictorial and descriptive record of personal reminiscences which must, in the nature of things, soon recede into history. Several of the authors have already reached the age of ninety years, and the white wings of memory will pass with them into the Valhalla of the Sea.

CHARLES W DOMVILLE-FIFE

Life in the Dying World of Sail, 1870-1910

BY ITS BEAUTY and grace the sailing ship invites that nostalgic sentimentality often bestowed upon relics of the past. Visitors who notice the inscription on the *Cutty Sark* at Greenwich are asked to share this veneration: 'Here to commemorate an era the *Cutty Sark* has been preserved as a tribute to the ships and men of the merchant navy in the days of sail. They mark our passage as a race of men. Earth will not see such ships as these again.' The image of the 'glorious' last days of sail is largely the creation of retired seamen-writers. In an unfinished essay written just before his death in 1924, Joseph Conrad summarises the era of the sailing ship with typical nostalgia:

> The last days of sailing ships were short if one thinks of the countless ages since the first sail of leather or rudely woven rushes was displayed to the wind. Stretching the period both ways to the utmost, it lasted from 1850 to 1910. Just sixty years. Two generations. The winking of an eye. Hardly the time to drop a prophetic tear. For the pathos of that era lies in the fact that when the sailing ships and the art of sailing them reached their perfection, they were already doomed. It was a swift doom, but it is consoling to know that there was no decadence.[1]

'Doom' without 'decadence' – like the death of a beautiful woman in her prime – is the seaman-writer's usual elegy for the sailing ship.

Such homage to the sailing ship in its decline remains incomplete without its counterpart – disparagement of the steamship. Old sailors could never forget that their paragon was being replaced by a tramp. Conrad again expresses the characteristic attitude:

> Cargo steam vessels have reached by this time a height of utilitarian ugliness which, when one reflects that it is the product of human ingenuity, strikes hopeless awe into one.

Some of the romance of the last years of the age of sail was stoked by the carefully-crafted black and white photographs of the period. Here, longshoremen idle away the time in this evocative photograph of Lowestoft docks taken at the turn of the century.

These dismal creations look still uglier at sea than in port, and with an added touch of the ridiculous. Their rolling waddle when seen at a certain angle, their abrupt clockwork nodding in a sea-way, so unlike the soaring lift and swing of a craft under sail, have in them something caricatural, a suggestion of a low parody directed at noble predecessors by an improved generation of dull, mechanical toilers, conceited and without grace.[2]

For men bred in sail, the steamship brought into life at sea both ugliness and the loss of a remote and specialised world of experience. Basil Lubbock complains that 'the calling of the sea is now a dull, monotonous business like any other trade and no longer a romantic profession'.[3] Felix Riesenberg celebrates the 'old' sea: 'The steamer and its relentless follower, the motor vessel, are robbing the sea of its hardships, but they are also rubbing away those romantic reflections which made the sea bearable, aye, a compelling thing without reason, or tangible reward. . . . Harsh as the sea was it then held virgin treasures not yet soiled by millions of smeary hands.'[4] Conrad further exaggerates the contrast between the worlds of sail and steam:

> The hand of the engineer tore down the veil of the terrible beauty [of sailing ships] in order that greedy and faithless landlubbers might pocket dividends. The mystery was destroyed. Like all mysteries, it lived only in the hearts of its worshippers. The hearts changed; the men changed. The once loving and devoted servants went out armed with fire and iron, and conquering the fear of their own hearts became a calculating crowd of cold and exacting masters. The sea of the past was an incomparable beautiful mistress, with inscrutable face, with cruel and promising eyes. The sea of today is a used-up drudge, wrinkled and defaced by the churned-up wakes of brutal propellers, robbed of the enslaving charm of its vastness, stripped of its beauty, of its mystery and of its promise.[5]

The sense of outrage recurs frequently in the writing of men who lived through the shift from sail to steam. Their disdain for the new way of life led them to glorify the old immoderately, and, in spite of patent distortions, their romantic image of the last days of sail still holds currency.

Had the transition from sail to steam been dramatically abrupt, there might be some grounds for accepting the romantic eulogy of clippers and tea races as a true image of sailing-ship life, but the changes in the pattern of sea commerce were gradual and irregular. No date can be isolated as a decisive turning point, and no single development can be labelled prime cause of the sailing ship's demise. The perfection of sailing ships and steamships occurred more or less simultaneously, beginning well before mid-century when the Tonnage Law of 1836 revised the measurement system to eliminate tax advantages for deep, clumsy ships. For the sailing ship, the discovery of gold in California (1848) and Australia (1851), the final repeal of the protectionist Navigation Acts (1849), and the advent of American competition (signalled by the remarkable tea voyage of the *Oriental* in 1849) spurred the development of extremely fast clippers in the 1850s and 1860s. But however much this was the 'golden' age of sail in the long-distance trades, steamships were significant enough to justify the founding of major companies (Cunard, the Pacific Steam Navigation Company, the Royal Mail Line, and the Peninsular and Oriental Steam Navigation Company) as early as 1840. The opening of the Suez Canal in 1869, by decreasing the gap between coaling stations, made the long-distance trades to India and the Far East practicable for steamers. Sailing ships suffered a depression after the Canal opened, but in the late 1870s they still proved more economical for bulk trades (coal, grain, wool, rice, and jute) which demanded neither great speed nor regularity. As Gerald S Graham suggests, 'even after the opening of the Suez

Early steam vessels in the dry-dock at Suez. The opening of the canal made it possible for the early steamships to voyage to the Far East, once the preserve of the clipper ships. (David MacGregor Collection)

Canal, much of the traffic to the Bay of Bengal, the East Indies, and Australia was still carried by the sailing ship. The cutting of Suez did *not* mark a turning point in the life of sail'.[6] The eventual supremacy of steamers also depended upon a slow process of technological improvement, particularly the development of strong iron hulls, screw propellers, and high-pressure steam engines. Not until the 1880s were steamers able to depress sailing-ship freights permanently, and bulk cargoes were carried under sail in the long-distance trades until the German submarines of World War I finally dispatched all but a few relics of the diminished fleet. It is clear that the disappearance of the sailing ship in the late nineteenth century was neither sudden nor complete.

The second part of Conrad's eulogy – 'doom' without 'decadence' – is also misleading. The sailing ship which held on to a decreasing portion of sea commerce in the last decades of the century was not simply a refined or improved clipper. The most important single change was a marked increase in size: the average tonnage of registered sailing ships rose from approximately 1,200 tons in 1860 to 1,500 tons in 1870, 1,800 tons in 1880, and 2,000 tons in 1890.[7] Such 'growth' in sailing ships would have been impossible without a technology based upon iron and steel rather than wood. The introduction of iron frames, riveted plates, steel spars, and wire rigging during the 1860s and 1870s permitted the building of larger ships which could still take the battering of heavy seas without working their hulls open and could stand the strain of the heavier masts and yards needed to drive larger hulls at a reasonable speed. The new sailing ship of the 1870s and 1880s, designed for cargo capacity rather than speed, had greater length, less beam, less freeboard (height of the deck above water), and a fuller bottom.

Though it seemed a boon to owners who found only bulk freights in the long-distance trades profitable, increased tonnage was largely responsible for decadence in the sailing ship. Larger, heavier, and clumsier than the clippers, these ships were not thoroughbreds: they were often overmasted to make up for increased weight;[8] their length sometimes made them cranky in manoeuvre and unmanageable when running before heavy seas; their low freeboard made work on decks which were almost constantly awash exceedingly dangerous. They simply do not represent what Conrad calls 'the *best* period of sailing-ship practice and service'; if, as he claims, 'the greatest achievements of Merchant Service seamen have been performed in ships of between 900 to 1800 tons',[9] the 1880s and 1890s were certainly an age of 'decadence' in sail.

The contradictions in Conrad's statements reflect a more general confusion about the social history of the sailing ship's last era. Nostalgia and romance are almost ubiquitous in the 'literature' of sail. Although economic conditions, regulations, voyage records, and disasters at sea can be reconstructed quite easily through parliamentary reports, ships' logs, and records of courts of inquiry, for the general atmosphere or 'feel' of sailing-ship life there are no sources of comparable reliability. 'To a man brought up in a shipping community,' writes William McFee, 'there is a faint feeling of nausea when reading sea poetry inspired by John Masefield . . .' He finds sea fiction, because it must inevitably distort 'truth', similarly unreliable:

The extreme clipper *Thermopylae*, lying at anchor in Sydney. Her generation of clippers created sensations with their fast runs out to Australia and back from the Far East. On her maiden voyage in 1868-69, she took sixty-three days between Gravesend and Hobson's Bay, Melbourne, and ninety-one days back from Foochow, laden with tea. The fine-lined clippers of her generation represented the apogee of sail. (David MacGregor Collection)

The four-masted barque *Pamir* was one of the famous Flying P-Liner sailing ships of the German shipping company F Laeisz and was built for the South American nitrate trade. Launched in 1905, she represented a generation of vessels quite different from the clippers. This photograph, showing her sailing light, gives a good indication of her huge size. She was the last commercial sailing vessel to round Cape Horn, in 1949.

The sea writer has to do with men whose mental processes are often simple to the point of imbecility and the only action possible consists in elemental conflicts with the sea. If the sea is behaving, as it frequently is, there is no story, and the writer has to invent astonishing aberrations of character.[10]

A A Hurst reverses this judgment:

Historians are seldom sound on matters of character [of sailing-ship seamen], since they usually have one axe or another to grind and, if one must depend on the written word for an assessment of these men, it is best to turn to the novels of the writers who knew the ships at first hand – Conrad, who sailed in the clippers; Jack London, who sailed in the *Dirigo* . . . and the like – to realise what manner of men they really were.[11]

Perhaps the typical disparity between fact and fiction, memory and nostalgia, verisimilitude and distortion can be illustrated by the comparison of another contemporary seaman-writer, Jan de Hartog:

The glory of the square-rigged ship has been immortalized by poets writing sonnets about long tricks at the wheel, and artists with beards singing sea-shanties in a jersey, accompanying themselves on the Spanish guitar. The advent of steam is considered to have been the advent of grime, trade unions, and class hatred between the bridge and fo'c'sle. It has corrupted the salts of yore from iron men on wooden ships into wireless-operators in flowered dressing-gowns . . . I sailed under canvas as a boy and in my memory the stalwart salts with the hearts of oak were moronic bipeds dangling in the branches of artificial trees in constant peril of their lives. The sea-chanties [sic] were ditties they were forced to sing by foreheadless bosuns, brandishing marlinespikes to mark time while pulling the ropes.[12]

Exaggeration and overstatement, in one direction or another, characterise the reports of amateur historian and professional writer alike. The way of life on board sailing ships – if it is to be re-created at all – must be pieced together from fragmentary and often contradictory scraps of insight, memory, and prejudice. What follows is an attempt to recast the image of experience in the lost world of sailing ships and to reassess seafaring in sail as a career.

*   *   *

When stripped of its superficial romance, the final era of commercial sailing ships is no less interesting to students of British social history. The sailing-ship voyage, by its isolation from what Conrad called 'land entanglements', embodied a world of experience almost completely alien to the environment of shore life – then or now. The ship imposed an inexorable captivity upon the men who lived and worked in her for months on end. The most telling feature of voyages in sail was almost complete isolation – an isolation which sealed off all contact with shore life and created a sense of estrangement and self-sufficiency.

Conrad frequently writes of 'land entanglements' with disdain, and Hurst describes a crew's revulsion to newspapers after a long voyage: 'We cast such offending rags on one side and rejoiced that we had forgone the dubious pleasures of civilization for so long.'[13] In the long-distance trades, sailing-ship men never expected a voyage of less than three months and often stayed at sea for six without once sighting land. Modern seamen who spend at most a week or two between ports on mechanised ships, in constant touch with the shore by radio, live in a different world. In the old world of long voyages, 'shore' affairs were remote and insignificant.

If sailing-ship men escaped the tumult and corruption of land civilization for the greater part of their lives, they could not avoid the confinement and boredom of a microcosmic society. Isolation for long stretches of time amidst primitive living conditions could reduce differences of personality to a low common denominator:

> A body of men thrown together aboard a sailing ship isolated from ordinary civilisation will gradually undergo transformation and take on a semi-barbaric character. When a score of people live in one small family for weeks, eating the same meals, sharing the same work, thinking the same thoughts, always complaining in concert, it would be strange if there was not evolved a certain common identity.[14]

Such 'identity' cannot be idealised as the estimable moral 'solidarity' of Conrad or the comfortable 'togetherness' of current sociological jargon. It was far more like the association of prison inmates (to follow Dr Johnson's analogy). Claude Muncaster, a retired seaman, writes that 'it was the unending character of the voyage, the want of variety, the scarcely bearable dullness when not able to lift the imagination beyond all present obstacles, which turned live men into sullen pessimism'.[15] Constant propinquity to the same men under the same conditions day after day is more likely to create dislike than 'solidarity'. Strained relations between men were often caused by the insufferable boredom of long voyages. Richard Henry Dana recalls the intellectual poverty of his voyage around Cape Horn:

> Any change was sought for which would break the monotony of the time; and even the two hours' trick at the wheel, which came round to us in turn, once in every other watch, was looked upon as a relief. The never-failing resource of long yarns, which eke out many a watch, seemed to have failed us now; for we had been so long together that we had heard each other's stories told over and over again till we had them by heart; each one knew the whole history of each of the others, and we were fairly and literally talked out.[16]

Seamen, claims Conrad, talk shop incessantly because their limited experience insulates them from other subjects. McFee explains their narrowness of interest as anti-intellectualism: 'Most of them were extreme conservatives in their thinking. They regarded anything strange and foreign with disfavor and suspicion. The great intellectual movements of the age passed them by.'[17] The prolonged isolation of the sailing ship, in spite of its freedom from the taint of 'land entanglements', was at best a mixed blessing.

Living conditions for both officers and men were no blessing at all. Modern seafaring (except in sailing yachts without auxiliary power) is not comparable because sailing ships lacked both heat and light. Although officers might have a cabin lamp and fire on nasty winter evenings, forecastles and deck-houses were usually cold and dark. The crew's quarters on the *Cutty Sark*, which were better than average, originally consisted of a single forecastle on the main deck. Within this relatively small, triangular compartment twenty-two seamen lived, each being allotted one bunk and space to store a sea chest. A single table with benches accommodated only one watch, or half the crew, for meals. There was no space and no privacy, but this forecastle was better than the deck-house which replaced it sometime before 1874 (to give the *Cutty Sark* more cargo space). The deck-house was more cramped than the forecastle and was usually awash in heavy weather even though the *Cutty Sark* took less water on deck than the heavier, clumsier ships built near the end of the century. Officers' cabins were more 'elegantly' furnished with a good bed and a chest of drawers, but they were equally compact.

The men of sailing ships expected neither comfort nor luxury. When Conrad writes of their 'healthy life', he is thinking of physically hardened men who knew little of the amenities of city life, who could 'bear the criticism of men, the exactions of the sea, and the prosaic severity of the daily task that gives bread – but whose only reward is in the perfect love of the work'.[18] Mates, as well as men, were picked for their brute strength by experienced captains, for junior officers spent much of their time supervising groups furling sails aloft or hauling braces on deck. The 'good' young third mate, Frank Bullen relates, tried to outdo his men aloft: 'If he can only beat the smartest man forward in getting out to

'The healthy life'. Men bend on a sail on the three-masted ship *Mount Stewart*. She was one of the last of the Australian wool clippers, built in 1891, but she was bigger and more full-built than the fast clippers of the earlier generation, and the gear was massive.

the weather earring, at reefing topsails or a course, he is delighted beyond measure.'[19] In the days before electric megaphones, officers were also valued for strong voices. The sailing ship required 'men of courage and grit, men of authority and resource, men of nerve strength and muscle fitness'.[20]

Above all else the sailing ship needed men of endurance. Any single voyage on the longer trades subjected men to racking heat and piercing cold, to storm and calm, to an almost constant soaking from spray and rain squalls. In conjunction with the natural hazards of constant exposure, overcrowding, ignorance of hygiene, tainted food, and sour water produced a high incidence of disease. Sea cuts and boils did not heal in bodily systems already contaminated by rotten food, and 'every windjammer seaman of the nineteenth century knew that he was liable to contract scurvy if he signed on too soon after a long deep-water voyage'.[21] The danger of scurvy (a partial starvation or vitamin deficiency caused by the absence of fresh fruits and vegetables) was increased both by hard labour at sea and by wild living ashore; the sailor's body never had a chance to recover from the last voyage. British ships – notorious the world over for poor and scanty food – occasionally met disaster through scurvy if they encountered head winds or calms. In 1897 the *T. F. Oakes* was reported to have arrived in New York over eight months out of Hong Kong with only the captain's wife and the second mate sailing her; all others on board were either dead or unable to move from scurvy.[22] Confined living quarters and lack of quarantine also caused the loss of ships and crews. The *County of Cromarty* was stranded on her maiden voyage in 1878 when all officers who could navigate were stricken with smallpox.[23] In an almost exact parallel to Conrad's first voyage as captain of the *Otago*, the crew and officers of the *Trafalgar* picked up Java fever in Batavia, and the ship was left in the hands of a few men during the voyage to Melbourne.[24] Taken together, these living conditions – cramped quarters, constant exposure, poor and sometimes rotten food, disease – do not suggest Conrad's 'healthy life'. Muncaster emphasises the 'wear and tear of human body and nerves aboard a sailing ship', and Riesenberg feels that 'continued too long, the harsh calling of the sea left its mark on bodies and minds'.[25] When a seaman was frequently 'worn out' at forty-five, his 'chances of becoming an inmate of an old sailors' home were not great'.[26]

Exposure alone cannot account for the latent debilitation of a long career at sea. When Conrad defines 'the work of merchant seamen' in terms of fidelity to duty and tradition – 'to take ships entrusted to their care from port to port across the seas; and, from the highest to the lowest, to watch and labour with devotion for the safety of the property and the lives committed to their skill and fortitude through the hazards of innumerable voyages'[27] – his grandiloquent tone, appropriate to a naval officer's commission, does not suggest the arduous labour of 'working' sailing ships. The passage from Europe to Australia brought weeks of incessant sail changes in the winter gales and heavy seas of the great 'Southern Ocean'; the passage around Cape Horn found men hauling braces on decks awash with seas which sometimes reached the almost incredible height of sixty feet. As the following description suggests, work aloft in bad weather was an extreme test of stamina:

'Lifelines', drawn by Anton Otto Fischer, the prolific marine artist and illustrator. This image captures so well the dangers and hardships of life on the deep-sea sailing ships. Artists such as Fischer and Arthur Briscoe painted for a public still enamoured with the romance of sail.

It looked madness to go on that yard; and maybe it was. It looked madness to try to reach it; and maybe it was. But we went, just the same. It is impossible to imagine the job that handful of tired out and sorely tried boys faced that night – and did. The whole foremast was shaking and quivering with the furious thrashing of the sail; the great steel yard quivered and bent; the rigging shook violently as if it wanted to shake us off into the sea boiling beneath. The loose ends of the broken sheet and the wire buntlines were flying around through the air, writhing like steel and chain snakes; if any had been touched by these it would have been the end.

Laying out along that yard, with the whole area of the sail flying back and over it, looked like facing death. Maybe it was, in a way; but nobody thought of that as, inch by inch, we fought our way out. The wet sail, which was over a thousand square feet of best storm canvas, was banging back over the yard; every now and then we had to drop beneath the yard, and lie balanced along the foot-ropes. I have not the faintest idea how we got that sail fast. I don't think anyone who was there has. We fought it times without number, and lost; but there came a time when we fought it, and won. But that was not before our bare hands – you cannot fight wet canvas with gloves – were red with blood and blue with cold.

A flying buntline end touched one of the German seamen in the head once, and brought swift blood. He reeled a bit, but carried on. Then he fainted, after a while, and because we could not take him down we had to lash him there. When he revived he carried on again.[28]

An experience like this recollected in later years is inevitably tinged with romantic nostalgia for the stirring moments of a lost youth. The tone of the passage is reminiscent of Conrad's apostrophe to the older generation of seamen who were 'men enough to scorn in their hearts the sentimental voices that bewailed the hardness of their fate'.[29] But the 'sentimental voices' were not entirely wrong. If ships had been properly manned, a few seamen would not have fought all night to furl a sail. The economic competition with steamships which led to larger and clumsier sailing ships also reduced the size of crews: for example, one ship which had originally put to sea with thirty-five hands sailed with only nine near the end of the century.[30] Undermanning made normal sail handling difficult and emergency work nearly impossible, increasing the strain on both officers and men and magnifying the inescapable dangers of seafaring. Skimpy crews, drained of energy by the watch-and-watch system (four hours on, four hours off), may explain the marked increase in collision losses during the latter part of the century: in 1870 alone, 1,788 sailing ships were involved in collisions.[31] Several stanzas of a song ('The Merchant Shipping Act') current among seamen show that they were no strangers to the idea of exploitation by owners:

> I'll sing about a sailor man that sails upon the sea
> In coasters and deep water ships, wherever they may be,
> Incurring needless hardships in earning others' wealth
> Now this is true what I tell you, for I've seen it all myself.
> Now sometimes it's all well enough, but other times it's hard
> To be hauling out to leeward with two hands upon the yard,
> You set two hands to steer the wheel, that leaves the watch with four,
> About enough to navigate a barge around the Nore.[32]

The strain of work on board undermanned ships was responsible for many personal injuries and deaths. A momentary lapse of attention could be fatal for men who spent much of their time working over one hundred feet above deck. Now only bridge and skyscraper construction workers face comparable hazards, and they do not have to contend with the violent swaying of their platforms. Even on calm days there was danger in temporary carelessness. Hurst somewhat romantically describes the psychological impact of these commonplace accidents:

Imagine a lofty barque, perhaps with all sail set and the sunlight and shadow playing over her fabric in delightful patterns of sheer loveliness as she sways steadily through a glorious summer's day with her three royals set: one or two men in the rigging, others working on deck, and the watch below washing or amusing themselves on the fo'c'sle head. Then there is a yell from aloft, wild and piercing with the shriek of ultimate fear, an instant of

At the wheel of the four-masted barque *Queen Margaret*. A helmsman would usually stand on the gratings; perhaps this position offered a better view. *Queen Margaret* was wrecked in 1913 when she stood in too close to the Lizard, was caught by the tide, and ran aground just off the point.

startled suspense and in a moment, before anyone can gather his wits together, there is a sickening, hollow thud as the body of a man hits the deck, after falling like a plummet for over a hundred and fifty feet. He may have fallen clear of everything, or he may have bounced on yards or rigging as he fell, but in either case it makes very little difference. Some, the very lucky ones, have lived to tell the tale, but usually they were dead – perhaps mercifully so.[33]

Sometimes a piece of gear failed without warning to bring instant death, as a seaman was killed on the *Grace Harwar* by a falling yard.[34] Men working aloft had more than their own lives at stake, for a clumsy lurch on a footrope or failure to subdue one end of a thrashing sail could send any number of shipmates flying to their deaths.

While serving as helmsman, the seaman's responsibility was sometimes crucial. If the ship were running before heavy seas, a moment of incompetent steering could let her 'broach to' (veer broadside to the seas instead of running before them), heel over and fill as the seas crashed aboard, and probably sink if the rigging were not cut away in time to relieve her. Even in less extreme conditions, careless steering could be fatal: when the helmsman of the *Star of Russia* luffed into a big sea one night in 1895, a whole watch was washed off the bowsprit.[35] Or an irregular sea might catch both helmsman and ship unawares: after losing two men off the bowsprit on such a random plunge, Captain Woodget complained, 'During the seven years that I had commanded the *Cutty Sark* I never knew her to put the boom under before'.[36]

A man did not have to be on the bowsprit to be washed away. The heavy loads and low freeboards of the late nineteenth century invited seas aboard: 'Every living seaman who has ever served in sail knows what it is like to be swept the length of a ship's main-deck in a flood of Niagara-like foam.'[37] 'It is the easiest thing on earth,' comments Villiers,

> to be swept overboard from the decks of a heavily running sailing ship, deep-laden, hard pressed by the sea and the wind. The ship scoops up a hundred tons of water over her lee rail. Then she lifts up that rail, and rolls the water murderously down to the other side, dipping that under the water also . . . you go slipping and sliding helplessly about the decks, and the sea empties you out, before you can help yourself, over the ship's immersed rail.[38]

Those who were swept off the deck rarely survived; even if the ship could be hove to before the man in the water disappeared, boats could not be launched in heavy seas, and those who managed to stay on board were battered mercilessly unless they jumped into the rigging quickly. J G Bisset describes a sea which boarded the *County of Pembroke*:

> About six that evening a tremendous comber broke over the stern and swept everything off the poop. The helmsman was picked up in the waist, half-drowned and with both legs broken. The Captain and mate saved themselves by jumping into the rigging. I happened to be standing just ahead of the mizzen-mast, and heard the mate yell: 'Hang on there!' At that moment two great walls of water, divided by the mast, swept past me carrying all manner of shattered deck fittings. I hung on like grim death and got nothing worse than a ducking and a severe fright. The cabin and the storerooms were flooded, and great gaping holes were left in the deck where the beautiful teakwood skylight and companion-hatch had previously stood.[39]

The heavily laden, clumsy ships of the last quarter of the century were so wet and dangerous in a seaway that they were dubbed 'half-tide rocks' by sailors. Captains ordered helmsmen lashed to the wheel for their own safety and strung weather cloths to 'blind' them (keep them from taking fright and leaving the wheel when huge seas rolled up astern). Everyone knew that a sea could bring mutilation or drowning instantaneously. The 'occupational hazards' – falling from aloft and being battered by seas on deck – made the sailing-ship man a poor insurance risk.

Ships themselves were little more secure than the men who sailed them. The large number of ships listed as 'missing' during the last half of the nineteenth century is unaccountable. Although Samuel Plimsoll blamed most of these losses on overloading or unseaworthiness, many ships disappeared without leaving a trace of their death throes. Sailing ships did not have the equipment to send out an SOS which would bring whole fleets of fast steamships to the scene; unless a distress flag or rocket were seen by a ship passing close, the sinking ship took her story down with her. But there were enough survivors to create a whole literature of disaster at sea in all its forms – leakage, capsizing, dismasting, fire, stranding, and collision. It is no easier to infer the quality of the experience from these reports of disaster than to reproduce the horror of an car accident from statistical summaries of road deaths and injuries. Knowing that no less than fifteen coal-laden sailing ships were posted missing in 1894 and 1895[40] is not equivalent to understanding the experience which Conrad evokes in *Youth*.

Of course, there are similarities in the way ships lose their masts or burn or break up on rocks, but each disaster is essentially unique. When Captain James Leslie of the *County of Roxborough* plotted his course to clear the Low Archipelago of the mid-Pacific in 1906, he had no way of anticipating the typhoon which thrust him onto the reefs of Takaroa Island. In 1878 the lack of a good longitude position put the *Loch Ard* ashore on the rugged coast of South Australia. Of the thirty crew and seventeen passengers on board, only one apprentice and one girl survived as the ship broke up, and they had the luck to be carried by currents into a small cove among the cliffs. When a typhoon in the Formosa Channel dismasted and sank the *Benjamin Sewall* in 1903, one boat of survivors reached a Japanese lighthouse, and the other fell into the hands of piratical natives who massacred all its occupants.[41] The *Craigburn* and a large part of her crew were lost in Port Philip Bay in 1891 because her captain refused to strike a bargain with the salvage tugs standing by. While becalmed off the Auckland Islands, the *General Grant* was sucked into a mammoth marine cave; as the swell built up outside, her masts bounced off the roof of the cave and ruptured the bottom planking. Only fifteen of the eighty-three on board survived, and they led a 'Robinson Crusoe' existence on a barren island for eighteen months before they were rescued by a whaling ship.[42] The story of disaster at sea was told in many similar chapters of storm, of freak circumstance, of incompetence, of panic – but it was told again and again. Neither men nor ships could escape the unforeseen. During his twenty years of seafaring, a life not 'adventurous in itself' by his own report, Conrad suffered personal injury from a falling spar, stranding, collision, fire, foundering, and a survivor's voyage in an open boat. Who would now think such a career unadventurous?

The 'careers' of sailing ships – even good ones – were no less susceptible to misfortune. Conrad's 'incomparable' *Torrens* is a good example because she was not a 'jinxed' ship. During her first fifteen years under Captain H R Angel she led a relatively uneventful life, but she was both dismasted at sea and on fire in port during the inaugural voyage of Captain W H Cope in 1890. In 1899 the *Torrens* became one of the few ships to survive collision with an iceberg; while loaded with explosives in 1903, she was towed into a small steamer in the Thames but did not blow up; finally, under Italian registry after 1906, she was twice stranded before she was broken up for scrap in 1910.[43] Other ships were not so lucky. The *Wanderer* (eulogised in Masefield's poetry) was known for maiming and killing her men in

The clipper ship *Torrens*, on which Conrad served
as Mate. She was a favourite passenger
ship out to Adelaide, where she was repaired after
her collision with an iceberg.

collisions. The *Inverclyde*'s spectacular history included dismasting, burning, capsizing, and sinking. The *Annesley* was a 'murderer' because someone, including one captain, had been killed on all but three of her voyages between 1898 and 1911.[44] Remarkable as they may seem, such mishaps were intrinsic to the routine business of long-voyage sailing ships.

Frequent disasters and almost constant breakage of gear cannot be entirely blamed on carelessness or professional incompetence. The quest for speed which began at mid-century forced sailing-ship captains into 'hard driving' or 'lugging sail'. Because this interest was not shared by the crew (carrying sail to the last minute made their work harder and more dangerous), it became a mark of distinction for captains rather than ships. As a dominating influence in the merchant captain's life, 'hard driving' can be dated quite precisely: it was a direct result of the struggle between British and American shipowners which began with the unprecedented voyage of the *Oriental* in 1849. When British shipowners bought or built faster ships, captains accustomed to the easy-going pace of the old East Indies trade suddenly faced more rigorous exactions: 'They had to watch their ships from hour to hour during the three months' race from China to England, rarely going below, getting very little sleep, and the result was that many eventually broke down'.[45] Soon owners were looking for a new kind of captain:

The China clippers needed the right men to handle them; sensitive men, who would treat them as the thoroughbreds they were, yet men of iron nerve, who knew not the meaning of fear, and who would drive their ships in all weather . . . with every hour an hour of racing and every minute one of tension. Men of infinite skill as navigators, who could find their way by day and night through the islands and rocks and banks and strong unpredictable currents of the ill-charted and little-known Eastern seas, and, by some daring moonlight passage through a shoal infested channel, steal a march on a more cautious rival.[46]

Some of the most successful captains of the early clippers were noted for their recklessness. 'Bully' Forbes, captain of the *Marco Polo* on her impressive maiden voyage of 1852 (sixty-eight days out and seventy-six back from Australia), was the prototype of the swaggering, hard-driving captain. Of the many legends which grew up around his name, some are certainly untrue. In an essay ('Legends') which lay unfinished on his desk when he died, Conrad chides Lubbock for repeating the tale of Forbes's 'padlocking his sheets, overawing his terrified crew from the break of the poop with a pair of levelled revolvers' as he carried tremendous presses of sail through heavy gales. Other legends are probably near enough the truth to indicate Forbes's character. As he left on his second voyage in 1853, he made the following announcement to passengers: 'Ladies and gentlemen, last trip I astonished the world with the sailing of this ship. This trip I intend to astonish God Almighty!'[47]

Whether or not such legendary exploits are true, the captains who made them do stand at the head of a lasting tradition. Throughout the remainder of the century, their successors were sensitive to reputations for carrying sail. In 1900 Bullen advised against too much prudence: 'Some men are so prudent, in other words, so lacking in courage, that they will shorten sail at the first premonition of bad weather, instead of reducing canvas as the weight of wind makes it impossible for the ship to carry it with safety.'[48] 'Hard driving' became an index of professional competence: 'The captains who were the most noted passage makers were invariably men who knew how much their gear would stand and when to carry sail and when to take in sail.'[49] Like any other tacit convention of renown, hard driving constantly disturbed the equanimity of captains. Captain Roberts of the *Kirkcudbrightshire* remembers his own quandary:

> I am inclined to believe that no ship ever made a smart passage unless the 'old man' erred a little on the reckless side. Many and many a time have I walked the poop all night blaming myself for having too much sail on the ship and knowing full well that if I tried to take anything in it would be sure to carry away. Often I vowed it would never happen again but somehow or other when the next gale came along it would just be a repetition of what had gone before.[50]

Among less analytic captains, the tradition provided a rigid if foolish standard of seamanship. Conrad explores the psychology of a former captain who was willing to risk disaster rather than mar his 'reputation':

> It was the pride of his life that he had never wasted a chance, no matter how boisterous, threatening, and dangerous, of a fair wind. Like men racing blindfold for a gap in a

hedge, we were finishing a splendidly quick passage from the Antipodes, with a tremendous rush for the Channel in as thick a weather as any I can remember, but his psychology did not permit him to bring the ship to with a fair wind blowing – at least not on his own initiative. And yet he felt that very soon indeed something would have to be done. He wanted the suggestion to come from me, so that later on, when the trouble was over, he could argue this point with his own uncompromising spirit, laying the blame on my shoulders. . . . [The thick weather suddenly cleared.] The unveiled, low sun glared angrily from a chaotic sky upon a confused and tremendous sea dashing itself upon a coast. We recognized the headland, and looked at each other in the silence of dumb wonder. Without knowing it in the least, we had run up alongside the Isle of Wight . . .[51]

With a little less luck, Conrad and all his shipmates would have been stranded and lost that day for the sake of a hidebound skipper's 'reputation'.

Daring seamanship, like fast skiing or bold horsemanship today, had become an unchallenged standard for merchant captains in the late nineteenth century. The tradition of hard driving established by the fast opium and tea clippers of the 1850s and 1860s persisted long after the speed trades had been turned over to steamships. Captains of the slower 'capacity' ships built near the end of the century struggled to maintain past reputations under nearly impossible conditions. Conrad sailed with a man of this sort (Captain William Stuart) in the *Loch Etive*:

No doubt the secret of many a ship's excellence does lie with the man on board, but it was hopeless for Captain S—— to try to make his new iron clipper equal the feats which made the old *Tweed* a name of praise upon the lips of English-speaking seamen. There was something pathetic in it, as in the endeavour of an artist in his old age to equal the masterpieces of his youth – for the *Tweed*'s famous passages were Captain S——'s masterpieces. It was pathetic, and just the least bit dangerous.[52]

Unquestionably, the anachronistic code of hard driving added acute strain to an existence already fraught with responsibility and hardship.

The captain's problems were by no means limited to matters of seamanship. The isolation and length of the usual sailing-ship voyage demanded both absolute authority and total responsibility. Captains could not evade burdensome decisions. For example, when an insane seaman began cutting away the rigging of the *Jessie Osborne* in 1875, the captain shot him to protect both ship and crew. In storms captains often had to order men to almost certain death: after the *Dawpool* had lost her main hatch off Cape Horn in 1891, Captain Fearon forced a reluctant crew to secure the opening on a deck awash with giant seas.[53] Merchant captains, like naval officers, were held accountable for all the mistakes of subordinates. Conrad's succinct dictum is apropos: 'It's the captain who puts the ship ashore; it's *we* who get her off.'[54] By this total responsibility and absolute power, the captain was set apart from all others on board:

The *Cutty Sark*, built in 1869, was one of the last clippers built and, after a spell in the tea trade worked in the Australian wool trade. By 1895 her days as a profitable carrier were numbered and she was sold into Portuguese ownership. Since 1954 she has been on display in Greenwich, beside the Thames, but in May 2007 she was badly damaged by fire during restoration.

The captain of a ship at sea is a remote, inaccessible creature, something like a prince of a fairy-tale, alone of his kind, depending on nobody, not to be called to account except by powers practically invisible and so distant, that they might be looked upon as supernatural for all that the rest of the crew knows of them, as a rule.[55]

Such radical loneliness spawned neuroses. Some captains, like the first skipper of the *Hinemoa*, went mad; others, like Captain Wallace of the *Cutty Sark*, committed suicide; many simply became drunks. Unlike the steamship, in which voyages are shorter and ties with the land much stronger, the sailing ship generated more than its share of Captain Queegs.

As the higher wages and better living conditions of steamships lowered the quality of sailing-ship men, the captain's difficulties mounted. Crews dredged up from waterfront saloons and brothels had very little motivation for the strenuous work on board sailing ships, and they were not readily amenable to discipline. Any crew which felt 'put upon' by officers or captain might become an unruly mob demanding its 'rights'. During the last quarter of the century, the disciplinary autonomy of captains shrank as Board of Trade regulations, court decisions, and union contracts multiplied. 'If the master or officers,' writes Bullen,

> worried beyond endurance, take the law in their own hands, their punishment and subsequent ruin is almost certain to ensue promptly. The rascals who have made the ship a hell afloat, confident in the tenderness of British law, and its severity towards all forms of oppression, pursue their rejoicing way, and if brought to court *may* be fined a trifle of wages, which, as they set no value upon money, does not punish them in the least.[56]

When a seaman named Allen was brought before a magistrate for assaulting Captain Barnes of the *Locksley Hall* in 1876, he was sentenced to only two days confinement while the captain got twenty-one for putting him in irons.[57] Although this judgement was reversed by the Home Secretary after a great outcry from shipowners, it does indicate the extent to which a captain's authority at sea had dwindled. After the turn of the century, the old ways of discipline in sail were totally anachronistic. In one ludicrous episode of the early twentieth century, the officers and crew of a sailing ship tried to settle a dispute about Sunday work by quoting the testament of union regulations. And an incipient mutiny on board the *Inverness-shire* in 1900 took the equally absurd form of a 'sit-down' strike.[58]

An older tradition of discipline at sea was not entirely blotted out by the red tape of 'labour relations'. It is somewhat odd that the 'bully' mate (so dear to the writers of second-rate sea fiction) had an American original. Brutality on American ships was so gross – assaults, maimings, murders – that the National Seamen's Union published the *Red Record* from 1888 to 1895 as a protest. In almost all cases which came before American courts, guilty officers were let off scot-free because the injured seaman could not organise a good defence; when the case against an officer was irrefutable, he usually disappeared before he could be brought to trial.[59] Captain Tweedie recounts the discipline of typical American ships:

> The Yankee bloodship had, as a rule, a remarkably strong afterguard who, in case of trouble, acted as one man. Besides the master, there were two, sometimes three mates, though only one would possess his certificate or licence. Then there was the sail-maker, the carpenter and sometimes a couple of hefty ordinary seamen. There were, in fact, enough hands aft to tackle the whole of one watch should occasion arise; nor would it be a plain straightforward fight with fists. The belaying pin was a favourite weapon, even a capstan bar was used at times, failing which, as a last resource, the gun came into play.[60]

In spite of more stringent and comprehensive regulations on British ships, some instances of comparable methods are recorded. The captain of the *Star of Russia* in 1887-1888 consciously imitated American practice. During a voyage from London to San Francisco and back, he beat two men, put two in irons on starvation rations for 'insubordination', and indirectly caused the deaths of three others by demanding unnecessary work aloft in bad weather.[61] And Sidney Smith, mate of the *Cutty Sark*, murdered a recalcitrant seaman when he refused duty during a hard gale.[62] The humane legislation of shore parliaments lost some of its compelling force in the insular world of long-voyage sailing ships.

Captains and mates do not deserve unmitigated censure for their occasional brutalities. Usually there was no other way of controlling an ugly lot of men. 'Where there is no weight of force behind an order, men will always be found to disobey or neglect it,' writes Bullen; 'and in the British Mercantile Marine it will often be found that a promising young officer's career is ruined just because he has once allowed a truculent bully to tell him to 'go to hell', and has not knocked that man down.'[63] When an officer did overstep the bounds of necessity, he was likely to get paid in kind. Hurst recalls the treatment given to one particularly obnoxious mate by a crew:

> Dark nights ashore have ever been the solution to problems of this sort, and when the mate of the ship went down to the lifeboat and sat waiting for the rest of the crew to go back on board one night, he found that they arrived in their full vengeance. The tiller was found to be a useful weapon, and the results of being battered beyond insensibility with this, together with other treatment of a similar nature, left him in a very sorry state. His aggressors then cast him adrift and made their way back to their own barque in the boats of the various other vessels in the roadstead. In the morning, the boat was found ashore on some rocks, with the still almost insensible and bloody form of the mate in it. He was long in hospital . . .[64]

The violent and lawless life of waterfront districts also reappeared at sea in the form of bloody mutinies. Among the fourteen men loaded on the *Leicester Castle* by a San Francisco crimp in 1902 were three Americans who later seriously wounded the captain and killed the second mate. Two Germans and a Dutchman murdered the captain, both mates, and four fellow-sailors on the *Veronica* in the same year.[65] Sailing-ship mutinies of the twentieth century resemble the notorious mutiny on the *Bounty* far more than such tame affairs as the recent 'legal' seizure of the Portuguese cruise-ship *Santa Maria* or the 'mutiny' of the British *Rangitata* in 1960.[66]

Taken as a whole, life on board nineteenth-century sailing ships was not the romantic existence which contemporary yachtsmen sometimes imagine. Long voyages marked by isolation, confinement, boredom, and miserable living conditions taxed the endurance of men who were already hard pressed by the gruelling nature of shipboard work. Near the end of the century, seamen were exposed to risks unknown to their predecessors as under-manned and overloaded ships made work aloft and on deck more dangerous, while the anachronistic tradition of 'hard driving' increased the probability of total disaster at sea. Unlike their counterparts in steamships, officers shared most of these discomforts and hazards in addition to the difficulties of controlling recusant crews with weakened disciplinary autonomy. If the sailing ship 'called' her men with an insistent voice, she called with the voice of a siren.

*   *   *

Why did men choose to spend their years amidst the hardships and dangers of sailing-ship life? Some, like Conrad, were lured by 'romance' and others were brought up to it by their fathers, but for most the sea was simply a means of livelihood. After stating that men's 'motives in going to sea were invariably economic', McFee recalls his own attitude towards the popular conception of a sea career: 'The Code of the Sea, in my time, was to get a job and keep it at all costs.'[67] The sea appealed to men from coastal regions who otherwise might have become 'drifters' – men without education, skill, or other means of support. After several voyages they had missed their chance for apprenticeship to 'land' careers and could get only the most menial work ashore. The two training ships for officers (*Conway* and *Worcester*) recruited the sons of gentlemen, so those lacking means or influence either went to sea as ship's boys or were trained in one of the eight Industrial School Ships (for paupers, waifs, truants, unruly apprentices, or potential 'delinquents'), the four independent ships (for the homeless and destitute), or the three reformatory ships (for convicted 'delinquents'). It is hard to disagree with the complaint of one MP that there were no opportunities for 'the children of respectable and honest parents' and that the ships which did exist recruited from 'the dregs of society'.[68]

In spite of questionable backgrounds and inadequate training, the heterogeneous crews of sailing ships sometimes performed well at sea. Hurst claims that even among the 'dying generations of professional shellbacks, sailing very large square-riggers with the minimum manning scales ever known in the history of sail', a 'sense of style' persisted throughout the century.[69] Muncaster, like Conrad, explains this unlikely perpetuation of 'craft' in aesthetic terms: 'In the seafaring art there is something beautiful and orderly. Always to me it was a source of wonder that the roughest sailor does his work with such thoroughness and neatness.'[70] On the other hand, there is a great weight of opinion confirming the adulteration of quality and competence in British seamen during the last half of the century. A statement made in 1872 by Sir Phillip Francis is typical:

> There is, from the nature of the business, a disposition for vagabonds to volunteer into the trade, not that they like the sea, but they wish to escape from the land. . . . Frequently an indifferent crew is got together, which are [*sic*] neither fit nor satisfied with its work. In the same forecastle, e.g., may meet, amongst a crew of eight or nine, an escaped pickpocket, a fugitive poacher and reduced field preacher. But this has always been so, more or less, and a handy man may soon pick up enough knowledge of his work to get along, if he has heart in it; but few of the class I am referring to desire anything else than to escape other evils to which they were exposed at home.[71]

Although the same kind of comment had been made about seamen in the Napoleonic era, there is no doubt that the controversy about 'deterioration' became heated during the late decades of the century. As parliamentary reports multiplied, contradictions increased. The Parker Committee of 1852 found that seamen had improved; in 1870, a committee of Liverpool shipowners decided that British seamen had deteriorated in skill, physical condition, and subordination; the Gray and Hamilton Report of 1872 discovered no fault

The *Cutty Sark* and *Worcester* lying at Greenhithe, on the Thames, in 1939. *Worcester*, a training ship for cadets, owned the *Cutty Sark* until the latter's move to Greenwich in 1951.

in the quality of seamen, but Gray reversed his position by 1874, claiming that the loss of life at sea was largely caused by poor seamanship. Thomas Brassey, who collated the findings of these and other reports, concluded that 'the alleged deterioration of the British seaman is not conclusively established', but he made an exception of 'the men employed in long voyage sailing ships'.[72] Evidently the controversy – like any question of quality – could not be settled judicially.

The plethora of investigations did draw attention to the unenviable lot of the sailing-ship 'hand'. On the whole, he had poorer health, scantier clothing, fewer possessions, and less education than his counterpart in steam. His one bargaining point with shipowners – skill – was gradually discounted after the abandonment of compulsory apprenticeship in 1854. This depressed competitive position was particularly anomalous in view of the need for skill on board sailing ships, whereas the steamer demanded 'only a burly labourer who is able to steer'.[73] Nevertheless the important differentiation between 'ordinary' and 'able' seamen was gradually blurred because it no longer reflected proven ability and experience:

Soon all distinction, *qua* ability, was lost . . . breaking down in the well-trained seaman everything like technical pride in his calling. Of what use was it to him to be a better man than others? It gave him no better standing – no better pay, and he found himself with the heaviest share of the work to be performed, whilst the ignorant lout stood idly by only fit to pull and haul or sweep the decks. Indifference and sullen carelessness was the result; many of the best men fell out of the ranks . . . and the ignorant *residuum* remained behind for the use of the British shipowner. . .[74]

Loss of status also brought loss of pay to the skilled seaman, for shipowners were not reluctant to take advantage of an undifferentiated labour force. During the last quarter of the century, the average wage for a sailing-ship seaman was 60 to 75 shillings monthly as compared to 90 or 100 for a deck hand on a steamship; even firemen, doing the filthiest and least skilled work imaginable, were paid more. And, as stevedores took over the loading and unloading of ships, the sailing-ship seaman was released immediately after docking to fend for himself until he could get another berth, which reduced his annual earnings even further.[75] It is no wonder that the more ambitious and hard-headed men left sail for steam.

As low wages gradually created a manpower shortage in sail, the trend might have been reversed, but shipowners found it easier to underman their ships and fill out crews with readily available foreign seamen. In 1851 only 4 percent of the men on British ships were 'foreigners', but the proportion rose to 13 percent in 1873 and 17 percent in 1895.[76] Foreign seamen were eager to sign on because pay in British ships was better than they could get elsewhere. Although captains quite often preferred Englishmen, they welcomed the greater competence and tractability of foreign seamen. Bullen summarises the attitude of captains:

If masters of ships are made to believe that, no matter how good the pay and provisions given, they can never rely upon getting, in the first place, sailor-men of their own race at all, and, in the second, men of their own nationality who will work cheerfully for their pay without a constant succession of worrying rows, it must not be wondered at if they prefer the foreigner, who comes already broken in, trained in seamanship, polite, and hard-working, no matter where he hails from.[77]

John Bull snobbery alone, without the backing of restrictive legislation, could not protect the inferior grade of native seamen who remained in sail.

Such outside competition for berths only complicated an economic position already deplorable, for the seaman's proverbial thriftlessness was abetted by an especially vicious method of procurement. In a report of 1874, the Duke of Edinburgh attributed the 'deficiencies' of seamen to 'crimping' and 'advance-notes'. Although crimping was illegal in British ports after 1854, it continued undercover at home and flourished in ports abroad, particularly in America and Australia.[78] Crimps, who were usually owners of waterfront boarding houses, acted as prime agents for procuring crews. Their existence depended upon two conditions peculiar to the sailing-ship trade: most ships spent long periods in port between voyages – unloading, refitting, and waiting for cargo; most owners, already finding

The port of Hamburg was one of the busiest in Europe during the era of sail, where
ships made fast to great wooden dolphins and discharged into lighters. Germany
established strong trade links with South America, particularly Chile, and, with the French, built square-riggers to exploit
the nitrate trade. They took out coal, cement and
general cargo and returned with the fertilizer.

profit margins lowered by the competition of steamships, could not afford to pay crews for time spent in port. Thus seamen who were paid off as quickly as possible dispersed, leaving the ship almost totally unmanned. Then cargo was loaded, captains had to find entirely new men, and they turned to the crimps to get them.

In their 'procuring', crimps used all the proven techniques of whore-house pimps.[79] Swarms of them boarded all incoming ships on the pretext of advertising their various boarding houses. By carrying bottles of whisky which pandered to a three-months' thirst in the forecastle, they easily led seamen to their houses, made them drunk, gave them prostitutes, and obtained their discharge certificates. If a ship were trying to hold her crew for quick sailing, crimps used the same methods to encourage desertion. Only in a boarding house could deserters hide under false names until their former ships had put to sea. Crimps gained power over both discharged men and deserters by letting them run slightly into debt, taking their certificates to a captain needing crew, and 'selling' the men for an advance-note covering two or three months' future wages. Because the note from the captain was not payable until the ship had been at sea for ten days, crimps made sure that their men got aboard – by getting them drunk or drugging them. In some busy ports they skipped the preliminaries and simply took a cartload of drunken seamen from ship to ship.

This whole system of selling men to ships would have been impracticable without advance-notes. The use of advance-notes was almost unavoidable for seamen. They were not paid off until three to five days after they were discharged from incoming ships; in the meantime, they could get credit for food, lodging, liquor, and women only from a boarding-house master. Caught between low wages and an understandable impulse for wild spending (after three or more months of confinement at sea), most seamen were in debt to the crimp for more than their cash wages before they had been paid. Even if the crimp did not 'shanghai' them at this point, they were forced to get an advance-note to pay their bills, and crimps often doubled their profit by discounting these notes at very high rates. Thus, after a few days ashore, most seamen had been duped and cheated of the scanty reward for months of hard labour. Stripped of money and thus of effective choice, they had no alternative to shipping out and beginning the whole cycle over again. The 'taint' of the land, one of Conrad's seemingly romantic notions, was a matter of bitter experience for many sailing-ship seamen.

Other European nations avoided the rather obvious evils of crimping by paying advances in cash, but England continued to use the note. The practice was sometimes rationalised in terms of seamen's spending habits: without advance notes, they would be unable to pay shore debts, get outfitted for another voyage, or provide anything for wives and children. So the argument went, but reform legislation in 1875 was defeated by the lobbying of crimps, who organised mass protest meetings to block any change. The new proposal, by substituting an allotment-note (payable only to seamen's relatives) for the advance-note, would have put them out of business immediately. After several futile attempts at compromise amendment, Parliament quickly defeated the bill.[80] Captains condoned the existing system, as owners did, because it provided an easy way of getting crews together. The seamen were the only losers. Why did they let themselves be duped? Most, spending the greater part of their lives at sea, had few shore attachments and were interested only in sprees during their brief spells on land. They knew what they were getting into when they followed boarding-house masters; if they did not like the consequences, they also knew that they could not avoid them. Without money, social status, marketable skill, or even the force of a well-organised group, sailing-ship seamen had no way of changing their lot.

At first glance the calibre and status of officers seems markedly superior to that of the men. Some of the captains of sailing ships were intelligent and cultured. Captain T Y

Powles of the *John of Gaunt* was a sportsman and skilled musician; Captain C C Dixon of the *Elginshire* was an amateur geographer, geologist, ornithologist, and photographer; Conrad describes one of his former captains (Captain Blake of the *Tilkhurst)* as 'a man of singularly well-informed mind'.[81] Elsewhere Conrad represents the officers of the Merchant Service as 'a steady hard-working, staunch, unromantic-looking set of men, belonging to various classes of society, but with the professional stamp obliterating the personal characteristics, which were not very marked anyhow'.[82] It is a mistake to categorise all officers so neatly, but Conrad does suggest one important distinction between the Royal Navy and the Merchant Service: the officers of the latter were not predominantly gentlemen by birth. Seaport towns provided the greatest number, and such men generally rose to command through the forecastle.

Practical experience was far more useful to the merchant-service officer than the more formal education given to naval officers. Even those fortunate enough to receive training on the 'gentlemen's' ships (the *Conway* and the *Worcester*) got a full taste of forecastle life during their apprenticeships. In most ships apprentices were not treated as midshipmen to be taught but as younger members of the crew to be 'used' for menial work and almost constant watch-standing. No distinction was made between pauper apprentices who would become able seamen and educated public-school boys who might eventually rise to command. The levelling tendency of this practice is obvious: the young man of influential family had an advantage only when it came to getting his first berth as an officer. Young men who reached the quarterdeck 'through the hawse-hole', as seamen put it, had some further advantages over their well-educated peers. They were much more likely to have the sea experience required by Board of Trade regulations (4 years for second mate, 5 for first mate, and 6 for master) at an earlier age. Because minimum ages for certification were very low (17 for second mate, 19 for first mate, and 21 for master), a boyhood spent at sea was the quickest way to command.[83] The examinations themselves, which Conrad describes so thoroughly in *A Personal Record*, stressed practical knowledge over theory, and the difficulties of celestial navigation could be overcome between voyages in one of the many cram schools. The career of Captain W H Angel is perhaps typical. As a native of Plymouth, he first became a ship's boy in coasters and then sailed on deepwater voyages as an ordinary and able seaman. After some tutoring in navigation, he passed the second mate's examination at 19, the first mate's at 20, and the master's at 21. The rest of his career was a succession of commands, each one better than the last.[84] Among men who had left school early and lacked the advantages of social status or family influence, such success was not unusual in a service which demanded skill and stamina above all else.

Although the officers of merchant ships cannot be stereotyped, as a group they were attacked throughout the last three decades of the nineteenth century. Some opinions of British Consuls in 1872 are worth quoting:

[H J Murray: Portland, Oregon] The masters frequently become morose and ill-tempered from being more or less isolated, and often give way to drinking, which soon subverts all discipline on board.

[E M Mark: Marseilles] England is not fairly represented abroad by the men who command her ships on the ocean; the grossest ignorance is seen; drunkenness largely prevails amongst them; they are reckless and frequently dishonest.

[William Ward: Memel] The most trouble is given by crews of vessels commanded by masters of an irritable, of a weak, or of a brutal character.

[Leopold March: Santander] How many [ships] have been stranded, run on rocks, brought in collision, taken to sea on the eve of stormy weather, the engine out of order in a manner discernible only to professional eyes, the cargo badly stowed, and finally inefficiently commanded in the hour of danger, all through the recklessness, stupidity, and lack of ordinary care, produced by dram-drinking and toping amongst the executive officers![85]

In the 'Report of the Royal Commission on the Saving of Life at Sea' of 1887, the increase in strandings and collisions was blamed on 'the neglect by the master or officers of the most ordinary rules and precautions of seamanship'.[86] Similar charges of low calibre and incompetence were made again and again. It is impossible to dismiss them entirely or overlook them as Conrad does in his many encomiums of British seamen. Models for the disreputable officers of the *Patna* (in *Lord Jim*) were to be found in the British Merchant Service.

No general explanation for incompetence or low calibre is adequate, but at least two causes can be isolated: slack enforcement of professional standards and the lack of a tradition comparable to that of the Royal Navy. Certification requirements (introduced by the Merchant Shipping Act of 1854) guaranteed a minimum of professional competence – the master's ability to find latitude and longitude, for example – but did not cure negligence because the penalties imposed for serious mistakes were rather mild. A year's suspension of certificate was not fatal to an officer's career – unless he happened to be 'romantic' like Lord Jim. Captain John Nichol was given command of the *Fifeshire* after a warning from the court which investigated the loss of his former ship, the *Glencairn*; a second court of enquiry suspended his certificate because he had stranded the *Fifeshire*, but he rose to command again in the steam tramps of another company.[87] A single mistake of this nature would have ruined an officer's career in the Royal Navy or even in the merchant navies of other European nations. Thomas Brassey claims that British shipmasters were inferior to their Scandinavian counterparts 'in point of education, professional knowledge, manners, and steadiness'.[88] Such summary judgments are difficult to substantiate, of course, but if British officers had not markedly 'deteriorated', they were seldom fit subjects for the praise heaped upon them by seaman-writers.

The economic changes which transformed the shipping industry also made the officer's career in the Merchant Service less lucrative. Commands, in particular, were no longer speculative ventures. In the first half of the century the captain of a 'John Company' ship might make as much as eight thousand to ten thousand pounds from each trip to India or China through commissions on freight, passage money, and personal traffic in goods. Many made their fortunes and retired after five or six voyages. Near the end of the century, the average annual wage for the captain of a small sailing ship was only one hundred and twenty pounds, and he was often forced to invest money in the ship as well.[89] Many owners would no longer allow wives and children on board, and in this case the captains found it very difficult to support them ashore.

The economic position of mates was far worse. When Conrad describes Mrs Bunter (in 'The Black Mate') living on a pound a week, he is not exaggerating, for the average monthly wage of mates in good sailing ships was six pounds. Conrad himself got only five as second mate of the *Narcissus* in 1884, and the chief mate was paid eight.[90] 'His pay is so small,' complains Bullen, 'that he *must* forego the delights of wife and children if he has only that pay to live on.'[91] Brassey blames parsimonious shipowners: 'It is not creditable to the shipowners that their officers should be in such abject poverty, that their children are found crowding into asylums originally intended to afford relief to the working seamen.'[92] The shipowners were directly responsible for the low pay of officers, but they were simply trying to counterbalance reduced freight rates with cheap labour, and they succeeded because sailing-ship officers had no effective bargaining position. Too many officers were certified for the decreasing number of berths available, and young men and foreign officers were willing to accept low salaries to get a berth. Bullen recalls one of his own experiences which illustrates the typical position of a mate:

Before my last voyage I had been prowling about the docks, looking for a ship, until I was in very low water indeed, and glad of almost anything. Yet, as I was married and had one child, there was a minimum wage below which I could not go without the prospect of my dear ones starving. Receiving information that there was a brig in the St Katherine dock wanting a mate, I hastened down to her, finding the master a pleasant, genial man, and English. I told him my errand, showed my credentials, and was asked what wages I wanted. I suggested £6 10s. per month, feeling as I did so that I might as well ask for the moon while I was about it. We finally agreed upon £5 15s. a month, which made my wife's income while I was at sea about 14s. a week. But I went home light-hearted enough in the feeling that I was no longer a dock-slouching mendicant, and that *something* was sure for at least twelve months.

The next morning, when I came on board to work, the skipper told me that he had received an offer from a German, fully certificated, to come as mate for £3 a month, and one from an Englishman, who said that, as he had money of his own, and only wanted to get his time in for master, he would come for *nothing*. 'I didn't take the German', said Captain W——, 'entirely because I had given you my word, but because I hold that it is a national crime to permit foreign officers to have charge of our ships, apart altogether from the shame of having them cut the already too scanty wages. And I didn't take the other fellow, because I wanted a man to earn his wages, and I knew that he was likely to earn what he offered to go for – nothing.' So I kept the berth, but, as the skipper truly remarked, had the owner known that he was paying much more for my services than there was any necessity for him to do, he would have been very angry.[93]

Sail and steam competed for little more than fifty years; by the time this photograph was taken, just before World War I, square-rigged sailing ships were eking out a difficult living mainly in the coal, nitrate and wheat trades where the huge distances still gave them a measure of advantage over steam. *Peking* was another of the Flying-P Line and is now a museum ship, docked at South Street Seaport, New York.

Rather than financial reward and security, experience and proven competence brought older officers the choice of taking what they had always gotten or being replaced by younger men.

Low pay was not the only disadvantage of the merchant officer's career. Working conditions degenerated near the end of the century. As rapid communications were established, captains lost a large share of their old independence to owners' port agents, in receipt of direct orders by wire, and to charterers' stevedores who supervised the loading of cargo.[94] Seniority for mates did not exist because they were signed on one voyage at a time to save the owner money while the ship lay in port. The young second or third mate's status was even less enviable. On a sailing ship, he was 'often scarcely removed from the foremast hands' in his work, handling braces, sheets, halliards, and buntlines on deck and working on the yards with the rest of the crew.[95] The distinctions between junior officers and seamen were never rigid on sailing ships. Boatswains, carpenters, and sailmakers might be promoted at sea, and officers long out of work frequently took berths in the forecastle. By the very nature of the occupation, officers who made only one long voyage a year were removed from their families nine months out of twelve. Taken together, these conditions of the profession – poor pay, discontinuous employment, slow promotion, doubtful status, and prolonged isolation – were not likely to attract bright and ambitious young men.

Life in the sailing merchant service of the late nineteenth century never matched the romantic image created by those exiled from its rigours. Caught in a limbo between old traditions and complete mechanisation, men who stayed in sail enjoyed neither the excitement of fast clippers nor the safety and luxury of modern steamships. The economic pressures which gradually transformed the British Merchant Service impoverished the sailing ship as a commercial carrier. The urgent demand for speed in the 1850s and 1860s had induced the perfection of the sailing ship, but the old naval architecture decayed as sailing-ship firms discovered that cargo capacity was the only effective weapon against the competition of steamships. Sailing these larger, clumsier, and more unmanageable ships built during the last decades of the century was no 'glorious' task because it entailed added hardships and dangers as well as longer voyages. The tangible rewards for the sailing-ship seaman decreased simultaneously. As steamships took over the more lucrative trades, both men and officers were paid less for the decreasing number of jobs available. Subject to 'technological unemployment', they had the prospect of doggedly hanging on in a dying profession or of 'leaving the sea to go into steam', as the old salts put it.

The men who remained in sail paid dearly for their inflexibility. They had to live through the death throes of the sailing ship, 'an age of apprentice-labour, rotten gear and patched sails, inadequate food and miserable conditions . . .'[96] In the metaphor of the seaman-writers who beguile the reading public with their image of 'the last days of sail', the 'ravishing mistress' was not blessed by death before she had become an old hag.

ROBERT D FOULKE

Overleaf: The boundless ocean: the last refuge of the square-rigger. This photograph was taken onboard *Moshulu*, the four-masted barque on which Eric Newby was apprenticed at the age of 19. He joined the ship in Belfast in 1938, sailing to Port Lincoln in Australia where they took grain before returning in the spring of 1939. His book of the voyage, *The Last Grain Race,* is perhaps the best evocation of life aboard the last sailing ships and is still in print. *Moshulu* herself is a restaurant ship in New York.

Introduction Notes

1. Joseph Conrad, *Last Essays* (London, 1955), p. 46.
2. Joseph Conrad, *Notes on Life and Letters* (London, 1949), p. 161.
3. Basil Lubbock, *Adventures by Sea from Art of Old Time* (London, 1925), p. 40.
4. Felix Riesenberg, *Log of the Sea* (New York, 1933), pp. 28–30.
5. Joseph Conrad, *An Outcast of the Islands* (London, 1949), pp. 12–13.
6. Gerald S Graham, 'The Ascendancy of the Sailing Ship, 1850–85,' *Econ. Hist. Rev.*, second series, IX (1956), 1, 75.
7. *Ibid.*, pp.79, 86; Basil Lubbock, *The Last of the Windjammers* (Glasgow, 1929), I, 119; R J Cornewall-Jones, *The British Merchant Service* (London, 1898), pp. 115–18. Before the turn of the century, a few *'freaks'* of over 3,000 tons were built to compete with steam tramps.
8. No less than eight new iron ships were dismasted on their maiden voyages in 1874. See Basil Lubbock, *The Colonial Clippers* (Glasgow, 1921), p. 248.
9. Conrad, *Last Essays*, p. 69.
10. William McFee, *Watch Below* (New York, 1940), pp. 3, 38–39.
11. A A Hurst, *The Call of High Canvas* (London, 1958), p. 11.
12. Jan de Hartog, *A Sailor's Life* (New York, 1955), pp. 107–08.
13. Hurst, *Call of High Canvas*, p. 250.
14. Claude Muncaster, *Rolling Round the Horn* (London, 1933), p. 155.
15. *Ibid.*, p. 202.
16. Richard Henry Dana, *Two Years Before the Mast* (New York, 1936), pp. 339–40.
17. McFee, *Watch Below*, p. 31.
18. Joseph Conrad, *Lord Jim* (London, 1946), p. 10.
19. Frank T Bullen, *The Men of the Merchant Service* (London, 1900), p. 146.
20. Lubbock, *Last of the Windjammers*, I, 1.
21. *Ibid.*, I, 3.
22. Charles W Domville-Fife, *Epics of the Square-Rigged Ships: Autobiographies of Sail* (London, 1956), pp. 54–65.
23. Lubbock, *Last of the Windjammers*, I, 218–19.
24. *Ibid.*, I, 4–6.
25. Muncaster, *Rolling Round the Horn* p. 182; and Felix Riesenberg in *A Conrad Memorial Library: The Collection of George T Keating*, ed. George T Keating (New York, 1929), p. 151.
26. Thomas Brassey, *British Seamen: As Described in Recent Parliamentary and Official Documents* (London, 1877), p. 220.
27. Conrad, *Notes on Life and Letters*, p. 197.
28. As quoted from Alan Villiers in Lubbock, *Last of the Windjammers*, II, 327.
29. Joseph Conrad, *The Nigger of the 'Narcissus'* (London, 1950), p. 25.
30. Brassey, *British Seamen*, p. 277.
31. *Ibid*, pp. 276, 279.
32. *Mariner's Mirror*, VI (1922), 31–32.
33. Hurst, *Call of High Canvas*, pp. 61–62.
34. A J Villiers, *By Way of Cape Horn* (New York, 1930), pp. 91–128.
35. Lubbock, *Last of the Windjammers*, I, 167.
36. Frank Carr, *The Cutty Sark and the Days of Sail* (London, 2007), p. 22.
37. Lubbock, *Last of the Windjammers*, I, 8.
38. Villiers, *By Way of Cape Horn*, p. 178.
39. Charles W Domville-Fife, *Square-Rigger Days* (London, 2007), p. 51.
40. Lubbock, *Last of the Windjammers*, 1, 34.
41. Domville-Fife, *Epics of the Square-Rigged Ships*, pp. 17–39, 66–79.
42. Domville-Fife, *Square-Rigger Days*, pp. 115–126; *Epics of the Square-Rigged Ships*, pp. 104–16.
43. Lubbock, *Colonial Clippers*, pp. 157–62; T W Pickard, 'Last of the Wool Clippers,' *Sea Breezes*, III (1947), 30–33.
44. Lubbock, *Last of the Windjammers*, II. 199–202, 305–06; I, 216–17.
45. E Keble Chatterton, *The Mercantile Marine* (London, 1923), pp. 162–63.

46. Carr, *The Cutty Sark*, pp. 3–4.
47. Lubbock, *Colonial Clippers*, pp. 29–32; *Last of the Windjammers*, I, 31, 38. For Conrad's comment, see *Last Essays*, p. 47.
48. Bullen, *Men of the Merchant Service*, p. 29.
49. Lubbock, *Last of the Windjammers*, I, 23.
50. *Ibid.*, I, 371.
51. Conrad, *The Mirror of the Sea* (London, 1946), pp. 89–91.
52. *Ibid.*, pp. 42–43.
53. Lubbock, *Last of the Windjammers*, I, 398–99; II, 95–97.
54. Conrad, *Mirror of the Sea*, p. 70.
55. Joseph Conrad, *Chance* (London, 1949), p. 288.
56. Bullen, *Men of the Merchant Service*, p. 49.
57. Edward Blackmore, *The British Mercantile Marine: A Short Historical Review* (London, 1897), p. 113.
58. Hurst, *High Canvas*, pp. 102–04; Domville-Fife, *Square-Rigger Days*, pp. 184–85.
59. Felix Riesenberg, *Vignettes of the Sea* (New York, 1926), pp. 116–26.
60. Domville-Fife, *Epics of the Square-Rigged Ships*, p. 141.
61. Domville-Fife, *Square-Rigger Days*, pp. 89–104.
62. Basil Lubbock, *The Log of the 'Cutty Sark'* (Glasgow, 1945), pp. 144–53. This notorious incident was the basis for part of Conrad's 'The Secret Sharer.'
63. Bullen, *Men of the Merchant Service*, p. 139.
64. Hurst, *Call of High Canvas*, p. 206.
65. Domville-Fife, *Square-Rigger Days*, pp. 77–88, 105–114.
66. When the crew broke open locked storerooms, hurled china overboard, went absent without leave in port, and refused duty at sea, Captain Hocken could do no more than pay off the troublemakers, and they filed a protest with the union! Richard Whitehead, *Evening Standard* (London), June 4, 1960, p. 3.
67. McFee, *Watch Below*, pp. 40–41.
68. Brassey, *British Seamen*, pp. 52–59, 67.
69. Hurst, *Call of High Canvas*, pp. 28–29.
70. Muncaster, *Rolling Round the Horn*, p. 49.
71. Brassey, *British Seamen*, pp. 28–29.
72. *Ibid.*, pp. 22–23, 30, 34.
73. Bullen, *Men of the Merchant Service*, p. 277.
74. Blackmore, *British Mercantile Marine*, p. 158.
75. Brassey, *British Seamen*, pp. 160–63, 167; Cornewall-Jones, *British Merchant Service*, pp. 269–72.
76. Brassey, *British Seamen*, pp. 35–37; Cornewall-Jones, *British Merchant Service*, pp. 269–72.
77. Bullen, *Men of the Merchant Service*, p. 282.
78. Brassey, *British Seamen*, pp. 2, 24.
79. *Ibid.*, pp. 24, 152–59, 178–200.
80. *Ibid.*, p. 204.
81. Lubbock, *Last of the Windjammers*, I, 45–48; II, 253–54; Conrad, *Mirror of the Sea*, p. 9.
82. Joseph Conrad, *Tales of Hearsay* (London, 1955), p. 85.
83. Blackmore, *British Mercantile Marine*, pp. 146–47.
84. W H Angel, *The Clipper Ship 'Sheila'* (London, 1919), ch. iii.
85. Brassey, *British Seamen*, pp. 293–96.
86. *Ibid.*, p. 124.
87. Lubbock, *Last of the Windjammers*, II, 255.
88. Brassey, *British Seamen*, p. 311.
89. *Ibid.*, pp. 321–23, 327.
90. Conrad, *Tales of Hearsay*, p. 114; Brassey, *British Seamen*, p. 358; 'Agreement and Account of Crew of the Narcissus' (reproduced in Jocelyn Baines, *Joseph Conrad: A Critical Biography*, London, 1960).
91. Bullen, *Men of the Merchant Service*, p. 87.
92. Brassey, *British Seamen*, p. 326.
93. Bullen, *Men of the Merchant Service*, pp. 225–26.
94. Blackmore, *British Mercantile Marine*, p. 253.
95. Cornewall-Jones, *British Merchant Service*, pp. 285–87.
96. Frank Knight, *The Sea Story: Being a Guide to Nautical Reading from Ancient Times to the Close of the Sailing Ship Era* (London, 1958), pp. 209–10.

1 My First Voyage

Half-deck of the *County of Pembroke* – A sea-sick cure – Pooped in the Southern Ocean
– Melbourne days.

EVEN after thirty-eight years the details of my first voyage linger vividly in my
memory. Born and bred in Liverpool, within easy reach of the docks, which in those
days held many fine sailing ships, it was perhaps natural that I should develop 'sea-
fever.'

As a boy I spent every spare moment at the docks, wandering around, lost in admiration
of the tall ships, or, with a few kindred spirits, paddling about in one of the leaky old boats
which were always to be found tied up astern of the small coasting craft. These adventures
usually resulted in our being chased by some irate ship's watchman or dock policeman,
when we would abandon the boat on the far side of the dock and scamper off till the hubbub
died down.

As may be imagined, boots and clothing suffered severely on these expeditions, and my
parents having forbidden me to go to the docks, I was sometimes hard put to it for an
explanation.

Finally, at the age of fourteen, I was taken from school and placed as an office boy with
a Marine Insurance Co. This somewhat curtailed my activities at the docks, but, to my
delight, it opened up a new world to me in the form of ships' log-books. Several of these
were always lying around the office for use in connection with claims, and in them I read
accounts of wrecks, strandings, fires, dismastings, hurricanes, cyclones, jettisons, shifting
cargoes, jury rigs, and other thrilling adventures.

After about three months of devouring these, I went home one evening and announced
firmly to my astonished parents that I wanted to go to sea as an apprentice. Nothing else
would suit me; I simply couldn't stay ashore any longer. They argued earnestly with me and
seemed to be obsessed with the idea that only ne'er-do-wells went to sea, and that no good
could possibly come of it.

I stuck to my guns, however, and threatened to run away, so after a couple of weeks they

---

EDITOR'S NOTE
Captain J G Bisset, RD, RNR, who has figured in many great dramas and tragedies of the sea, gives here an
account of his early life in famous sailing ships at the beginning of the century.

Queen's Dock in Liverpool.

gave in, and my father set about the task of getting me a berth. Through a friend in the shipping business, I eventually signed indentures with the firm of William Thomas & Co., of Liverpool, and was appointed to their barque *County of Pembroke* as apprentice. The premium was £20, to be returned after four years' faithful service, plus another £20 as wages, which was to be paid in the following manner: £3 for the first year, £4 for the second, £5 for the third, and £8 for the last year of serving. Not princely sums, but wages then meant nothing to me, so long as I got to sea.

For three weeks prior to sailing I worked by the ship with the other two apprentices and the first and second mates. At last I had achieved my ambition of going on board a ship freely without being chased by watchmen and police.

We worked from 6 AM to 6 PM daily, taking in stores, cement-washing the fresh-water tanks, bending sail, whitewashing the biscuit tanks, scrubbing the cabins, and a thousand-and-one other jobs in preparation for sea. It was hard work, but I gloried in it; and, as I walked home in the evenings in a filthy dungaree-suit and a badge cap stuck jauntily on the side of my head, I hoped all the other boys I met were duly envious of my lot.

The other apprentices, Bill and Tom, had been two years at sea, so they knew the ropes and were able to indulge in numerous jokes at my expense, but they were good fellows and we got on well together. At long last came sailing day. The tide served at 4 AM, so, with the rest of the crew, I joined the ship the night before. Having said a fond good-bye to my mother and younger brothers and sisters, I set off in an old four-wheel cab, accompanied by my father and elder brother, with my sea-chest, canvas bag, and 'donkey's breakfast' piled on top.

I was fourteen and a half years old and had never been away from home before, and the parting was a sad one. We spoke very little in the cab on that account, and also because the rattling of the iron-tyred wheels on the cobble-stones made speech and hearing almost impossible. Drawing up close to the ship, they helped me to get my dunnage on board, and then my father put a small Bible into my hand, and, in a broken voice, bade me read it regularly, and not to forget to say my prayers. My brother hugged me and implored me to bring home a monkey or a parrot!

Then they drove away, and I was left on the cold, deserted quay, feeling not a little miserable and lonely.

A few minutes later, raucous voices proclaimed the arrival of Bill and Tom and several others of the crew, all more or less tipsy. Hurriedly opening our straw beds (called 'donkey's breakfasts') and throwing a few blankets on top of them, we turned in to get some rest before tide-time. Bill and Tom were soon snoring loudly, but sleep positively refused to come to me. It was my first experience of a straw bed, and it smelt like a damp stable. Thoughts of my family sleeping in comfort ran through my head, and it was only a sense of shame that kept me from stealing ashore and running home.

Eventually I must have dropped off through sheer exhaustion, but it seemed as if I had only been asleep a few minutes when there came a great banging at the 'half-deck' door, which was thrown open with a bang to admit the mate, a huge figure clad in oilskins and sea-boots, and carrying a hurricane-lamp. 'Now then,' he roared, 'show a leg there, young feller-me-lads! Get out of it!'

Tom and Bill were out like scalded cats, but I, feeling like death, decided that the call couldn't possibly include me, so turned over and tried to sleep again. A moment later a great horny hand reached under the blankets and, grasping me firmly by the ankle, drew me sprawling on to the deck. 'Skulking, eh?' snarled the mate. 'Skulking on your first voyage! By God, if you're not out of here in two minutes, I'll flay the hide off you, you young ——!' And with a burst of profanity he lumbered out, and could be heard going through the same performance in the forecastle, which was divided from the half-deck by a thin wooden bulkhead.

Tom had lighted an evil-smelling oil-lamp which was secured to the bulkhead by a large rusty nail, and by its smoky light we scrambled quickly into oilskins, for the rain could be heard pattering dismally on the deck overhead. A few minutes later the mate roared: 'Turn to!' and all hands tumbled out on deck. Having divided them into two shivering groups, he sent one aft with the second mate, and took the others forward, with orders to 'Un-moor'.

Tom joined the mate's group, and I stayed with him. It was 4 AM and pitch dark, with a bitterly cold east wind and driving rain. I had never been out at such an hour or in such weather before, and I was frozen stiff. Sticking close to Tom, I pulled on ropes, wires, and chains with numbed fingers, and only a hazy notion of what it was all about.

Finally, we were put to heaving round a capstan on a heavy, wet rope, and I discovered that we were gradually pulling the ship out into the middle of the dock. After much shouting and cursing, we passed through a narrow lock and came to rest behind two large dock gates butting on to the river. By this time it was growing daylight, and having put a few lines ashore to hold her, the mate gave the welcome order, 'All hands to breakfast,' accompanying it in my case with a lusty kick that lifted me off my feet.

Breakfast consisted of a huge mug of coffee, half a loaf of stale bread, and margarine. It tasted horrible to me, but, cold and ravenous, I managed to force some down, and actually felt better for it. We had barely finished this repast when the mate roared: 'Make the tug fast!'

The dock gates were now open, and the tug *Sarah Joliffe* backed in and passed us a long

The first leg of voyage: a tow out of harbour to the open sea.
Here a brig is towed by the paddle tug *Imperial*.

The three-masted barque *County of Pembroke* soon after her launch in 1881.

towing-wire which we made fast on the forecastle head. She then forged slowly ahead, and casting off our ropes we moved out into the river, and our voyage had commenced. I had hoped that some member of the family might have come down to see us depart, but I suppose they didn't know about such matters, and probably it would only have made me more miserable. The only people to see us off were a few dock labourers, who gazed idly, and I thought somewhat pityingly, as we drew away, then went calmly back to their work of shutting the river gates.

As we dropped down-stream on the ebb tide I leaned over the rail and watched the old familiar landmarks slipping past – buildings and other objects that I had only seen previously from ferry boats. Goodness knows when I would see them again, for our voyage might last anything from one to three years. I was already beginning to feel a little homesick. My day-dreams were soon rudely shattered by the mate, who cursed me for an idle young scoundrel and set me to work.

At noon we were sent to dinner, and I was told off to bring it from the galley. The cook was a very old Welshman, with a dirty white beard. Grumbling in high-pitched tones, he handed me three deep tin dishes, known as 'kids', stuck one on top of the other. The bottom one contained a quantity of watery vegetable soup; the second one some potatoes cooked in very dirty jackets; and the top, a loathsome-looking piece of boiled mutton with horrible yellow fat, and surrounded with chunks of carrot and turnip.

I was told to put the kids on the deck, as there was no table, and we sat round on our sea-chests and helped ourselves on to enamel plates. The carpenter and sailmaker lived in the half-deck, making five in all. They had first cut at the meat, followed by Bill and Tom, and

County of Pembroke ashore and wrecked in Algoa Bay, South Africa,
after the great gale of 1903.

I came last. I swallowed some soup and a potato, but the mutton was beyond me, and even to this day the sight of boiled mutton gives me a feeling of nausea.

After dinner I returned the kids to the galley, swept up the half-deck, and we sat round smoking and yarning. It seemed to be a point of honour with 'Chips' and 'Sails' never to make two consecutive voyages in one ship. They had been all over the world, and I listened spell-bound to their yarns. In the middle of a most exciting one the tug blew a series of blasts on its steam whistle, and the mate came along bellowing out to 'Make sail'.

Some of the men jumped aloft to loose topsails and foresail, and shortly, after much hauling, shouting, and cursing, I saw our white wings spreading above us, and we started laying over to the breeze. A few minutes later the tug was cast off, and as she steamed under our stern she blew three long blasts, which is the seaman's method of bidding farewell the whole world over. Now our last link with the shore had gone, and my heart went with her.

All hands were now ordered aft, and the mates picked watches. Six men each, and Bill and I were appointed to the mate's watch, and Tom joined the second mate. It was now about 2 PM, and much to my relief, for I was feeling very sea-sick, our watch was sent below till 4 PM. I threw myself into the bunk fully dressed, and fell asleep. At a quarter to four Tom called us. I turned out, but after a violent spasm of sickness, climbed back again, and prayed that the ship might go down quickly and take me with it.

At eight bells Bill tried to shake some action into me, but gave it up as a bad job and went on deck. Five minutes later the door was flung open, and the familiar roar of the mate greeted me: 'Come on, young feller-me-lad! Out of it I'll —— well cure you,' and with that he took me by the scruff of the neck and dragged me out on deck.

The ship was slipping along at good speed and lurching heavily, so that every now and again she buried her lee scuppers and flooded the deck with water. Grabbing an enamel pannikin from the galley, he scooped up a pint of sea-water, and said:

'Drink that; it'll make a sailor of you.'

Assisted by vigorous shakes and threats from the mate, I swallowed it all, hoping it would make a corpse of me!

Then I was handed over to Bill, with orders to keep on deck. It was a drastic cure, but once I got rid of that salt water I began to feel better, and by 6 PM, the end of the dog-watch, I was actually feeling hungry. Incidentally, I have never been sea-sick since that day.

From 6 to 8 PM we were below, and during that time ate our supper, which consisted of biscuits and margarine, smeared over with marmalade and washed down with tea, without milk.

At 8 PM we again went on deck in oilskins and sea-boots, for it was blowing a whole gale, and water was coming aboard both fore and aft. The mate ordered me to keep on the poop out of harm's way, and Bill piloted me along the main deck in the inky darkness, and left me sheltering behind a weather cloth that was stretched across the mizzen rigging. He explained to me that one of my duties was to watch the clock in the companionway and strike the requisite number of bells every half-hour.

The roar of the breaking seas as they crashed on to the main deck, the howling of the wind in the rigging, the driving spray, the darkness, and the violent lurching of the vessel, all combined to make me a bit scared, and not having got my sea-legs, I several times found myself in a heap in the lee scuppers. On one such occasion, as I crawled back to windward, cold, wet, and miserable, I found the Captain standing there with the mate. Seizing my shoulder, he told me in a kindly way how to stand with my legs apart, and to hold on to the mizzen rigging for support.

About 9 PM, with the gale increasing, it was decided to take in the fore upper topsail, and the mate ploughed his way forward and roused out all hands. Very soon I heard the men shouting as they pulled and hauled, followed by the angry flapping of canvas as the yard was lowered. Then the shouts came from aloft as the men grappled with the stiff, wet canvas in their efforts to pass the gaskets round the sail.

It was a mystery to me how, in such pitch darkness, the men knew from that amazing tangle of ropes and wires which ones to pull on to furl the sail, and also, how they had the nerve and ability to go aloft in that furious wind, and work on the violently swaying yards without breaking their necks. I began to feel that I would never make a sailor.

At last the watch was over, and at midnight Bill and I groped our perilous way forward to the half-deck and, throwing off our wet oilskins, turned in. Our entrance woke up 'Sails', and he and Bill lay there smoking reeking pipes for ten minutes, and discussed the weather. Then the lamp was blown out, adding a further stink to the already stuffy room, but in a few minutes they were both snoring peacefully. I lay there thinking of home and its comforts, and wondering why in the name of fortune I had chosen to come to sea. Eventually I slept for what seemed to be about five minutes, and was then roughly shaken by Tom, who announced that it was one bell (a quarter to four AM), and time for us to 'show a leg'. Wearily we turned out, donned the wet oilskins again, and went on deck for another four hours.

Thus I was introduced to the four-hourly watch-and-watch system, which I endured for nearly seven years as apprentice and second mate in sail, and which became such a habit with me that even to this day I rarely sleep for more than four hours at a stretch.

The bad weather continued for nearly three weeks, by which time we were in the region of the N.E. trades, that carried us nearly to the Equator. On striking fine weather my nautical education commenced, and for the first time I was allowed to go aloft. Before starting, the mate gave me some good advice, which I have never forgotten. 'Hold on to the shrouds and never to the ratlines', and 'Keep one hand for the ship and one for yourself.' Following this advice has several times been the means of saving my life, especially when up aloft furling sail in cold, bad weather, when one is inclined to throw caution to the winds in order to get the job done.

Once having been aloft and seen the working of the yards and sails, I soon became familiar with the names of all the ropes, wires, chains, blocks, and other paraphernalia which constituted the make-up of a sailing ship. Such names as halyards, sheets, clews,

Changing the main topsails on *Queen Margaret*, the four-masted barque. Changing from fine-weather sails to heavy duty ones and *vice versa* were the regular tasks of sailors entering and leaving the Southern Ocean.

vangs, braces, tacks, downhauls, lifts, backstays, dead-eyes, reefs, cringles, foot-ropes, sheer-poles, lanyards, bullwhangers, and earrings, became part of my vocabulary, and in the dog-watches I learned various knots and splices, and also how to box the compass.

After leaving the 'trades' we struck the doldrums, an area of calms, heavy rain squalls, and baffling winds. Advantage had to be taken of every puff of wind to get through this area, and consequently the yards were being constantly hauled round from one tack to another, and the sails clewed up in the calms to prevent them flapping to pieces as the ship rolled about in the long swells. We had several weeks of this, then picked up the S.E. trades, which carried us towards the Cape of Good Hope and the 'Roaring Forties'. As the trades fell light, we sent down our fine-weather sails, and replaced them with a heavy suit, ready for bad weather.

Rounding the Cape, we commenced to run the easting down, and encountered a succession of westerly gales, before which we made good progress. But the *County of Pembroke* was a poor ship to run, for she had a low poop and was liable to take a purler over the stern, especially if unable to carry enough sail to keep her ahead of the seas.

In one exceptionally heavy gale we ran too long, and the sea rose to such mountainous heights that it seemed impossible to heave the ship to without rolling the 'sticks' out of her. It was decided therefore to keep her running, and to trust to God that she kept before it. About six that evening a tremendous comber broke over the stern and swept everything off the poop. The helmsman was picked up in the waist, half-drowned and with both legs broken. The Captain and mate saved themselves by jumping into the rigging. I happened to be standing just ahead of the mizzen-mast, and heard the mate yell: 'Hang on there!' At that moment two great walls of water, divided by the mast, swept past me carrying all manner of shattered deck fittings. I hung on like grim death and got nothing worse than a ducking and a severe fright. The cabin and storerooms were flooded, and great gaping holes were left in the deck where the beautiful teakwood skylight and companion-hatch had previously stood.

Fortunately the glass commenced to rise about this time, so by superhuman efforts we managed to set a reefed foresail, and she ran safely through the rest of the gale. The holes in the deck were covered with planks and canvas, well spiked down, and all hands got busy bailing out the storerooms and saving as much of the food as possible. Despite every effort, the helmsman died the next day and we buried him at sea. It was to me an impressive and heart-rending experience.

By the time the gale had blown itself out, and we had everything shipshape again, all hands were exhausted by exposure and loss of sleep, and the Captain ordered rum to be served instead of lime-juice. We apprentices, not being entitled to grog, got a tin of condensed milk between us, much to the disgust of Bill and Tom, who liked a glass of grog as well as anybody.

I had now become quite a useful young sailor; able to go aloft in all weathers and to do a job of work with the rest. It took me some time to get used to the poor food and the monotony of salt beef one day and salt pork the next, with no fresh vegetables. But sea air and hard work agreed with me, for I grew like a mushroom and became as strong and active as a monkey. Eventually, after one hundred and ten days' sailing, we arrived in Melbourne, where I found about thirty letters awaiting me from the family and friends, wishing me good luck on my first voyage and tendering me a lot of good advice.

Despite this, however, I fell away from grace, although in a fairly innocent way. One night I had been ashore, and when returning about 10 PM I heard some of our sailors singing inside a public-house. Peeping in I saw a crowd of men and women dancing and singing to the music of a very ill-played piano. One of the sailors saw me and invited me in for a glass of beer – my first. In return, I offered to play the piano for them. This delighted everyone, and soon I was rattling off any tune they wanted in fine style, and the dancing grew fast and furious.

Several glasses of beer had accumulated on top of the piano and I was having a grand time. Suddenly there was a hush, and a loud, raucous voice yelled: 'Out of it, young feller-me-lad! Damn your eyes, what the hell are you doing in here?' It was the mate! A huge hand seized me by the back of the neck, and I was propelled rapidly out of the door and down to the ship, assisted by sundry cuffs and kicks.

The following day I was severely reprimanded by the Captain and had my leave stopped for a week. I had broken the terms of my indentures by entering an alehouse or tavern, and this place had evidently an even worse reputation. Furthermore, it was solemnly explained to me that I was a disgrace to my parents, and would eventually end on the gallows. Thus ingloriously terminated my first adventure ashore, but, thank God, I have enjoyed a good many since.

After a month in Melbourne discharging general cargo and loading grain, we set sail for Falmouth for orders. Rounding Cape Horn in the depth of winter, we experienced a lot of heavy weather, and on the 125th day dropped anchor in Falmouth harbour. We lay there for over a week, and then, to the delight of all hands, got orders to proceed to Liverpool.

During the voyage I had grown so much that none of my clothes would fit me, and I was in a quandary what to wear to go home when we reached Liverpool. In the end the Captain advanced money for me to get a suit in Falmouth. I had it built to my own specifications, and I realise now that it must have been a rather remarkable-looking affair. It was of blue serge, with fancy purple lining, a velvet collar, skirted coat, and bell-bottomed trousers, a rig generally affected in those days by coasting sailors. Topped off with a new wide-awake hat, I felt no end of a dog, and longed to get ashore to show it off to my landlubberly acquaintances.

We towed round to Liverpool and entered the same dock as we had left ten months before. I scampered home in the evening and burst unexpectedly on the assembled family. What a warm welcome they gave me to be sure, and how they pressed round hugging, questioning, loving, and admiring me – and what a hero I felt. But through it all I can never forget the pained look that crossed my mother's face when she first caught sight of those bell-bottomed trousers. The next day I was rushed off to a tailor.

2 My Second Voyage

An iridescent sea – A tragedy in the 'Roaring Forties' – Algoa Bay during the Boer War
– Burning of the *Mariposa* – The *Brambletye* – Newcastle, NSW, at the close of the
century – Portland, Oregon – Pitcairn Island and home.

THE ship was then laid up in the Salthouse Dock for six weeks, discharging and
loading. During that time we apprentices got a fortnight's leave and then returned
to work on board. I must confess that at the end of those two weeks the comforts
of living at home made me think of swallowing the anchor, but my parents in their wisdom
said: 'No. You've made your bed; now you must lie on it, so off you go and be a man.' I
thought this was a bit heartless of them, but I know now that they did it for my own good.

My mother packed my bag and chest with a good supply of clothes, and, unbeknown to
me, hid amongst them some dainties in the shape of chocolate bars, apples, packets of tea,
and tins of condensed milk, all priceless treasures to any apprentice. Saying good-bye was
such a tearful business that I began to think they might relent at the last moment, but they
stuck to their guns, although I know my mother was heart-broken.

On the 15th September, in the year 1899, we set sail for Port Adelaide, South Australia.
The same master, Captain John Williams, of Sarn, Pwllheli, was in command, but the
mates and the rest of the crowd on board were new to the ship. In the half-deck we had Bill,
Tom, myself, and a first voyager named Jack O'Connor, hailing from Drogheda. His
parents had purchased for him a complete, brand-new outfit at Lewis's, and it included,
amongst a lot of other strange and useless items, a cracker hash bag and mallet! The other
occupants of the half-deck were a Welsh sailmaker and an old Russian-Finn carpenter with
a deeply lined face and a long, overhanging grey moustache. He was a penniless old
wanderer, carrying very few tools, and fitted into the category known to seafarers as 'jack-
knife carpenters'.

There was a seamen's strike on in Liverpool at the time, for a rise of pay from £2, 10s. to
£3 per month. Our men were really blacklegs and signed on secretly for £2, 15s., but they
turned out to be a very good crowd. The Captain drew £12 per month, the mate £6, 10s.,
and the second mate £4. As we apprentices drew no pay, we thought everybody else was well
paid and wondered what all the grumbling was about. Money meant nothing to me in those
days. I had never had any, so did not know what I was missing. We had a fine run down to
the trades, and the crew were soon licked into shape by the mate, a fiery little Welshman

with a tongue like a whip-lash, and the second mate, a hefty young man who had the reputation of being a bit of a bruiser in his native town of Portmadoc. They were well backed up by Captain Williams, a just man of strong personality, with whom it was dangerous to argue.

Having kept well to the eastward in the trades, the Captain decided to run down between the Cape Verde Islands and the mainland, taking advantage of the south-moving current. The night we were to go through the passage the ship was running with a spanking breeze, and a rough sea on the starboard quarter. It was pitch dark, with no moon. The mate had the eight-to-twelve watch, and as I went aft at 11 PM, to strike six bells, he and the Captain were pacing the weather side of the poop. Suddenly there was a wild yell from the forward lookout of 'Breakers ahead!' and, as I looked, the sea was lit up with a bright phosphorescent glow, the tops of the waves clearly defined in long white rows.

'Hard down!' roared the Captain to the helmsman. 'Run forward, Mr Mate, and slack away the weather fore braces, then call all hands.' As he spoke, he dashed to the weather main braces and slacked the yards on to the backstays as she came round to the wind. For the next few minutes pandemonium reigned. The hands tumbled out like scalded cats, and rushed to gather in the slack of the lee braces and ease off the weather sheets, which caused the courses to set up a thunderous flapping. In the middle of this, as the ship flew up into the wind, a heavy sea poured over the weather rail and flooded the decks with a mass of jelly-like substance that squelched between our toes as we floundered about in obedience to the mate's incessant orders.

Braced sharp up on the port tack under such a press of sail, she lay over with her lee scuppers awash, and spurts of glowing water splashing round our legs as we clued up the royals. For about ten minutes she scudded along in a ghostly light comparable to that of a full moon, then, as suddenly as she had entered it, she passed out into black darkness again. When everything was snugged down, and the hands were coiling up the tangled gear, I went up on the poop and heard the Captain and mates excitedly discussing the matter. 'Never saw anything like it before,' said the Captain. 'By my reckoning she's thirty miles from any land, but I'm not taking any chances. All hands stand by to 'bout ship. We'll go outside Cape Verde Islands and be sure of it.'

'Aye,' said the mate. 'By damn, it's better to be sure than sorry,' and, leaning over the forward rail, he shouted: 'Stand by to tack!' The men took up their stations, then came the orders: 'Hard down. Let go jib sheets. Let go an' haul. Roundy-come-roundy, my hearties!' Like a great yacht, she spun on her heel and stood off to the north-westward to wait for daylight. Next morning, with the atmosphere as clear as a bell and nothing in sight, we stood south again, and during the day passed the islands at the safe distance of fifteen miles. There is no doubt that the night before we had passed through a great shoal of jelly-fish, but it put the wind up everyone for a while.

Losing the trades in six degrees north, we spent the next couple of weeks man-handling

Opposite: The four-masted barque *Beatrice* running before a gale.

her through the doldrums, hauling the yards round at all hours of the day and night to take advantage of every puff of wind. Flat calms, burning sun, bursts of tropical rain, baffling airs, and thunderstorms, all combined to make life a misery. One night a large steamer hove in sight and almost ran us down. The mate told me to take the stern light from its screen and wave it about to attract attention. I waved it so violently that it went out. Cursing me for a fool, the mate hurriedly struck a blue light, and the steamer sheered off at the critical moment, missing us by the length of a marline-spike.

Eventually we struck the south-east trades, which carried us almost to the Cape, and we commenced running our easting down. We made good progress before heavy westerly gales, and on the hundredth day out from Liverpool passed Amsterdam Island, lying half-way between Cape Town and Adelaide. Shortly after this a tragedy occurred. One evening, just before dark, the ship was running under two lower topsails and a reefed foresail. With a very low glass, and tremendous seas crashing up under her stern and threatening to poop her, the Captain decided to heave-to for the night. Rousing out all hands we took in the foresail with much difficulty, for the wind had reached hurricane force, then, standing up to our waists in water at the braces, we pointed the yards, and the Captain, watching his chance, brought her safely round on the port tack.

Soaking wet, the men of one watch then went below, while those on deck struggled to the forecastle head to set the fore topmast staysail. We had finished the job and secured all the gear, when Evans, our youngest able seaman, crawled up to windward to take a turn with the chain tack that had got adrift and was dangling over the side from the end of the cat-head. The mate bellowed to him to leave it alone, but at that moment the ship dipped her nose in it, knocked us all off our feet, and Evans disappeared over the weather bow. We rushed to the rail and saw him struggling in the water, weighed down by his heavy sea-boots and oilskins.

'Get a lifebuoy,' yelled the mate; and two of us rushed down to the locker under the forecastle head. Meantime, they grabbed the jib downhauls off their pins, where they had been securely hitched to prevent their being washed adrift, and endeavoured to fling the stiff, water-sodden rope over the side. But the wind caught it as if it had been a silk thread and blew it in under the bows. Working feverishly, and in imminent danger of being washed overboard, we secured the lifebuoy to a dry length of line from the locker, and the mate directed it overboard with a mighty heave, only to see it fly back like a kite right across the ship. By now, owing to the great drift of the ship, poor Evans was thirty feet away and we could do nothing to save him. Then, as we gazed despairingly, a giant comber broke over his head and we saw him no more.

The sailmaker, frantic with excitement, dashed aft to implore the Captain to do something. All hands followed and, shouting above the roar of the wind, the Captain ordered them down into the cabin, where they could hear what he had to say. As they stood, with the dim grey light from above glistening on their streaming oilskins, bracing themselves against the violent lurching of the ship, the Captain explained the situation. 'The ship's having a hard fight to live in this gale,' he said. 'A boat wouldn't live one second, even if you could get it over the side without being smashed to matchwood. And if you got it over the side, who could pull it to windward against this sea? The ship won't sail to windward. You all know that. She's hove-to now and drifting to leeward like a crab. I know how you feel about it, and if any man's got any suggestions, out with 'em quick.'

The men shuffled uneasily, then old Murphy spoke up. 'Thank you, Capt'n. We realise there's nothin' could be done, but we feel more satisfied now you've told us. Poor Evans 'as gone west any'ow. I saw 'im sink with me own eyes, God rest 'is soul.' 'Well spoken,' replied the Captain. 'Evans was a fine seaman and a good man; we're all very sorry for him and for his parents. Now carry on with your watches and don't make yourselves miserable thinking about it. That'll do.'

Muttering sympathetic words to each other, the men clambered up the companion and made their perilous way forward. The sudden snatching away of a good shipmate from such a small community of superstitious seamen is an event not easily forgotten, and for some days a gloom hung over the ship. The weather fined up at last, and without further incident we arrived off Adelaide on the 123rd day out. We stayed moored in the dock for a month discharging general cargo, and during that time, thanks to many kindly families who invited us to their homes in the evenings, we boys had an enjoyable time and were kept out of mischief.

Since leaving England, the South African War had broken out, and we now received orders to take aboard grain, flour, and fodder, and proceed to Algoa Bay. We loaded at two small places, called Port Germain and Port Pirie, and finally sailed about the middle of February. Rounding Cape Leewin, Western Australia, we edged north to avoid the westerlies and made a fairly good passage of 65 days. About the longitude of Mauritius the glass fell to about twenty-seven inches, accompanied by a long swell from the north-east and a sky of terrifying appearance. It was the hurricane season, and we snugged down to lower topsails for about twenty-four hours, expecting every moment to be struck by a cyclone. Our luck held, however, and the storm passed north of us.

Algoa Bay is an open roadstead, and it was crowded with shipping, both sail and steam, waiting to be unloaded. There was a grave shortage of lighters, and of course the steamers got them first. The ship lay there six weeks before a hatch was uncovered. During that time we apprentices rowed the Captain ashore every morning in the gig, and went back for him in the evening, or whenever he ordered. We took the opportunity of slipping ashore, two at a time, and watching thousands of horses and mules being unloaded from lighters on to the small jetty. The congestion was beyond belief. The town, Port Elizabeth, was full of soldiers and Kaffirs, and, despite the war, everyone seemed to be having a good time.

One Sunday afternoon a steamer called the *Mariposa* hoisted the signal NM, meaning 'I am on fire'. Our Captain decided to go over and see if he could lend assistance, as he knew her Captain. We got alongside and found twenty other boats there on the same errand. She was loaded with hay, and her forward holds were well alight. Her Captain shouted down to us that he had a live pig on board and asked whether we would like to have it. 'Sure,' called our Captain, and a few seconds later a great squealing hog, weighing 300 lb., was flung over the side. It was too big to get into the boat, so the Captain leaned over the bow and put a bowline round its neck with our painter. In doing so, he lost his gold presentation watch

The full-rigged ship *Brambletye*, of 1876. Here she is seen off Port Elizabeth, South Africa, during the Boer War, loaded with explosives.

over the side. There was some good-humoured chaffing from the other boats, and the Captain, feeling very angry and slightly ridiculous, transferred himself to a friend's boat that was passing and left us to tow 'Dennis' back to the ship.

It was a two miles' pull, but we got him there, more dead than alive. After hoisting him aboard with a davit fall, the cook quickly put him out of his misery and we had glorious feeds of fresh pork for several days. The *Mariposa*'s fire got the upper hand and she had to be abandoned. A naval party put a charge in her cables, blew them apart, and towed her ashore, where she glowed like a live coal for the next three days and nights. She must have been of tough build, for she was eventually towed to England and repaired.

Lying in an isolated bay about ten miles away was the full-rigged ship *Brambletye*, loaded with explosives. We pulled the Captain over there one fine morning to visit his friend Captain Porter, who had his wife on board. The *Brambletye* had been there five months and, as we pulled alongside, we could see that she was covered with a sheath of barnacles over a foot thick. As she rolled gently this rose out of the sea on either side and made a noise like water lapping a shingle beach. She had a nucleus crew and there seemed to be no prospect of her being unloaded. That night we brought Captain Porter's wife back with us, and the next day she sailed for England on a Castle boat. Two months later the *Brambletye* was unloaded and, having scraped the barnacles off as far as possible, she made Newcastle, New South Wales, in 95 days.

We took a month to discharge and take in ballast, then sailed for Newcastle also. The passage was uneventful, except that I had the first real fight of my career, and that with our first-voyager, Jack O'Connor. He was a big chap, but slow, and I was getting on fine till I

Newcastle, New South Wales, from where coal was exported around the world. *Moshulu*, the four-masted barque is moored in the foreground.

split the knuckle of my little finger against a brace block instead of against his head, and I carry the scar to this day. I nearly fainted with the pain, and the men stopped the fight, but not before Jack had presented me with a lovely black eye into the bargain.

On arrival we found Newcastle in the throes of a coal strike, and lay alongside, up the Dyke, for three months before getting a load of coal. During that time we shifted the ballast from end to end of the ship, and scaled and painted the bottom to within six feet of the keel. In the run of her we applied hot white lead and tallow to make her slip through the water. We discharged the ballast in baskets, the motive-power being an old horse on the jetty. Newcastle was a famous place for sailormen in those days, and readers who have been there will remember such well-known spots as Temple West, the photographer; Ingalls, the tailors; the 'Black Diamond Saloon', in Hunter Street; the 'Flags of All Nations', in Carrington; and the numerous chop-houses that used to supply 'all you can eat for sixpence'.

Bill, the oldest apprentice, was out of his time in Newcastle. He fell in love with some girl, married her, and got a job ashore there. I have never heard of him since.

From Newcastle we sailed with a cargo of coal to Carrisal, in Chile, a small harbour in 28 degrees S. and 71 degrees W. On the way there the ship was beset with a plague of fleas, said to have been brought on board with the coal. There were millions of them and we got little sleep. On bright days we would bring our blankets out in the sun and slay hundreds as they jumped in the warmth. In the course of a couple of months they entirely disappeared, much to our relief. Carrisal was a one-horse town and we lay at anchor about a mile off to discharge our coal. The crew were allowed on shore on Saturday nights. They had a couple of good binges on poisonous red wine that made them deathly sick, then gave it up as a bad job. We hoped to get orders to load nitrate for home, but freights were low and instructions came to take in ballast and proceed to Portland, Oregon. We made the run of 4600 miles without incident, and were towed up the Columbia river for a distance of 100 miles by the large stern-wheeler tug *Harvest Queen*, which was lashed alongside on our quarter.

Portland was a gay town in those days, with a flourishing red-light district and hundreds of flash saloons. Crimps and boarding-house runners abounded, and our men, who had by now about eighteen months' pay due to them, were warned to watch their step. If they got drunk it was ten chances to one they would find themselves shanghaied on to some old hooker bound for God knows where, with a broken head, no clothes, and a couple of months' 'dead horse' to work off. We lay at the mills, a good way down the river, and discharged our ballast, then loaded a full cargo of flour. Captain Williams left us in Portland and joined one of the Company's larger ships, called the *Kate Thomas*, whose Captain had died. We were sorry to see him go, for he had taken a kindly interest in the crew. In his place we got the mate of the *Kate Thomas*, who now assumed the title of *Captain* Sager. In due course we sailed, bound for Queenstown for orders.

Three of our men had been shanghaied, and the only substitutes we could get were three miners who had never been to sea before. They were carried on board drunk, and the boarding master, having collected eighty dollars apiece blood-money from the Captain for what he described as three experienced ABs, put an armed guard on board till the tug-boat left, in case they should attempt to get away. Poor chaps, they had no fight in them for over a week, due to the drugs that had been administered, and could not be brought to believe that they were on a ship bound for Europe.

Captain Sager turned out to be a most generous man, with little of the old shell-back about him. It transpired that he intended leaving the sea at the end of the voyage, having inherited a sum of money sufficient to keep him in comfort for the rest of his days. With this fact in mind, he laid in stores at Portland with a lavish hand, regardless of the feelings of the owners when the bills were presented. It was lucky for us that he did so, as we took 152 days to reach Queenstown, a distance of approximately 16,000 miles.

The average 'lime-juicer' skipper would have bought three months' stores and MADE them spin out, blaming the weather – and the cook – for short rations. That is the reason why British sailing vessels were known all over the world as the hungriest ships afloat. We left Portland about the middle of June and positively dawdled south in light airs and fine weather. Sager was by way of being a great sportsman, and spent all his waking hours trying to catch something. He had a rifle, harpoon, grains, and several fishing-lines; and his bag during the trip consisted of sharks, porpoises, dolphin, albacore, bonito, turtle, albatross, mollyhawks, boobies, and Cape pigeons. He never killed the birds, but got endless amusement from watching them waddle awkwardly about the poop.

Drawing south of the Line we found ourselves in the vicinity of Pitcairn Island, so the Captain made for it, intent on getting a supply of fruit and vegetables. We arrived there one fine afternoon and lay-to about three miles off shore with the main yards backed. We could see coral growing on the bottom and feared shoal water, but, putting the lead over, found twenty-one fathoms. Four boats came off, bringing about thirty men and women with good loads of pumpkins, breadfruit, oranges, bananas, melons, coconuts, beans, sweet potatoes, and curios in the shape of coral branches, and empty coconut-shells decorated with painted flowers and the words 'Souvenir de Pitcairn'. One of the boats had brass name-plates on either bow bearing the word 'Victoria'. It had been presented to the islanders by the Queen many years before.

The natives were well-built, copper-skinned folk, and spoke both English and Kanaka. They all had long, splayed toes, the result of never wearing footgear; and many of them had a vacant far-away look in their eyes. The head man, an old fellow of about seventy, with a long white beard, carried a large book in which he asked the Captain to write some details of the ship and sign his name. It contained records going back over a hundred years. Several of the men and their wives were invited into the cabin for tea. They politely refused, however, but took away a few of the cook's rock cakes and probably regretted it later, for they did not belie *their name*. The men, despite their vacant looks, drove hard bargains and were keen to get clocks or watches, which they called 'time-pieces', as well as clothing and Bibles, in return for their baskets of mixed fruit and curios.

Having been away from home for so long, no one had much to barter, but sea-chests and bags were ransacked and everyone made some sort of a deal. The Captain secured a good general supply for the ship by the simple method of opening the after-hatch and handing out three bags of flour from the cargo. As for myself, I was practically stripped to a gant-line, having sold everything possible during the voyage in order to get money to go ashore. A thorough search revealed that the only saleable article I possessed was a Bible. This had been presented to me by my father at the beginning of my first voyage and was inscribed: 'To Jim from his Father on the occasion of his going to sea. October 1898.' I must confess that the Bible was by no means dog-eared. As I re-read the inscription, however, a feeling of home-sickness came over me, and I felt loath to part with what seemed like a link with home. But there was my tempter, quick to note my reluctance, adding a few oranges to his fascinating basket of fruit, and, finally, throwing in his *pièce de résistance*, a painted coconut-shell, and I succumbed. I comforted myself with the thought that, while he was marooned on a lonely island, and unable to help himself, I would soon be able to get another Bible, and, furthermore, the fruit was necessary to my health.

In later years this incident was recalled to my memory by hearing the following story. A young man starting out on a sea career was given a Bible by his sorrowing mother. 'Read it every day, John,' she implored; 'and on Sundays read my favourite portion, the eleventh chapter of Isaiah.' Promising faithfully to do so, he set sail. But he fell on evil days, deserted his ship, became a beachcomber and a ne'er-do-well, landed in gaol, wandered all over the world as a good-for-nothing hobo, contracted fever, and eventually, after five years' suffering and privation, arrived home a broken man. His mother, shocked and heart-broken, took him into her poor home and nursed him back to health with loving care. 'Did you read your Bible every day, John, as you promised?' she inquired. 'Yes, mother,' he replied. 'And during all my wanderings your Bible is the one thing I managed to keep by me. You'll find it in that small bundle of clothes I brought home.'

Eagerly she searched his miserable belongings and unearthed the precious Bible, opening it at her favourite chapter. There to her dismay she found the ten-pound note she had placed between the leaves five years ago, as a farewell gift that she could ill afford.

The islanders gave us a cheer as we made sail and stood south toward the dreaded Cape Horn. We struck a succession of easterly gales, and battered about that desolate region for nearly a month before getting the welcome order to steer north. The remainder of the trip was uneventful and we arrived at Queenstown on the 152nd day after leaving Portland.

Captain Sager went ashore and celebrated his arrival by going on a glorious binge. He could hardly be persuaded to come on board at the end of a week, when we were ordered to tow round to Dublin to discharge. On the way there, in a muddled state, he made up the crew's accounts of wages, and clean forgot to deduct the slop-chest money for items purchased by the men during the voyage. The sum amounted to about £80 and belonged to Captain Williams, who had handed over the slop-chest and bills to Sager in Portland, on the understanding that it would be refunded to him on the pay-off.

The crew, in festive mood under the influence of several pints of Dublin porter, accepted their money without question, especially as it appeared to be well on the right side, and cleared off to their homes – or elsewhere – before the mistake was discovered. Later on, I believe, Captain Williams recovered about half of it from men who lived in his neighbourhood, and Sager refunded the rest from his own pocket, so all was well. The ship lay for a month in Dublin with only the two mates and us three apprentices standing by. I was appointed cook, and, although it was a fairly easy job, I soon learned that it was a thankless one. The mates, after wolfing some of my most appetising dishes with gusto, would vow that I couldn't cook hot water for a barber's shop!

The cargo discharged, the *County of Pembroke* towed to Liverpool in ballast and the voyage of twenty-five months was over. I returned home a big hefty lad, with the love of the sea in my bones and no more thoughts about swallowing the anchor. I was to be the oldest apprentice next voyage. That was something to look forward to.

The pilot witnessed the departure of ships to every corner of the world, and guided them safely back into port. Here, the French four-masted barque *Fennia* drops the Mersey pilot prior to her last voyage. In February 1927 she encountered appalling weather round Cape Horn and was almost completely dismasted. She made Port Stanley in the Falkland Islands where she remained until being broken up in 1977.

3 Starvation

In the full-rigged ship *County of Cardigan* – Wages and articles – Graft – Sailortown in old-time Callao – The barque *Scarsdale* – The calaboose – Prisoners to clean streets – Ways and means – Iquique – Nitrate – Anisou – Starvation – Scurvy – The bum-boat at Queenstown.

ONE blazing afternoon the full-rigged ship *County of Cardigan* sailed into the roads at Callao, Peru, and dropped the mud hook. She had come from Newcastle, New South Wales, with 2000 tons of coal, and had been 110 days making the passage across the Pacific instead of the normal 60 or 70. The food was running short and the fo'c'sle hands were hungry and discontented. The after-guard, comprising the Captain, two mates, boatswain, sailmaker, carpenter, and steward, was just strong enough to keep the unruly elements in subjection.

The *County of Cardigan* had sailed from Liverpool some twenty months before this story opens. The crew, with one or two exceptions, had stuck by her and accumulated back wages to a considerable extent. In the beginning she was not a badly fed ship, when compared with the 'lime-juicers' of those last years of sail. The stores provided by the owners had long since been consumed, however, and the Captain was now doing the victualling. In the process he was cutting things down to the bone, and all aboard considered that he was lining his pockets as well. Moreover, he was a hypocritical old skinflint and had been heard to boast that he 'kept the Sabbath and everything else he could lay his hands on.'

After lying at anchor for four days, orders came for the ship to move alongside the coal wharf. This was good news, for everyone was longing for a run ashore, and it was feared that she might have to discharge in the roads, when such a delight would have been frowned upon. The sailors, hungry and discontented as they were, managed to raise a chanty as they hove round on the windlass capstan, the chanty men cheering their drooping spirits by inventing extempore verses about the lovely maidens and gallons of rum that awaited them in the fair town of Callao.

The anchor was broken out after an hour's hard labour, and with a couple of tugs fast ahead and astern the *County of Cardigan* was jockeyed alongside a berth at the coal wharf, not very far from the town. The sailors immediately fell in aft and requested the Captain to advance them some money to go ashore. As I have said, the men had good pay-days coming to them, but in those days there was a clause in the Articles of Agreement that no man had

The full-rigged ship *County of Cardigan*

any claim on his pay till the voyage was completed. It was the custom, however, when a ship was in port, to advance each man ten shillings on Saturday night, providing it was due to him.

The Captain had anticipated this request, but he had a shrewd idea that if he advanced them money on this particular night they would not be fit to start discharging coal in the morning. 'Send a couple of them down here as spokesmen,' he said to the mate; 'I'll fix 'em, the lazy loafers,' and he seated himself importantly in a chair at the head of the cabin table. Two men, a Britisher and a Swede, shuffled in and removed their caps. 'Well,' barked the Captain, 'what the hell do you want?' 'Ve thought,' replied the Swede, twisting his cap awkwardly before him, 've bin so long at sea, ve like to get some money to buy some tings.'

'Tings, eh?' mocked the skipper. 'You've been buying "tings," as you call 'em, in every port. Take ma advice and leave 'em alone. What have you got to say, Barnes?'

A truculent-looking character with an evil squint jumped in with both feet. 'We got money comin' to us, 'aven't we? We're not b——y convicts. We want our rights.'

'Oh! it's rights ye want?' roared the skipper. 'Rights! Let me remind you, Barnes, if you get your rights ye'll get no money, for the articles say ye're not entitled. But I'll no be hard on ye. After knock-off time on Saturday every man will get money – if ye behave yourselves. Mind that, now – *if ye behave yourselves*. I'll have no skulking. See to that, Mister Mate. The men that work hard will get money. Now get to hell out o' here, and let's have no more old buck.'

The mate hustled them out of the cabin and they went forward to tell the bad news, which was received with groans and curses. 'All the Old Man is thinking about is gettin' the coal discharged,' explained Barnes. 'I'm goin' ashore anyway. Whose comin'?' Only three of the younger men decided to accompany him, the other six able seamen preferring to wait for Saturday. These four ransacked their belongings to find something suitable for sale, and finally went ashore with a couple of old blankets and a few trifling curios, which they disposed of for five *pesos* in a near-by marine store. Armed with this they went to a low-down café, hoping to be able to join in whatever fun might be going. After a couple of rounds of drinks they were broke again, but the wily proprietor, with an eye to securing their custom on Saturday night, stood them another drink, then they returned on board feeling that they had made a good connection for future festivities.

Next morning all hands were called at five-thirty, and at six o'clock the second mate came forward and ordered 'turn-to'. The main hatch was stripped of its tarpaulins, and with the aid of a crane and large iron tubs, holding one ton each, they started discharging the coal. It was gruelling work digging down into the main hatch. The tub was landed in the centre, and eight men distributed themselves round, gradually filling it, either by lifting in large lumps by hand or scrabbling around with their very inadequate shovels.

Eight o'clock brought a welcome three-quarters of an hour spell for breakfast. This consisted of rank coffee, hard biscuits, and a few lumps of fried gristle, which the cook

Discharging coal by dolly winch on the west coast of South America.
This was gruelling work under the tropical sun of the 'flaming coast'.

optimistically called beef. Work then proceeded till noon, when a halt was called for dinner. This was the big meal of the day. Watery soup, boiled bullock-meat, and a few sweet potatoes. At one o'clock they turned to again, and worked till six, with a ten-minute break at four o'clock for a 'smoke'. With the stifling heat, the clouds of coal-dust, the unaccustomed job of shovelling, and the furious driving of the second mate and boatswain, the men were almost dead at the end of the day, and after swallowing a tasty repast similar to that which had been served for breakfast they washed some of the dust from their faces and turned in.

The next day was a Saturday, and work finished at one o'clock, by which time the men had burrowed down to the 'tween decks and were able to slide their shovels under the coal, making the work slightly easier, although the dust was more concentrated in the confined space. In the afternoon all hands were mustered aft to get their weekly money, the mate having reported favourably on their work. The Captain, attired in his one and only shore suit of heavy, rough tweed, worn with a pink shirt and a brilliant tartan tie, sat at the head of the cabin table grasping in his hand a canvas bag full of *pesos*. He paid the petty officers and apprentices, then the ten able seamen filed in. Casting a baleful eye over the tattered bunch he addressed them as follows: 'The mate tells me ye've wor-r-ked fair to middlin' so I'm going to let you have some money. But mind this. Any man that's no here for work on Monday morning will get no money next week. Sign here.'

Each man received five *pesos* and signed his name on a sheet of paper, under the direction of Mack, the steward, who was acting as Captain's clerk and being very officious about it. Two of them couldn't write, so Mack inserted their names, which they each attested by a shaky cross. Having got their money the men hung about the cabin door whispering together.

'What's the matter noo?' shouted the Captain angrily. 'D'ye think the money's no good? Out with it, if you've got anything to say.'

An elderly seaman named Price was pushed forward. 'Well, sir,' he began, 'we were wondering if you'd let us have a tailor. We're all in rags and want some clothes.'

'Oh! it's a tailor ye want,' said the Captain, adopting a knowing look. 'A tailor! What's the matter with using some o' they five *pesos* to buy clothes, eh?'

'Well, sir,' replied Price, appealing to the others for support, 'there's lots of other things we want as well.'

'I know,' said the Captain, wagging an enormous forefinger at them. 'I know fine what ye mean by that. Tak' my advice and be careful. Ye're in a heathen country noo, an' ye'll maybe get more'n ye bargain for. I'll consider the matter during the week. Now get away oot o' here and behave yourselves.'

They went away chuckling together like schoolboys at the prospect of having gained a point. But the Captain was chuckling too. He would arrange with some rascally slop-chest merchant in Callao to allow the men to spend thirty shillings each, and in settling the bills he would get a good commission. Whatever the men bought would be held by the merchant, and delivered on board in parcels just before the ship sailed, so that in the event of a man deserting, the skipper would still have the goods. The men, of course, would make a bargain too. They would probably buy no goods at all and get one pound cash in return for thirty shillings of their pay. But with the old-time shell-back it was a case of 'Come day, go day, God send Sunday'; and as long as they could get money to squander they cared little what it cost them.

That night all hands went ashore intent on an orgy of wine, women, and song. On the way they met some of the crew of the barque *Scarsdale*, who assured them, from past experience, that THE place to obtain such commodities at the cheapest possible price was 'Liverpool Joe's', and they accordingly led the way to that delectable haunt. It stood on that notorious street, the Calle Pura, in the heart of the sailortown of old-time Callao, and proclaimed itself to the world by means of a large slat of dunnage-wood stuck over the door, on which the boss himself had painted the words: 'LIVERPOOL JOES. WELCUM'.

Bursting in like a gusty breeze from the ocean, the men found themselves in a large square room, dimly lit by a few gas-jets enclosed in wire cages. An expanse of rickety wood-flooring was cleared for dancing in the centre, and was surrounded by a number of spidery tables and chairs, at which several highly decorated Peruvian *señoritas* were seated like gaily plumaged birds of prey.

Across the far end of the room ran a metal-covered bar, behind which stood Joe himself, with a cunning smile of welcome on his wasted features. He was a Liverpool man who, in his youth, had been a wind-bag sailor. He had drifted in, much as his customers had done to-night, fallen in love with the daughter of the house, married her, and eventually succeeded to the business. It was better than going to sea.

The crew of the *Ladye Doris*, the steel full-rigged ship, after discharging coal at Iquique.

His wife, now prematurely aged, fat, and podgy, sat behind the bar, raking in the meagre cash and keeping an eye on the bottles. 'Come in, boys,' called Joe. 'Come in and have a good time. What ship?' They clustered round the bar, and Joe engaged them in a spirited line of sailor-talk as he dispensed the drinks. They began to feel at home. After a couple of snorts of *pisco* all round, Joe started the automatic piano. Very soon the *señoritas* were whirled into a dance and all was merry and bright. Towards midnight some of the older hands decided to return on board. The money was running low, and they had visions of coming ashore on future nights for a quiet drink after working hours. Barnes and his three associates, now very well-oiled, scorned the idea of going on board. 'Come on, lads,' he shouted thickly, 'let's go to the place we were in on Thursday night and have some fun. To hell with the ship!'

They lurched down the ill-paved street, singing lustily, a proceeding which attracted the attention of the police, and after wandering aimlessly through several back alleys they found the dive, which was known as the *Alcazar*. Staggering in, they reeled up to the bar and greeted the proprietor with great good humour. 'Hello, me old ropeyarn,' began Slim, a lanky Australian, 'let's have a bottle o' *vinto, pronto.*'

'Ah-h-h-h!' roared the proprietor, 'you wanta da vino, eh? To-night you go to Liverpool Joe and spend all a da money; now you coma here with no money and wanta da vino,' and with that he brought a huge brown fist down on the bar in a menacing manner.

''Oo said we ain't got no money?' yelled Green, a brawny Irishman. 'Sure we got lashin's of it. 'Ere, boys, let's 'ave a tarpaulin muster an' we'll buy the b——y place.'

Fumblingly they searched all their pockets, and succeeded in mustering something less than a *peso*.

'We bin robbed,' wailed Gill, a rat-faced Cockney from down Limehouse way. 'We bin robbed by some o' these perishin' dagoes – blarst their ugly mugs!'

'Wat you say?' bellowed the proprietor, producing a murderous-looking black-jack from under the counter, as a crowd from the tables surged up to the bar.

'We dagoes, eh? You call us dagoes?'

'Yes!' roared Barnes. 'A lot o' lousy, rot-gutted dag——'

Before he could finish, the black-jack came down with a thwack on top of his head and he bit the sawdust with a moan. Like a flash the place was in an uproar. Slim, Green, and Gill attempted to put up a fight, but they were borne under by superior numbers, and a few minutes later the police rushed in and dragged them off to the calaboose. Here they were flung into a stinking cell, with a dozen other drunks, and were soon snoring soundly.

At six o'clock the following morning the prison bell clanged loudly, and Gill woke up with a start, to hear cell doors being thrown open with a clatter. ''Ere,' he shouted, giving his three mates a shake, 'they're goin' to chuck us art'.

'Where the 'ell are we?' groaned Barnes, sitting up and rubbing a hefty lump on his aching head.

'We're in the calaboose, an' it's Sunday mornin',' said Gill.

'In the calaboose, are we? Then that's torn it,' announced Barnes, who had previous experience. 'We don't get out o' here till we've done some work, believe me.'

'Work!' snorted Green, passing his hand over a badly swollen jaw. 'They'll get no work out o' me. I'll see 'm in hell first. I'm goin' to 'ave another sleep.'

A few seconds later a well-directed stream of water from a fire hose drove them into the prison courtyard, and Slim and Green, being loudest in their protests, were pounced on by half a dozen muscular warders and secured by the wrists to a bar running over the top of a treadmill. A dozen other prisoners were fastened in the same manner, then the mill was released and commenced to revolve, its function being to pump water from a well up to a row of supply tanks on the roof. Green's theory about doing no work very soon collapsed. It was a case of keep on treading, or hanging by the wrists and having one's ankles pounded by the wooden steps. He tried both methods and decided that to keep on treading was the least painful.

Barnes and Gill suffered a worse indignity. They were fastened by the ankles with a long length of small chain to the stern of a garbage-waggon, drawn by a mule, and sent forth with broom and shovel to do a bit of street-cleaning. If they showed any sign of slacking, the mule was put to a jog-trot for a while, and they either had to run or be dragged along the street feet first. They cleaned the Calle Pura and several back alleys, working miserably past Liverpool Joe's and the Alcazar, the occupants of which were now apparently sleeping soundly in their beds. Towards 10 AM their labours led them near the dock gates, when who should happen along but the Captain and mate of the *County of Cardigan*, out for a morning stroll. Catching sight of his men, the Captain stopped, and pointing to them with a huge, knobbly walking-stick, remarked good-humouredly to the mate: 'Well, if that does'na beat cock-fightin'. They canna find enough wor-r-k to dae on the ship, so they come oot to wor-r-k for the police. A queer bunch, and no mistake.' And off they strolled in comfortable fashion.

By noon the men had returned to the calaboose and were mercifully released. Footsore and weary, bruised and battered, crestfallen and famished, they staggered on board, and, having wolfed every scrap of food they could find, threw themselves into their bunks till the following morning.

Remembering the Captain's words about money, they all turned to at 6 AM, and, having acquired a coating of coal-dust over their black eyes and other abrasions, they felt better able to face their shipmates. Towards the end of the week the main hatch was cleared of coal and they began to load 700 tons of stone ballast for the run down to Iquique.

Having no money, and nothing to sell, the men were forced to spend several evenings at the Seamen's Mission, but in due course Saturday came round again, and the Captain, after delivering a heavily sarcastic lecture on good behaviour, allowed them another five *pesos* each. Slim and Green had heard about a Chinese gambling saloon in the town where they had a good chance of 'doubling their money'. Barnes and Gill were rather dubious, but agreed to accompany them and ''ave a go at it'.

They managed to squeeze into this filthy den, which was crowded with a cut-throat-looking mob. After some jostling they got near enough to a roulette-table to place their stakes, when Gill discovered that his pocket had been picked. He started to raise a rumpus and was promptly thrown into the street by two burly chuckers-out. Here he was joined ten minutes later by the other three, who had been reduced to one *peso* between them. Cursing their luck, they retired to a small dive, spent the *peso* on drinks, and returned to the ship. There was nothing for it except the Mission again, but on the following Wednesday – the ship being due to sail on Saturday – the Captain announced that each man would be allowed to purchase goods up to the value of ten *pesos* at Pedro's, the tailor. He would settle the bills, and the goods would be sent on board and distributed by him, AFTER the ship sailed.

This was hailed as exceptionally good news, and the forecastle decided that the 'old man' was not such a bad sort after all. That evening all hands invaded Pedro's store. Some purchased very inferior goods at very inflated prices and others demanded cash. At this Pedro threw up his expressive hands in dismay.

'No, no,' he cried. '*Capitan* he tell me no give cash. Men must buy clothes, 'e say. No can give cash.'

'Oh, come off it!' roared Barnes. 'You and our old man 'ave it all worked out. 'Ow much cash will you give?'

'Me very poor man,' wailed Pedro. 'Suppose I give cash, *Capitan* 'e no pay me. What I do? What I do?'

'I'll tell you what to do,' shouted Slim, chasing Pedro to cover behind his counter. 'Cut out the snivelling and say 'ow much you'll give'.

'No can give more than five *pesos*,' said Pedro, in a hoarse whisper. '*Capitan* he kill me.'

'A b——y good job if 'e did, you lousy old skinflint,' said Barnes. 'Five *pesos* for ten! Generous old swine, ain't you? What you say, boys? Shall we take it?'

After much lurid discussion four of them signed on the dotted line and took the money. Then, having consigned Pedro and his store to every possible disaster and misfortune they could think of, they ambled off to Liverpool Joe's for a spree. Joe wasn't expecting any cash customers on a Wednesday night, but he soon got in some *señoritas* and started the piano going, so making sure they didn't get away till their money was exhausted. They returned on board about midnight, half-seas-over, perfectly happy, and broke again.

On Friday evening the last of the coal was discharged. The ship was towed out of Callao on the following morning and sail was set for Iquique, a run of about 600 miles down the coast. After leaving port the Captain distributed the parcels of clothing with the air of a man presenting Christmas parcels to orphans, but there was a grim smirk on his face as he hid away fifty *pesos*, representing his commission on the deal with Pedro.

After a fine-weather passage of nine days the *County of Cardigan* sailed into the open roadstead of Iquique and dropped anchor. Here she was to load saltpetre in bags and proceed to Queenstown for orders. The saltpetre came off in lighters, holding about a hundred tons each, and was hove on board, one bag at a time, by means of a hand-winch worked by four men, with a fifth as relief. There were a dozen ships loading, so work proceeded slowly and, during the long spells between the departure and arrival of lighters, opportunity was taken to heave up the stone ballast and dump it overboard.

Toiling under a blazing sun from 6 AM to 6 PM daily, with poor food and no opportunity of shore leave, the men grew surly and quarrelsome, and the mates had to do some hard

This well-known photograph of Iquique shows sailing ships loading nitrates. Some of them, only part loaded, are well out of trim.

driving to keep them in hand. The Captain sized up the situation and purchased a quantity of cheap firewater known as *anisou*. The men got a tot of this at 11 AM and another at 4 PM on working days, and their spirits revived somewhat.

Two or three times a week the Captain would be rowed ashore, a distance of about two miles, in the gig, with the four apprentices at the oars, to return a few hours later with a supply of provisions consisting of pumpkins, sweet potatoes, wild honey, and horrible-looking lumps of fresh beef. He took care to let it be generally known on board that such things were terribly scarce and it was only by tremendous exertions on his part that he was able to have the best-fed ship in the port. He and Mack, the steward, made a great parade of taking stock of the ship's stores to make sure that she would not run short on the way home. 'It'll be fine weather off the Hor-r-n at this time o' the year. We ought to make Queenstown in a hundred days,' he decided. After five weeks in the burning heat of Iquique the ship finished loading, and the men eagerly hove round the windlass capstan to the tune of the fine old chanty: *Rolling Home! Rolling Home! Rolling Home to Merry England!*

The ship made a good passage down to the latitude of Cape Horn, then the Captain's predictions about fine weather fell to pieces, and for three whole weeks it blew a succession of violent easterly gales that drove them away to the westward. During this period the starboard lifeboat and the Captain's gig, of which he was extremely proud, were reduced to matchwood by a heavy sea; and a harness cask containing about three weeks' supply of salt beef was washed overboard from the poop. Eventually the easterly gales blew themselves out, the wind drew round to the south-west, and the ship began to make up some of the lost distance. Exactly two months to the day after leaving Iquique observations placed the vessel well to the westward of Cape Horn, and the welcome order was given to 'square away' and run to the north-east. After weeks of exposure to icy gales, constantly sleeping in wet clothing and with oilskins worn to tatters, the crew were showing signs of exhaustion, but now they were cheered by the prospect of running up into fine, warm weather, and having rounded the dreaded Cape, they felt that at long last they were on the final leg of the homeward voyage, although there was still about 7000 miles of sea to cover.

After making good progress for several days, however, the wind suddenly chopped round to the north-east again and came on to blow hard, with mountainous seas. Head-reaching under close-reefed foresail and topsails, the Captain spared neither himself nor his crew in desperate efforts to avoid losing ground, but, despite it all, during the next two weeks the ship was driven back to the latitude of the Cape. Things were beginning to look serious and, having taken stock of the rapidly dwindling provisions, the Captain was on the point of deciding to run for the Falkland Islands when the wind came fair again and he carried on.

This time the ship got a good slant and ran right into the south-east trades, which carried her up to the vicinity of the Equator. Now one hundred days out, the crew were living on less than half-rations, which was barely enough to keep body and soul together. It was three months since anyone had eaten fresh meat or vegetables, and salt food makes the blood thin.

The ship was in the doldrums, a region of calms, light baffling winds, and sudden bursts of tropical rain. Anxious to get out of this sweltering, lifeless area, the Captain had the men hauling the yards round day and night in an endeavour to profit by every breath of wind. No sooner would she be braced up on one tack than the wind would fly round to another quarter and the work had to be done all over again. Or it would fall calm and the sails had to be brailed up to prevent them slatting to ribbons as she rolled about in the confused swells. Everyone was weak and tempers were frayed. Green, voicing an angry protest, was knocked down by the mate. His head struck a ringbolt and he lay in his bunk unconscious for two days. The boatswain and his cronies were at loggerheads, and the apprentices fought among themselves like cats. The Captain and steward quarrelled constantly, each blaming the other for the lack of food, and throwing some of the onus on the cook by accusing him of waste. Their heated words in unguarded moments, about faked bills for provisions and unequal division of the spoils, reached the mate's ears, and he began to realise that it was the Captain's meanness and rapacity that had led them into this terrible state.

One day the hands fell in aft and demanded to see the Captain, who, in a foul temper, met them at the brake of the poop. 'What's the trouble now?' he rasped. Hardy, the oldest of the seamen, stepped forward as spokesman. 'We want you to put in somewhere and get some food. We can't go on like this much longer. We're breaking out in boils, and soon we won't be able to work the ship.'

Deciding to take a high hand, the Captain roared back: 'So ye're dictating tae me what I shall do wi' the ship, eh? Ye weak-kneed, miserable bunch o' hoboes. You're getting the same food as I am, an' I'm no complainin'.' At the sight of their pinched faces, however, he softened a little. 'God Almighty sent the weather, and stores'll no last for ever. Its bad luck on all of us.'

There were some dozen Chilean nitrate ports. This is the anchorage at Pisagua just north of Iquique, and shows well the barren coast where the Andes mountains meet the sea.

'Yes,' assented the mate. Not because he agreed, but he could realise a very particular need for discipline at this juncture. 'We've got to work the ship home,' he added. 'It's the only way out.'

'Ye're absolutely right,' said the Captain; 'but some of these amateur navigators think they know all about it. I tell ye, men, there's no port we can go to that's any better or nearer than Queenstown. If we fall in wi' a ship I'll get some provisions, never fear. Get the lifeboat ready against we do. That's all I have to say. Now get away forrard and leave the handlin' o' the ship to them that knows best about it.'

After the men had shambled forward, the Captain warned the mate to go easy with unnecessary work and to reserve the men's strength for handling sail.

A few days later they hit the north-east trades and began to make good progress. Being a steady wind, all hands were able to get sound sleep and rest under dry conditions. Meantime the grub was running very low, however. Tea, coffee, butter, sugar, and flour ran out, and everyone lived on hard biscuits, pea-soup, and quarter-rations of salt beef and pork. The Captain rummaged through the cabin lockers and produced a few tins of sardines, salmon, and beans. He gave them out fairly, but they only served to whet the men's appetites for a good square meal.

The trades died away about thirty-five degrees north of the Equator and a fair wind sprang up, which carried them towards the Azores. One day the ship fell in with a Swedish barque and signalled for provisions, only to find that she was in the same state of semi-starvation and had nothing to spare. Tightening up their belts, the men hung over the rails, searching the horizon for the sight of a steamer. Their eyes had sunk into their heads and their bodies were as thin as rails. Several days of calm weather prevailed, and the Captain, reduced to a shadow of his former self, began to ponder over the idea of making for Fayal. The salt beef and pork ran out completely, and they were now living on pea-soup and biscuits, of which there was still a fairly good supply. Fortunately there was also plenty of water, an empty tank having been filled by the rain in the doldrums.

The men now started to eat slush. This was the fat skimmed off boiling salt beef and pork. It had been collected in two casks during the voyage and was used for mixing with tar and for greasing down the masts. Biscuits soaked in water and fried in this made a sickly, horrible meal, but it was better than nothing. The Captain tried to prevent them using it by saying that they would get boils, and possibly scurvy, but finding that the mates and petty officers were eating it too he desisted, alarmed by their fierce resentment.

At last a strong southerly wind sprang up. It put Fayal out of the question, but it was fair for Queenstown, and with every stitch of canvas set, the course for Southern Ireland was continued.

Two days later smoke was reported right ahead. The Captain was all excitement. 'Run up a signal,' he ordered, 'an' call all hands.' The second mate consulted the signal-book and hoisted the flags N.V., meaning: 'Short of provisions. Starving.'

A few minutes later the mate appeared on the poop. 'Get the boat swung out,' shouted the skipper. 'All hands on the job. There's a steamer comin' along. We'll get some grub.'

The mate went forward to rout out the watch below and came back to report two men sick.

'Sick!' ejaculated the Captain. 'The lazy loafers. An' a steamer in sight. A fine time to go sick. What's the matter wi' them?'

'Scurvy, I think,' said the mate. 'They look pretty bad.'

'Scurvy, eh? They've been eatin' that slush, that's what's the matter. I warned the lot o' ye aboot it, didn't I? Here! What flags have we got flying?' He had glanced aloft and seen the two flags indicating an urgent signal. The second mate told him their meaning.

'God Almighty!' he cried, rapidly thumbing over the signal-book. 'D'ye want yon steamer to report us as starvin'? What would the owners think o' that? Put up U.A.K., meanin': "Can you spare me some provisions?" Ma God, I have to think of everything. Stand by the braces to back the main yards.'

The steamer drew close, flying the signal to send a boat. She proved to be a Spaniard, called the *Toledo*, a small ocean tramp, sea-scarred and rusty. The yards were backed and the *County of Cardigan* came to rest with the *Toledo* a quarter of a mile to leeward. 'Into the boat,' shouted the Captain to the second mate. 'Take six men and a boy with ye and bring back all ye can get – includin' a bit o' tobacco if they have it, but I never knew a Spaniard yet who smoked good tobacco.'

The boat was lowered, and at once started leaking so badly that a couple of buckets and another boy were hastily shipped to assist with the baling. She shoved off, and in a few minutes had disappeared round the stern of the *Toledo*.

There was a short pause; then the *Toledo*'s propeller began thrashing the water, and the tramp gradually drew away, revealing the boat pulling back to the ship. 'She's very deep,' remarked the Captain; 'must have a good load by the look o' her.' But the good load proved to be mostly water, which the two apprentices were baling overboard as if their lives depended on it. She drew alongside and passed up ten pieces of salt beef (about thirty pounds), a small bag of potatoes and onions, a five-pound box of dried raisins, and six packets of Spanish cigarettes.

'That's all they had to spare,' explained the second mate as he clambered on board. 'And her skipper says he'll send the bill to our owners when he gets to St John's.'

'Aye,' replied the Captain slowly, staring ruefully at the small collection of stores. 'He'll send the bill in all right, and charge sea-prices too, the auld scoundrel. I know these foreigners. Get the boat hoisted.' And he shepherded the steward and the cook aft with the precious foodstuffs.

With infinite labour the boat was cleared of water and got on to the skids without damage. Then the Captain sent for the mate. 'Now look here,' he said, 'when ye get the yards trimmed, and the ship on her coorse, bring the sick men aft to the spare cabin. Who are they, by the way?'

'It's old Price and the Swede,' answered the mate. 'They say they've had scurvy before, and that leaves them more open to it.'

'Aye, that's so,' agreed the Captain. 'Bring them aft an' I'll doctor them accordin' to the *Medical Guide* an' we'll keep a small stock o' these potatoes and onions for them, an' they can have a double whack o' lime-juice. It's running mighty short, but they can have mine. An' here, gi' these filthy cigarettes oot to the crew. Tobacco, they Spaniards call it! More like rope yarns.'

The mate went away, and returned shortly with Price and the Swede, who were put to bed. They were pale and sallow and complained of sore mouths and leg swellings.

'We'll have ye as right as trivets in no time,' said the Captain; 'but, in the meantime, ye'll get no more o' that slush.'

That evening every man got a boiled potato and an onion for supper, with the promise of some salt beef the next day, after it had been boiled in the pea-soup. The cook, who had been idle for several weeks, except for making the soup, which was nothing but split peas and water, now got busy putting the beef in pickle and setting a piece to soak for next day. He also concocted a marvellous plum-duff of soaked biscuits and raisins – which looked like a football, and tasted worse.

The Captain estimated that under normal conditions they would make Queenstown in eight days, and the salt beef was to be given out at two ounces each man a day, to last that time. The potatoes and onions, except the stock for the invalids, lasted only three days. Head winds and calms upset these calculations, and it was not until the morning of the fifteenth day after sighting the steamer that the *County of Cardigan* finally anchored in Queenstown Harbour, having been 162 days on the voyage from Iquique. By this time both officers and men were like skeletons. Everyone was suffering from painful boils and possessed scarcely enough strength left to go aloft and furl the sails. Strangely, the sick men were, however, rapidly recovering.

Queenstown (now Cobh) harbour on the south coast of Ireland. Before the age of the ship's radio,
Queenstown and Falmouth were important orders ports.

As the mud hook plunged to the bottom the bum-boat sheered alongside. It was the usual thing for ships to arrive short of provisions, and the proprietor of the marine equivalent of the coffee-stall had brought off a plentiful supply.

'The top o' the morning to yez, Captain!' he shouted. 'You'll be lettin' the men have a bum-boat to-day, and thim so hungry?'

'Aye,' replied the skipper, raising his voice so that he could be heard along the decks. 'Let every man and boy have a loaf of bread, a half-pound o' butter, and a pot o' jam at my expense. After that they can spend up to a pound a man, and five shillings to the boys, while the ship lies here.'

As he concluded these words he indulged in a prodigious wink, which the bum-boat proprietor rightly interpreted as meaning 'commission as usual'.

Within five minutes the food as ordered by the Captain was distributed, and, in addition, a tempting display of eatables for sale was laid out on the main hatch. There were crusty loaves, sausage-rolls, pork pies, slices of bacon, eggs, various kinds of jam and tinned stuffs. It seemed almost too good to be true. That evening, despite the fact that they had been stuffing themselves all day from the bum-boat, the men sat down to a mighty dinner, and turned in feeling at peace with the world. The *County of Cardigan* waited eight days at Queenstown for orders and then proceeded in tow to Liverpool.

4 The 'Leicester Castle' Affair

The *Leicester Castle* arrives – Stories of mutiny – Shipping criminals as sailors at 'Frisco
in 1902 – Blood-money – Fire-arms in British ships – The 'dead horse' – Flying-fish days
– Pitcairn Island – The night of tragedy – Murder – Mutineers leave on a raft –
Investigation by HMS *Shearwater* – A mystery of the Pacific.

ON the 5th December 1902 a large square-rigged ship arrived at Queenstown, from San Francisco, with such an amazing story of murder and attempted piracy on the high seas that the local residents crowded down to the waterfront to gaze at her as she lay serenely at anchor in the harbour. And this notwithstanding the fact that they were accustomed to the sight of sailing ships, big and small, hungry and otherwise, Queenstown being one of the two famous ports (Falmouth was the other) at which homeward-bound sailing vessels called for orders.

This particular craft was the Liverpool three-masted, full-rigged ship *Leicester Castle*, of 2000 tons register. Hardly was her anchor on the bottom and the canvas furled before a rumour spread through the town that her Captain carried four bullets in his body as the result of a murderous attack upon him; that the bullets had been in him for several weeks, and he had carried on like that while bringing the ship home.

A crowd of idlers gathered to watch him come ashore, but promptly dispersed when he sprang nimbly from the agent's launch, looking the picture of robust health. Trudging homeward in the drizzling rain, these people declared one to another that the man who had spread the rumour was a liar. But they were wrong. Captain D Peattie, of Paisley, Scotland, *was* carrying four bullets in his body, and they had been there for 94 days!

That, however, was not the only amazing feature in the altogether amazing story which this Liverpool ship had to tell. The singularly brutal and unprovoked nature of the attack upon the shipmaster, and the killing of one of his officers, was another. Then there was the desperate and almost hopeless means of escape adopted by the assailants, and their motive. For a whole week the story became the one absorbing topic of conversation among the

EDITOR'S NOTE
In the following four chapters Captain R Barry O'Brien describes, in the words of the principal participants: A mutiny in the full-rigged ship *Leicester Castle*; Life aboard the hell ship *Star of Russia*; The tragic voyage of the barque *Veronica*; and, A Shipwreck to Remember.

A harbour-side scene at San Francisco.

people of Queenstown; and the theories advanced for the crime were remarkable for their diversity.

The series of happenings – so remarkable for the twentieth century – began in July 1902. The *Leicester Castle* was at 'Frisco. It was a good period for shipping. Cargoes were plentiful and freights were high. The ship had just completed loading a cargo of wheat and was lying at anchor in the bay, with sails bent, hatches battened down, and everything else ready for sea.

She needed, however, fourteen hands to complete her complement of twenty-eight all told. Here was the difficulty, for conditions ashore were even more prosperous than at sea, and this had resulted in a shortage of sailors. For days Captain Peattie had haunted the British Consulate and the shipping offices, hoping to pick up the men. But he had no luck in the one or the other place, and was obliged in the end to seek the aid of the boarding-house masters, who held a monopoly of sea-going labour and could always be relied on to find a crew of sorts for any vessel.

One of these rascals did the trick, and on 25th July everyone on board the *Leicester Castle* was delighted to see a launch come alongside with the rest of the crew. This boarding-house keeper of old-time San Francisco was undoubtedly a rascal, as were the rest of his kind, but he must have had some decent streak in him, unless it was merely to guard himself against possible unpleasant consequences, for on coming aboard he went straight aft to the saloon and warned Captain Peattie about one of the new men.

'I ain't sayin' he'll make any trouble, Cap,' he explained. 'He's been quiet enough all the time he's been at my place. But he carries a gun. I thought I'd better tell you that.'

'Thanks,' replied Captain Peattie. 'Is there anything else about the fellow which you feel you ought to tell me?'

The boarding-house master shook his head, and the Captain told the mate to muster the fourteen men aft.

Eleven of them produced satisfactory discharges, and were obviously seamen. But the remainder had no papers of any kind, and little more in the way of clothing than what they stood up in. The man about whom the Captain was warned was one of these three. His name was Hobbs, he said, and he hailed from Illinois. Thirty to thirty-five years of age, he was a thick-set, muscular man, with dark, evasive eyes and a rather sinister face. The other two men were also Americans. One gave the name of Sears, the other of Turner. Sears said he hailed from Idaho, Turner claimed Oregon as his birthplace. Sears was a pleasant-looking young fellow of about twenty-two. Turner, in countenance and demeanour, was more in keeping with Hobbs.

'You three fellows may be sailors, but you don't look it,' Captain Peattie remarked dryly, running his eyes over the group. 'Let's have the truth,' he added. 'Have any of you ever been to sea before?'

'Sure,' replied Hobbs, scowling. Sears and Turner nodded, but said nothing. A few questions were put to the three men, and they answered them fairly well. Captain Peattie, however, was not satisfied.

Leading the boarding-house master to one side, away from the men's hearing, he said: 'You'd better take these three Americans back ashore, and bring me off three proper sailors in their place. To me they look like cow-punchers, and we've no use for men of that type.'

The wily citizen of the waterfront shifted his big cigar from one corner of his mouth to the other.

'Say, Cap, this ain't London or Liverpool,' he remonstrated. 'It's 'Frisco, where gen-u-in-e sailormen are about as scarce as them gold nuggets you Britishers think our side-walks are paved with.'

Captain Peattie smiled sarcastically. 'If I held a ten-dollar bill under your nose you'd manage to do what I ask, no doubt,' he said.

'You're ab-so-lute-ly wrong, sir,' replied the American, shaking his head emphatically. 'Just now there ain't another honest-to-goodness sailorman in the port. You've got the lot. Really, Cap, you 'aven't got much kick comin'. Aboard the last hooker to sail from here there wasn't a single man who knew how to steer, or splice.'

As the result of his own fruitless search Captain Peattie realised that there was probably a good deal of truth in what the boarding-house master said. He nodded. 'All right, I'll make the best of them,' he answered. And with that he dismissed the new men, and led the way below.

A few minutes later, having received his written authority to collect 280 dollars from the agent on the ship's account – 20 dollars for each man – the boarding-house master departed. Captain Peattie returned on deck, and at once sent for Hobbs.

'I understand you've got a revolver in your possession?' he said, without any preliminaries. 'You must hand it over into my custody.'

The man cast an angry glance towards the launch, chugging its way shoreward; then slowly brought his eyes back to the Captain's face.

'It belongs to me, doesn't it?' he replied sullenly.

'No matter,' said Captain Peattie. 'Aboard this, or any other British ship, members of the crew are not allowed to carry fire-arms. You must hand over your revolver. I'll give it back to you at the end of the voyage.'

Hobbs hesitated for a few seconds; then, with a shrug, pulled out of his pocket a big Colt, which he handed to the Captain. He was about to walk away, but the latter halted him.

'I take it you've got some ammunition as well?' Captain Peattie asked.

Open the breech and you'll find it,' retorted the man insolently.

Captain Peattie kept his temper, but pin-points of fire glowed in his eyes. 'I'm referring to the rest of the ammunition,' he snapped, and there was a steely ring in his voice.

'I haven't got any more, sir,' replied Hobbs, in a more civil tone.

'Are you sure of that?'

The man nodded, and Captain Peattie told him he might return forward.

A less diplomatic shipmaster might have insisted upon searching the man's clothing and effects, but the *Leicester Castle*'s Captain did not see any point in making a mountain out of a molehill. After all, ammunition by itself wasn't much use to anyone. He had the revolver, which was the principal thing. Going down to his cabin he locked this up among the rest of his fire-arms, and with that he considered the incident closed. The new men were signed on later in the day, and on 26th July the vessel sailed.

The first month of the homeward passage passed off uneventfully. Fine weather was picked up after leaving port, and was carried down into the north-east trades. The *Leicester Castle* made no pretence of being a clipper, but she was a well-found, well-fed, and thoroughly comfortable ship. She had been afloat for twenty years, and among seamen was known as a 'happy ship'. During the time he had been in command Captain Peattie had always made a point of keeping her as such. Unnecessary 'work-up' jobs were strictly discouraged, and in no circumstances would he allow his officers to haze the men. I mention this to show that what subsequently happened was in no way the result of ill-treatment of the crew.

The captain's cabin in the four-masted barque *Lynton*. Captain E Gates-James and his wife pose for the photographer in San Francisco around 1900. There was a world of difference between the captain's quarters and those of his crew in the fo'cs'le.

A month out from port the Line was crossed. Everyone had thoroughly settled down to shipboard routine by then. The 'Frisco days were forgotten; those who had been shipped there had worked off the 'dead horse' (the month's advance-pay they had been obliged to sign away to the boarding-house master for their board and keep), and were now once more working for themselves.

After being in the doldrums for only two or three days the ship picked up the south-east trades. Fine, leisurely days followed as, with yards braced up for the port tack, she stood down into the South Pacific. Model and coir-mat making began in earnest. Those who had no particular hobbies indulged in sing-songs during the dog-watch. One man had a mandolin, another a concertina, a third a mouth-organ, and between them they put up some pretty good orchestral efforts. Taken as a whole, the ship's company appears to have been an exceptionally happy lot during those lazy 'flying-fish days'.

There were three notable exceptions, however. Neither Hobbs, Turner, nor Sears ever took part in the other men's amusements. They kept strictly to themselves, and were not very popular in consequence. Nevertheless, they did their work well enough, so the after-guard had no fault to find with them.

As the voyage progressed it became more and more evident, by his increasingly morose demeanour, that Hobbs had something on his mind. Only on one occasion, however, did he actually betray any particular concern about anything. That was on 2nd September. The ship was approximately in latitude 20 degrees south, longitude 130 degrees west – roughly 300 miles north of Pitcairn Island, and much the same distance, north-eastward, from the Gambier Islands and the Maratea Group, belonging to the Low Archipelago.

While at the wheel that afternoon one of the sailors had asked the officer of the watch whether they were likely to sight any of these islands, it always being a source of interest during a long voyage to get a glimpse of *terra firma*.

The officer in reply had said that, if the wind remained easterly, they might sight Pitcairn; but should the wind come away from the westward, as it looked like doing, the old man would probably shape a course direct for Cape Horn, and that would take them away from the islands.

Back in the fo'c'sle, after having finished his two hours' 'trick', the sailor was narrating

The four-masted steel ship, *Tarapaca*, ghosting in light airs.

this conversation to his mates, when Hobbs came in. 'What was that you were saying about the islands?' the American demanded, halting and fixing his dark, unfriendly eyes on the speaker. There was something in his tone and whole demeanour – a kind of suppressed excitement – which caused the other men to pause at what they were doing and to glance at him. But his face was as impassive as a block of granite.

The helmsman repeated what he had been told. A few moments later Hobbs returned on deck, where he was joined by Sears and Turner. Standing by the mainmast the three men remained in deep conversation until long after the sun had dipped below the rim of the horizon.

There was no moon and it was intensely dark when Captain Peattie came on deck that evening for his customary stroll before turning in. All day the south-east trade wind had been gradually falling away, and now the ship was crawling along at a bare three knots. The weather was exceedingly hot and sultry, and the men of the watch below as well as those on deck were sleeping out in the open. Captain Peattie paced the poop for half an hour; then stood yarning with Mr Nixon, who was in charge of the deck, until ten o'clock. At that hour he said good-night to the officer and went down to his cabin.

He had been lying in his bunk, reading, for a quarter of an hour or so, when, at ten-thirty, there was a knock at his door.

'What is it?' he asked, lowering his book on to the counterpane.

'Beg pardon, sir,' came Sears' slow, rather pleasant drawl. 'A man has fallen from the foreyard and broken his leg.'

Captain Peattie thought it rather strange that a man should not be able to look after himself aloft on such a fine, quiet night. He wondered, moreover, what the fellow had been doing up there at all. However, he made no comment.

'All right, I'll be there in a minute,' he answered, jumping out of his bunk and pulling on his trousers and shirt.

Thus clad, with a pair of slippers on his feet, he passed out of his cabin and entered the saloon, where he lit the lamp suspended above the long table, to have sufficient light to see what he was doing when the injured man was brought in. Sears by now had crossed the saloon, and was standing against the port inner doorway, from which a short fore-and-aft alleyway led to the outer door and the main deck.

'Where is the injured man?' the Captain asked, glancing round at the young American, on whose pale, rather perturbed-looking features shone in the light from the lamp.

'Outside, sir,' he replied, jerking his thumb over his shoulder. 'Tell the second mate to bring him in here,' ordered Captain Peattie briskly, at the same time removing and folding the cloth on the table.

There was a shuffling movement in the companionway outside, and a second later Hobbs passed stealthily through the starboard doorway into the saloon, placing himself between the Captain and the latter's cabin.

This sudden and well-timed entry could be accounted for only by assuming that Hobbs had been crouching in the companionway, listening to what was being said, and all ready to act.

Captain Peattie noticed that Sears disappeared as Hobbs came in. Wheeling round to demand an explanation for such extraordinary behaviour, he was greatly surprised and dismayed by the look of savage ferocity on the man's face. It was clear that Hobbs meant murder, and he did not waste a moment in giving definite proof of this fact.

'Now then, Captain,' was all that he said, as, whipping out a revolver, he fired at comparatively close range.

The bullet struck Captain Peattie in the breast, just above the heart. With great courage he rushed at his assailant and struck him a blow in the face. Hobbs stepped back, and fired again. This second bullet embedded itself in the biceps muscle of the Captain's right arm. Nevertheless, the outraged shipmaster again closed and attempted to tear the revolver from his grasp. Weak from shock and loss of blood, he was, however, no match for the big, powerfully built assassin. The man thrust him away with comparative ease, and fired again – three shots in rapid succession. Two of these bullets lodged in the Captain's chest above his ribs, the third grazed a forearm and then splintered the mirror over the sideboard.

Captain Peattie reeled across the floor and collapsed in a heap. At that moment the chief mate, who had been asleep in his cabin, came to the door of the saloon. Hobbs instantly levelled the revolver at him. Slamming the door the officer ran out on deck, calling to the men to hasten aft.

Possessed either with a diabolical blood-lust, or else wishing merely to finish off his victim without wasting any more bullets, Hobbs thrust the revolver into one pocket of his reefer and snatched from the other a heavy wooden mallet, purloined from the sailmaker's store. With this he now started to belabour the prostrate man on the face and head.

The Captain's shouts for help had been heard by Nixon, the watch officer, who happened to be some distance away, on the fore deck, and he came running aft. There was a look of horror on his face as, with fists clenched, he dashed into the saloon. The man-killer must have heard and seen him coming, for, dropping the mallet, he snatched the revolver again. A shot rang out, and Nixon, a fine young Scotsman from Edinburgh, fell dead with a bullet in his heart.

Suddenly there came the rush of many feet, and realising that the game was up, that his plan, whatever it might have been, had failed, Hobbs ran out of the saloon.

Beck, the steward, and Dunning, an apprentice, were the first to reach the wounded man. Across the saloon doorway lay the dead second mate, whose fists were still clenched in impotent rage. The floor, ceiling, and panelling of the saloon were spattered with blood, and some of the swivel chairs were broken. Beside the table, in a pool of blood, lay the Captain. At first, both the steward and the boy-apprentice thought that he also was dead, but suddenly he spoke to them, telling them to fetch the mate.

Accompanied by most of the sailors, all of whom had armed themselves with belaying-pins, iron shackles, cobs of coal, or whatever had come nearest to hand, the chief officer arrived on the scene at that moment, and took charge of the situation. The Captain was lifted and carried to his room, where first aid was rendered by an able seaman named Brennan, who had served with an Ambulance Corps in South Africa during the Boer War.

The ship's fire-arms, including the Colt taken from Hobbs, were still in place, and the

The full-rigged ship *Leicester Castle*. This ship was the scene of a mutiny on the high seas that has few rivals.

chief mate now took charge of them, giving orders that the sailors were to remain aft during the rest of the night, and that the door and ports leading into the saloon from the main deck were to be closed and secured. The man at the wheel reported that he had seen Hobbs come up the companionway and run down the poop ladder on to the main deck. It was assumed from this that the murderer and his two accomplices were somewhere at large on the fore deck. To do the chief mate justice, as he was subsequently criticised in some quarters for not attempting an arrest at once, it must be pointed out that not only was the night intensely dark, but that the mutineers might all be strongly armed. Moreover, the men under him, though apparently well-intentioned, were a mixed lot – Dutchmen, Scandinavians, Russian Finns, and the like – some, or all, of whom might have failed him at the crucial moment, thereby adding disaster to tragedy.

The mate's intention was to strongly hold the poop until daylight, then to sally forth and round up the desperadoes. It so happened, however, that he was saved this trouble. Shortly after midnight the men on the poop were astonished to see the three mutineers come drifting past the ship, along her starboard side, on a raft. They were evidently in an angry and ironical mood, for one of them shouted something derogatory about 'lime-juicers', as British sailing ships were known, and another – it was Hobbs' voice, the men declared – bawled at the top of his voice: 'Hurrah for the American flag!' The mate gripped his revolver and levelled it, but quickly curbed the impulse to fire. And a few seconds later – almost before the men on the poop had recovered from their surprise – the raft was lost to view in the darkness astern.[1]

The chief mate's second act, as the raft went drifting past, was to heave the ship to. Lighted lamps were then brought, and the fo'c'sle and fore deck were thoroughly searched for any clue the fugitives might have left. It was ascertained that their raft had been constructed from a dozen spare grain shifting-boards (twelve feet long, by one foot wide, by three inches in thickness), which had been kept under the fo'c'sle head. The planks had evidently been placed side by side, and two deep, and then securely lashed with the ends of the running gear, which had been cut away at random. Thus built, the raft would have presented a fairly solid structure. To render it still more buoyant, however, the desperadoes had torn from the forward boats their cork fenders. They did not use one of these boats because the two on the forward skids were not under davits, and therefore were far too heavy for three men to launch; while the ones farther aft, the lifeboats proper, were much too near the poop. It was assumed that before being lashed the planks were propped up against the bulwarks, and that the completed structure was toppled overboard by means of a watch-tackle. The fact that the ship had barely steerage-way made the task of launching the raft comparatively easy. But, even so, it was an exceedingly daring and clever get-away.

Further examination revealed the fact that the three mutineers had provisioned themselves for a week or ten days. They had taken all the food and tobacco they could lay their hands on, and most of the other men's clothing, as well as their own. Two deck buckets were missing, and it was concluded that these had been filled with fresh water and taken away on the raft.

The chief mate kept the ship hove-to until daylight, then put her back on her course, the lookout-men aloft having failed to see any sign of their quarry. Captain Peattie was in a critical condition for several days, but thanks to his fine constitution and Scottish tenacity he gradually recovered. He contemplated making for Valparaiso (about three weeks' sail) for medical aid and additional hands, but decided to carry on. Considering that he had four bullets in his body, one perilously near his heart, it was an extremely courageous decision to make.

Very bad weather was experienced rounding the Horn, but after that the ship had a good run home. When the affair had been reported at Queenstown, the *Leicester Castle* was boarded by the District Inspector of the RIC, the Chief Constable of the port, and a detective-inspector; and statements were taken down from several members of the crew. One man testified that, shortly before the shooting, he had seen a hundred rounds of ammunition in Hobbs' bunk. Unfortunately, he had not reported the matter, or thought very much about it.

Asked as to his theory regarding the murder and attack upon himself, the Captain stated

---

[1] When I first heard it I disbelieved this incident about the raft. It seemed too utterly incredible that such a thing could have been constructed in so short a time. Still more so, that three perfectly sane men could have been so lost to reason as to entrust their lives to it in the middle of the Pacific. I regarded the story as a far-fetched sailors' yarn, but having looked up the *Leicester Castle*'s records, and read Captain Peattie's report, I am satisfied that it is true in every detail.

that he considered it to be a case of piracy. The mutineers intended to kill him, he said, and get into his room, where he kept the fire-arms. Hobbs had plenty of ammunition, he pointed out, and if he had succeeded in getting his hands on his own Colt he would have murdered every man who did not side with him. The arrival of Beck and Dunning, however, caused him to realise that the plot had failed, and he took desperate measures to escape the hangman.

Ironically enough, the bullet which killed Nixon was fired from the latter's own revolver. This had been stolen from his room shortly before the tragedy. The chief mate heard someone moving about in the next cabin, and called out to ask who it was. Turner replied, saying he had been sent below to get the second mate's pipe and tobacco, which seemed a perfectly reasonable explanation.

Thus Sears and Turner were both implicated in the crime, the latter by stealing the revolver, the former by acting as a decoy and getting the Captain out of his cabin with a false message. No doubt Hobbs, who was clearly the arch-criminal, purposely involved them in that way.

The question 'What was the motive?' naturally arises. This, I am afraid, must be left to conjecture. The general opinion seemed to be that all three men were wanted for some other crime, and that they adopted the wild idea of capturing a ship on the high seas, and sailing her to some lonely Pacific island, far beyond even the long arm of the law. Subsequent inquiries at 'Frisco, however, failed to throw any light on the mystery. The American police had no record of the men in the names they had given, but who can say that these were their *real* names, or even that they belonged to the States they claimed.

With the arrival at San Francisco of the British sailing ship *Howth*, on 13th December 1902, it was believed at first that the fugitives had been located, for the vessel reported that while she was off Pitcairn, on the night of 25th September, fire-signals were observed ashore. The Captain thought that the islanders were endeavouring to attract his attention and, after hearing of the *Leicester Castle* affair, he jumped to the conclusion that they had the mutineers on the island and were anxious to get rid of them.

Largely on the strength of this information, HM sloop *Shearwater*, Commander C H Umfreville, was instructed to leave Honolulu for Pitcairn and the adjacent islands to search for the fugitives. She rejoined the Flag at Coquimbo early in February 1903 without having found any trace of them, however. With that they were presumed to be dead.

Personally, I think there can be no doubt as to the outcome of the men's desperate bid for freedom. They were three hundred miles from the nearest land, in the loneliest stretch of ocean over the seven seas, and they had no means of propulsion. Being really landsmen, they were no doubt lulled into a false sense of security by the fact that the sea was smooth and the wind negligible. They may have learned, moreover, and been influenced by the fact, that the current was setting southward towards Pitcairn. Even so, they stood barely one chance in a thousand of making the island, for sooner or later the wind must have freshened, and the merest lop on the surface of the ocean would have been sufficient to wash them off their precarious perch.

What agony of mind and body they suffered before the end is best left to one's imagination. Try to visualise the scene. A small raft, twelve feet long by six feet wide, with three cowering men huddled on it. A blazing tropic sun overhead. An empty waste of water all around, its quicksilver-like surface stabbed here and there by quickly moving black fins. The waters in the vicinity of the South Pacific Islands are literally infested with sharks, and a number of the brutes had been seen from the deck of the *Leicester Castle* on the day of the tragedy.

At Queenstown the ship was ordered to proceed to Manchester, where her cargo was discharged and the crew were paid off. The tragedy resulted in a great outcry against the crimping system in San Francisco, whereby undesirable aliens of every kind were foisted with impunity on British ships. The Commissioner of Navigation for the State of California suggested legislation by Congress, requiring the boarding-house masters to be properly licensed and placed under the jurisdiction of a responsible executive committee, of which the British Consul should be a member.

Nothing was done in the matter, however. The pernicious practice continued to flourish until the last square-rigger out of the port spread her white wings and sailed away.

5 Hell Ship

'Hell ships' and 'Lime-juicers' – A hell-ship officer becomes Captain of the full-rigged ship *Star of Russia* – Outward bound 1887 – Christmas at sea – A seaman in irons – Torture – Psychology in the days of sail – A sea bully – Gale off Diego Ramirez – 'Hazing' – 'Frisco in 1888 – Sailors' Home – British Consul investigates – Shanghaied – 'Cracking on' – A hurricane in the Southern Ocean – Apprentice lost – The end of a 'boy-killer'.

AMERICAN sailing ships, in their prime, were renowned – or rather ill-famed – the world over for the brutal treatment their crews received on board them. There were exceptions, no doubt; but the majority of these Yankee packets richly deserved the title of 'hell ships', 'blood boats', and the like. Their hard-case skippers and bucko mates, possessed by some diabolical and inhuman blood-lust, were experts in the art of 'working-up' and 'man-handling' refractory crews; and many cases are on record of their beating a man to death with their belaying-pins or knuckle-dusters, or of subjecting him to such methods of refined cruelty that he went mad, or jumped overboard to escape from them. In rare instances these human gorillas were brought to justice and executed, or sent to penal servitude for long terms. But so difficult was it for the prosecuting attorneys to collect evidence against them – an instance of which I shall give in this narrative – that in the majority of cases they went free, to perpetrate fresh outrages elsewhere upon long-suffering and down-trodden sailormen.

During my own sailing-ship days I was with a number of men who, at one time or another, had served in these American ships. Nearly all of them bore some mark – a scar, a permanent limp, or maybe merely a tendency to insomnia – to remind them of the fact. One old shipmate I recollect in particular, who had served in a number of Yankee packets, had an ugly white scar running from his left temple, across the empty socket of his left eye, down to his mouth. A blow from a knuckle-duster had inflicted this hideous wound, and the old fellow was as proud of it as a war veteran might be of his VC.

To have served in an American 'hell ship' and survived was regarded as a great honour. The experience lifted a man out of the ruck aboard a British 'lime-juicer', singled him out as a hard case, stamped him as a man of iron – to be looked up to, respected, and admired by his less fortunate (?) shipmates. Indeed, I honestly believe that the old sailor I have mentioned would far sooner have had his ghastly scar, which never failed to send a shudder through me, than all the proverbial gold in China.

The American ship *Gatherer* was one of the
most notorious 'hell-ships' of the 1880s and '90s.
The terrible treatment of sailors aboard such vessels was a
contributing factor in the formation of
The Sailors' Union of the Pacific, established
in San Francisco in March 1885.

Captain X, with whom this narrative is concerned, was a Yankee 'hell-ship' officer *by adoption*, and as such was a scoundrel of a far deeper dye than many real American captains and officers brought up from boyhood in the American Merchant Marine. A Britisher by birth, X had begun his sea career in the famous 'Stars' of Belfast. After serving in the *Star of Denmark* he entered the American Merchant Marine. For the next six years he served in a number of notorious Yankee packets, including the *Gatherer* and *Harvester*, than which it would have been hard to find two more unwholesome 'blood boats'.

He returned to the British Mercantile Marine saturated with Yankee ideas; and, merely remembering him as a very capable officer, his old firm gave him command of the *Star of Russia*, a fine-looking full-rigged ship of 1892 tons register.

Until then this vessel had been commanded by a Captain Simpson, a wise and considerate shipmaster who had been so popular with his men that several of them had stuck by the old ship for many voyages. Captain Simpson was given command of the company's first steamer, and no sooner had Captain X taken his place in the *Star of Russia* than all her old hands realised that their happy days were over.

The vessel sailed from London, bound for 'Frisco, on 5th December 1887, and before she was clear of the English Channel the new Captain had made it known that he intended to run the ship in real Yankee fashion, and that when he spoke he expected everyone to flap their wings and fly.

'But this ain't an American ship, thank heaven!' remonstrated a young American named McLean. 'She's a Britisher, sir: a lime-juicer! Look at the old red duster at her stern.'

There was something rather funny in this – an American standing out for British justice and fair play; a Britisher upholding Americanism – but Captain X hadn't the pride of race, imagination, or sense of humour to see it.

'The flag at her gaff, or the port of registry on her stern, doesn't cut any ice with me,' he answered. 'Out here, on the high seas, I shall run her in my own way. That'll be Yankee fashion. If any of you want to know any more about this, just let me hear you question an order, or see you walking when you should be running, and you'll damn soon learn!'

Three days out from the Channel the skipper began to put the screw on the men. Their afternoon watch below was suspended. This meant that instead of working twelve hours a day, which was what the customary four hours on duty and four hours off amounted to, they had to work sixteen hours, with only eight for eating, sleeping, and recreation. The men put up with this injustice for a week or ten days; then they rebelled.

This was four days before Christmas. People ashore were buying presents, holly, and their Christmas fare; were exchanging the compliments of the season with one another; and the atmosphere of Yuletide festivity stole across the sea and entered the *Star of Russia*'s gloomy fo'c'sle.

'I'm damned if I'm going to do any work this afternoon,' declared McLean, while he and his watch-mates were having their dinner.

'Nor me,' replied another sailor, amid murmurs of approval from his shipmates.

The full-rigged ship *Star of Russia*, shown here under British colours.

The mate appeared at the door and ordered the men out to holystone the decks. They held a hurried consultation and, having elected McLean as their spokesman, went aft in a body to interview the Captain.

'How much longer do you intend to work us like slaves, Captain?' demanded McLean, meeting the skipper's scowl boldly. 'The ship's articles don't say we're to work in our watch below, and we contend that, except in cases of emergency, you have no right to make us.'

'So you'd teach me my business!' snarled this hybrid Captain.

'Nothing of the sort, sir,' answered McLean. 'I'm merely standing up for our rights.'

'Your *rights*!' Captain X gave a snort of derision. 'Since when, pray, have fo'c'sle scum like you had any rights aboard ship? You're here to do as you're told. If I say you're to work sixteen, twenty, or even twenty-four hours in the twenty-four, you'll do it – no matter what the articles, the Board of Trade, or the Merchant Shipping Acts say.'

'I'm damned if I will!' retorted McLean angrily. 'I've reminded you before, sir, and I'll do it again, that this is a British ship – not a blasted Yankee "hell ship"!'

'Put that man in irons!' thundered the Captain, and, before McLean could resist, the mate and second mate pounced on him, pinned him to the deck, and snapped a pair of handcuffs on his wrists.

Snatching a belaying-pin from the rail, the Captain turned towards the other men.

'Well, what's it to be?' he demanded. 'If you intend to obey the orders, get hold of those holystones. If you're still going to disobey ——'

He did not finish the sentence, but the venomous glitter in his eyes and the savage ring in his voice told the sailors quite clearly that he would not hesitate to use violence. Glancing at one another nervously they turned and, without a word, picked up the holystones. Five minutes later McLean was bundled below into the dark lazarette.

The Captain visited him there an hour later. The place was lit by a solitary hurricane-lamp, and by its miserable light McLean could see the gleam of triumph on the shipmaster's thin-lipped, brutal face.

'Well, how do you like being down here among the rats?' he sneered.

'I can stand it,' replied McLean. 'It's first trick to you, Captain. I'll play my cards when we get to 'Frisco.'

The words were uttered contemptuously, and in a sudden wave of fury the Captain seized the helpless man by the throat, shook him violently, and then flung him to the deck. Half-stunned, McLean did not stir, and dropping on to his knees beside him the Captain handcuffed his hands *behind* his back.

That evening the steward brought down a pannikin of water and a dry biscuit. But he did not assist the captive to eat or drink, because he had been instructed not to. McLean was not hungry, but he suffered from great thirst. Lying on his stomach he endeavoured to drink like a cat, and accidentally knocked the pannikin over. All that night he suffered from acute cramp in his arms and shoulders, and next morning, when the Captain again went below to gloat over him, he begged to have his arms handcuffed in front of him. The skipper acceded to the request only after the poor fellow had sworn that he would never again question any order.

McLean was kept below in handcuffs for three days. During that time his daily fare consisted of three pannikins of water and three dry biscuits. The rats scampered around him continually, adding to his misery. On Christmas Day he was brought up to the saloon to have the charge against him in the official log read over to him. This was a tissue of lies, accusing him of having attempted to incite the men to mutiny. He declined to make any reply to the charge when invited to do so. The Captain informed him that he would be reduced from able seaman to ordinary seaman, that his tobacco would be stopped, and that in future he would not be allowed to steer or keep a lookout – a punishment calculated to humiliate him in the eyes of his shipmates. Then he was ordered back to the fo'c'sle, and when they saw how his sturdy, independent spirit had been utterly crushed his shipmates were shocked beyond measure. Never very robust physically, McLean became morose, went off his food, lost weight, and finally fell ill. The Captain insisted that he was malingering and refused to let him lie-up, but the sailmaker, a wise old sea-dog with a knowledge of human nature, declared that the poor young fellow was breaking his heart because of the shame of having had his spirit crushed.

During the next month, while the *Star of Russia* ambled southward through the tropics, the Captain employed all the little tricks he had learnt in Yankee ships to make life a hell for the men. The decks were holystoned and holystoned again, until they were as smooth as glass. The paintwork was washed and re-washed, until the sheen of the bare iron shone through it. When the supply of holystones and washing-soda began to run low the cables were dragged up on deck and chipped; then the sailors were sent down to scale the damp, rust-stinking chain-lockers – eight or nine men being herded into one locker, so that the air they breathed was foul and there was scarcely elbow-room.

Such insane ill-treatment of the crew, of course, did not make for efficiency, but Captain X, like most sea bullies of his kind, did not worry about that. His purpose was thoroughly to cow the men, so that they would eat out of his hand during the rest of the trip, and desert the ship directly she reached port, leaving their wages behind them.

One day, in the first week of February, McLean, who was suffering from acute rheumatism, went aft to ask for some liniment. His arms were badly swollen and on his right wrist was a large sea-boil. The steward, a spineless fellow, referred him to the Captain, who merely laughed at him and told him to go forward and tie a piece of canvas round the sore. McLean used one of his handkerchiefs instead, then rejoined his shipmates in the port chain-locker. His hands were so badly swollen, however, that he could not wield his chipping-hammer and scraper; so he returned on deck and sat down on the fore hatch.

The Captain saw him there and ordered him to take a pot of slush and grease down the fore t'gallantmast. He protested that it was a job for a man who could use his hands properly. The Captain then asked him if he would prefer to go back in irons to the lazarette. The very thought of the rats and gloom down there made the young fellow shudder, and he obeyed the order. The ship was pitching considerably at the time and more than once he narrowly escaped falling to the deck.

On another occasion the bullying master tore a bandage off McLean's arm, saying he would have no malingering. The two mates do not appear to have been brutal men, but how it was they failed to call a halt to their superior's inhuman conduct is more than I can understand. One can only surmise that, like the sailors, they were thoroughly scared of him.

There were an exceptionally large number of severe gales off the Horn that year, and the *Star of Russia* came in for her share of them. It was blowing hard from the westward when she sighted the Diego Ramirez – that cluster of rocks lying off Cape Horn – on 16th February; and before night closed in all hands were called out to reduce sail. The mainsail was hauled up first, and while one watch was aloft trying to furl it the Captain suddenly gave vent to one of his frequent outbursts of violent temper.

The men aloft found that they could not get the weather side of the sail on to the yard, as its clewgarnet was too tight, and a young sailor named Marshall sang out to those on deck to slack this off. It was a perfectly reasonable request, but the Captain, who hated anything in the shape of criticism, resented it.

'Too tight be damned; let the lazy swabs exert themselves,' he rasped, waving back a sailor who had moved towards the rope.

Unaware of this interference, or that he had annoyed the Captain, Marshall let out another shout, injecting a note of irritation into his voice.

'Are you all deaf down there?' he bawled. 'Slack off the weather clewgarnet, can't you! We can't get the sail on to the yard.'

Still there was no response and, letting go of the bunch of canvas he had been clinging on to, Marshall shouted to his mates on the mainyard to 'leave the damn thing and come down on deck.'

The Captain, who was aft, heard the loudly uttered injunction, and, darting down the poop ladder, he strode forward.

'What the devil do you mean by shouting orders?' he demanded of Marshall, as the young sailor leapt out of the rigging on to the deck.

'I wasn't shouting *orders*,' replied the latter, in an aggrieved tone. 'I was merely——'

He got no further, for an iron fist shot out like a ramrod, catching him on the point of the jaw and sending him reeling into the scuppers. Completely knocked out, Marshall lay where he had fallen for a few seconds; then, recovering consciousness, he leapt to his feet.

'You'll pay for doing that, you swine!' he shouted, snatching at a belaying-pin. Before he was able to get his fingers on it, however, the Captain struck him again, and he fell a second time, covering his face with his hands to save it from the shower of savage kicks aimed at him. Only when he lay still, bleeding and groaning, did the brutal skipper desist.

There was no sleep for anyone that night. The Captain had decided that the men needed a fresh lesson in discipline, and he saw that they got it. With oaths, threats, and kicks they were kept on the hop until daylight broke, furling, reefing, and then setting sail again. There was not an ounce of fight or 'comeback' in any of them when at last the watch below was dismissed.

The next morning, striding up to Marshall while he was at the wheel, X said: 'So it's you, my fine buck! Well, what have you to say about that clewgarnet to-day?'

'Nothing,' replied Marshall. 'What I've got to say will keep until we get to 'Frisco.'

'And then you'll go whining to the British Consul, I suppose?' sneered the Captain. 'A damn lot I care for him, or any other consul!'

Two days later, in a fit of fury over little or nothing at all, the Captain very nearly pitched three men – named Johnson, Browne, and Keers – off the main upper t'gallantyard. They had gone aloft to furl the main upper t'gallants'l, but as the sail was bellying backwards over the yard they could not get out along the foot-rope to smother it. Keers sang out to the crowd on deck to haul in on the weather brace, which would have pointed the yard into the wind and spilled the air out of the sail. It was as natural a request as Marshall's had been, and to the Captain's way of thinking just as presumptuous.

'Leave the brace alone!' he snapped, as half a dozen men moved towards it. Then, suddenly darting along the deck, he threw it off its belaying-pin *and actually let the brace go.*

The result of this criminal act was that more wind than ever rushed into the sail; and the yard gave a tremendous jolt upwards, almost throwing the three men off it.

'Perhaps *that* will teach them to keep their tongues between their teeth,' he jeered, turning on his heel and striding aft. No one had the temerity to question his brutal and insane act.

A week later his continual hazing of the men resulted in a tragedy. The ship was still off the Horn, beating to and fro in the teeth of the furious westerlies. Huge seas flooded the decks, repeatedly gutting out the fo'c'sle, petty officers' and apprentices' quarters. For three days no one had tasted a hot meal. The sailors' bedding was as sodden as their clothes, for water continually seeped through the seams of the straining fo'c'sle-deck head. The elements were certainly doing their best to make everyone's life a hell, but this was not enough for the Captain, whose passion for inflicting misery was an abiding obsession with him. Coming on deck on the morning of 28th February he saw the watch puffing disconsolately at their damp pipes, and instantly he flew into a temper.

'Can't you find something better than that for the lazy hounds to do, mister?' he demanded of the second mate, who was in charge of the watch on deck.

'We've just finished hauling tight the weather braces, sir,' replied the officer. 'I dismissed the men for a bit of a spell-o.'

'A spell-o be damned!' exploded the skipper. 'Do you think this is a Sunday school, mister? Bring the loafers aft and set the cro'jack.'

The second mate glanced at his superior with surprise, for the cro'jack had been furled only a few hours before – there was far too much wind for it. He knew better than to argue, however. The carpenter, sailmaker, and bosun, who were day men, turned out to bear a hand with the sail, and while its sheet was being hove down a big sea broke aboard in the waist, sweeping the sailmaker overboard. The second mate threw a lifebuoy to him; but he might as well have saved himself the trouble, for within a few seconds the sailmaker had been swept out of sight in the smother of foam. Later on in the morning, while a fierce squall was raging overhead, the cro'jack split from head to foot and blew into ribbons.

This needless loss of life evidently made some impression on the Captain, for during the next two or three weeks he let-up on the crew considerably. Everyone knew that, sooner or later, he would break out afresh, however. And he did – over so trivial a matter that no rational skipper would have taken any notice of it.

Star of Russia under sail. In 1887-88 she sailed from London to San Francisco in 128 days.

A deck bucket was missing and, obsessed by the conviction that someone had thrown it overboard deliberately, he had all hands mustered aft.

'One of you has thrown that bucket overboard,' he said, sweeping the row of faces in front of him with his small, unfriendly eyes. 'Unless the guilty one owns up, I shall put you all on your pound and pint, and stop your tobacco. Speak up, now. Who was it?'

The sailors glanced interrogatively at one another, then suddenly Marshall spoke.

'I lost the bucket, sir,' he said quietly.

'Ah!' exclaimed the skipper triumphantly.

'But not intentionally,' Marshall added. 'I was drawing some water from over the side——'

'That's a lie!' the Captain shouted. 'I know your type. You're the sort of fellow who would find pleasure in slashing into ribbons a brand-new topsail. You threw that bucket over out of spite. Now, didn't you?'

Marshall shook his head, and his lip curled contemptuously.

'You must be judging me by——' he began, but a sailor at his side nudged him, and he stopped. The Captain, no doubt, guessed what he had intended to say, however.

'You think you're smart, don't you?' he snarled. 'Before I'm through with you, you'll wish you'd never been born. I'll wipe that smirk off your face. See if I don't!'

From that moment young Marshall was singled out for particular ill-treatment. He was made to work in his dog-watch below, as well as his afternoon watch below, so that he had little more than four hours in the twenty-four to himself. All the dirty and unpleasant 'work-up' jobs the skipper could think of were given to him. He was made every day to clean out the pigsty and the hencoop, and the messy job of scouring out the empty paint and tar drums was allotted to him as well. One day, while the ship was rolling her rails under, he was ordered to take a pot of slush and grease down the three t'gallantmasts. He managed to do the fore t'gallantmast; but he very nearly lost his grip and fell while doing the main t'gallantmast. White-faced and trembling, he came down on deck and refused to go aloft again.

'I know what your game is, Captain!' he shouted hysterically. 'You're hoping I'll fall and kill myself. But I'm not going to give you that satisfaction. If you want the mizzen t'gallantmast greased down, do it yourself!'

Such defiance was bound to result in one thing.

'Put that impudent swab in irons!' the Captain thundered, and five minutes later Marshall was in captivity in the lazarette.

He was kept there in handcuffs for three days, during which time his daily fare consisted of the usual three dry biscuits and three half-pints of water. On the fourth day, the weather being comparatively fine, he consented to finish the job, and so was released. Subsequently he was brought aft to have the charge against him in the official log read over to him. As in McLean's case this was a pack of lies, and his reply was a statement to that effect. It became known to the Captain a little later that the sailor was keeping a diary, and one day the latter was taunted about this.

'I suppose you've got all your grievances written down?'

Marshall nodded.

'Yes, all of them,' he replied grimly. 'I've forgotten nothing.'

'Well, when you get ashore, go and get them published in the newspapers,' jeered the skipper; and then, snapping his fingers in the defiant young sailor's face, he added: 'That's what I think of the Press!'

On 10th April 1888, at 1.30 AM, the *Star of Russia* anchored in 'Frisco Bay, 128 days from London. During the rest of the night all hands were kept hard at work, giving the sails a harbour-stow, washing down the decks, and doing a thousand-and-one other jobs.

'The swabs will desert directly the boarding-house masters arrive, so we may as well get the last ounce of work we can out of them,' the skipper confided to the mate. His prophecy proved correct, for hardly had the ship reached her discharging berth than the sailors began to clamber down the ends of ropes into the boarding-house masters' boats, which lay alongside.

Lolling over the poop rail, a cigar clenched between his teeth, X watched the familiar scene with much interest. Occasionally his lip curled contemptuously, as well it might, in view of the men's apparent anxiety to leave their hard-earned wages behind them.

Unknown to the Captain, Marshall, McLean, and Keers had quite a different purpose in view, however. Before leaving the ship they had solemnly vowed to make him answer for his brutal behaviour to them. Their intention was to prosecute him in the United States courts, and directly they got ashore they went straight to a lawyer for advice. The lawyer took down their statements, made an appointment for them to see him again, and warned them to keep clear of the boarding-house masters in the meanwhile. Two alternatives were open to them in consequence: to stay either at the Mission to Seamen or at the Sailors'

Home. Fearing that it might prove a little dull at the former, they decided to go to the Sailors' Home. It was an unfortunate decision, for the concierge of the Home, though reputed to be a benevolent foster-father of merchant seamen, was just as desirous of picking up a little easy money as any unsavoury crimp in the port.

The skipper of a Yankee homeward-bounder made him a good offer for the three men's services, and there and then he started to talk them out of their intention to prosecute Captain X.

'You wouldn't stand an earthly, b'ys,' he told them. 'In this here port the skipper always gets the better of the men in law cases. You'd lose yer case and earn yerselves a bad name in the bargain. 'Taint worth it, b'ys. Forget about the *Star o' Roosia*. Here's a packet offerin' you thirty bucks a month, and you only received fifteen a month aboard that British lime-juicer.'

'What about the lawyer who's got our case in hand?' asked Marshall, weakening.

'Forget about him, too,' replied the benevolent gentleman.

'He'll only fleece you, and then chuck yer case when your money's gone. I guess I know all about 'Frisco lawyers and judges. They're that darned crooked they can't lie down in bed.'

In this way the wily rascal gradually talked the men over, and next morning they presented themselves at the US Shipping Commissioner's Office to sign on in the Yankee ship's articles.

Meanwhile the lawyer had been having a talk with the British Vice-Consul, who, learning that the three sailors were over in the Shipping Commissioner's Office, sent for them.

'We'll come as soon as we've signed on here,' Marshall told the messenger from the British Consulate.

'No, come first,' was the reply; and, followed by his two shipmates, Marshall left the building.

The British Vice-Consul told the sailors that they would have every assistance in bringing a charge against Captain X, if they wished to do so. It was entirely for them to decide, he said. If the charge was brought, he would summon the Captain to appear at the British Consulate and proceed with an investigation immediately. He went on to explain to them that if the matter was not very serious the Consul would have the power of settling it. But that if it was serious – and it appeared to be – the case would have to be tried by a Naval Court, composed of the Consul or Vice-Consul, a British Naval Officer, and three British shipmasters.

The sailors left to talk the matter over with their late shipmates, and that was the last the Vice-Consul saw of them. Marshall was shanghaied aboard the *John o' Gaunt* that night; and when McLean and Keers recovered consciousness, after having been sandbagged and doped, they were bound out through the Golden Gate aboard the Yankee packet.

Still determined, however, to get to the bottom of the trouble, if he could, the British Vice-Consul dispatched a messenger to bring in the remainder of the *Star of Russia*'s late crew. Unfortunately, none of them were to be found; and from this fact it was inferred that they all had been shanghaied back to sea.

The *Star of Russia* left 'Frisco, for Queenstown, on the 23rd July 1888. She had a brand-new crew, and scarcely had she passed through the Golden Gate before the Captain started his old tactics. The fact that the British Consul had been unable to bring him to book made him more contemptuous of the law than ever. All the way through the tropics he hazed the new men in real Yankee-ship fashion; and one dark, dirty night off the Horn, weary and dispirited at being hounded from one 'work-up' job to another, a young sailor, named Bowden, aged twenty-four, fell from the fore rigging to the deck and was killed.

The other sailors declared that the Captain was to blame and swore that they would have him brought to justice as soon as the ship reached port. But at Antwerp, to which place the *Star of Russia* was ordered from Queenstown, they got no farther with their grievance than the first row of garish grog-shops, where painted-up harlots condoled with them over their hardships and took the first opportunity of relieving them of their cash.

Captain X had again escaped the penalty he so richly deserved; but it was generally believed that the owners took him severely to task over his conduct and warned him that if there was any more trouble in the ship he would have to go. However that may be, he certainly was a changed man when the *Star of Russia* left Antwerp for Melbourne on the 20th February 1889. The vessel cleared the English Channel without anyone having been man-handled and a week or two of the passage passed off uneventfully.

It was too much to expect, however, that a man of such violent disposition would remain

'Running before a gale', portrayed by Anton Otto Fischer.

like a lamb for long. There were other ways of working off his tremendous energy; and suddenly he decided to try to make a record passage, which would please his owners and give him the excuse to make things mighty uncomfortable for all hands.

Strong favourable winds aided his purpose and, having crossed the Equator 19 days out from Flushing, the *Star of Russia* went tearing southward with every stitch of canvas spread and the men standing by the sheets and halyards the whole watch through.

She crossed the meridian of the Cape on the 13th April, 50 days from Flushing; and then, taking full advantage of a freshening gale, the Captain began to drive her in earnest. By dawn next day it was blowing a whole gale, before which, under every rag except the royals, mainsail, and cro' jack, she reeled in a mad, headlong flight, yawing two, three, and sometimes four points on either side of her course.

The chief mate, who had been in the ship as long as the Captain, and understood her thoroughly, did not approve of such reckless 'cracking-on'.

'It's lunacy,' he confided to the second mate. 'She's not one of those square-built bread-barges you can drive until the cows come home. Presently she'll be taking the bit in her teeth and then anything may happen.'

As a matter of fact, the records of her previous voyages should have warned the Captain that the *Star of Russia* was not a ship to trifle with. She was one of those fine-lined, heavily sparred vessels which seemed to have a mania for broaching-to in heavy weather. Her old log-books told of many such occurrences, with loss of life. About 1895 she distinguished herself in particular by drowning her mate and the whole of the port watch except the helmsman. Had it occurred before he assumed command of the ship, Captain X might have learnt a lesson from this tragedy. This, however, is a moot point. Personally, from what I have learned of the man, I do not believe it would have made the slightest difference. Some men are too bombastic and pigheaded to learn from the experience of others, and Captain X appears to have belonged to that type. He had made up his mind to knock spots off all the other ships bound to Melbourne, and he merely laughed derisively when to the sweating and labouring helmsmen the mate pointed, in an eleventh-hour attempt to make him realise that the ship was becoming unmanageable.

'Surely you don't expect me to reduce sail just because you've got a couple of clod-hops at the wheel?' he sneered, strutting up and down the poop as if he owned the sea.

'They know their business, those two men, sir,' the mate replied. 'They're the two best helmsmen in this ship, and you'd be lucky to find their equals in any other ship. They should have been relieved an hour ago, but I'm hanging on to them for fear the next couple will broach the ship to.'

Eventually the Captain did consent to take in the t'gallants'ls and to reef the foresail; then, on the 18th April, by which time it was blowing a hurricane, he ordered the mate to take in the three upper topsails as well.

A night of terror followed as the ship tore through the black void, with the wind screaming in her rigging and huge, white-crested combers boiling-up along her sides and crashing aboard in the waist. There was no thought of heaving-to now. It was too late for that. All hands realised that she would have to run it out as best she could.

Star of Russia (far right) when part of the Alaska Packers' fleet, carrying salmon from the company's canneries in Alaska. The Alaska Packers' Association was the last American shipowner to operate a large fleet of sailing ships. They purchased *Star of Russia* in 1901 and from then on renamed each ship they bought with the prefix '*Star*'.

'So long as the maniac doesn't get the notion of clapping on some more canvas she'll be all right,' opined the sailmaker, a grizzled old shell-back who had been at sea in the 'fifties. But at 8 PM on the 19th April, much to everyone's consternation, the Captain did get that very idea into his head.

'I think she'll stand the mizzen upper topsail, mister,' he remarked to the mate, sweeping his restless eyes over the bare masts and spars aloft.

'In this wind,' the mate shook his head vigorously, 'it would drive her under, sir.'

'Nonsense!' retorted the Captain scornfully. 'It'll help her to keep ahead of the seas. Send a couple of hands aloft to loose it, mister. And tell the rest to stand by the halyards.'

The gaskets of the sail had been cast adrift, and the men on deck were clustered round the fourfold halyard purchase, slowly hoisting the yard, when suddenly the ship indulged in one of her fancy tricks – swooping against her helm round to windward.

The men at the wheel managed to check her wild swing before she broached-to completely. But as she commenced to pay-off, back towards her course, an enormous breaking wave came roaring down towards her quarter.

'For heaven's sake, hang on, everyone!' bawled the mate, in a frenzy, clasping the rigging with both hands.

Scarcely was the warning out of his mouth than, with the shock of an avalanche, the giant wave crashed aboard, tearing the men from their holds and sweeping them in a heap along the deck into the very eyes of the ship. Bruised and battered, and all but drowned, they picked themselves up and began to make their way aft again. They were all under the impression that the ship was foundering, as well they might have been, for the damage done would have sunk a less well-found or staunch vessel.

Two of the lifeboats had been lifted bodily off their chocks and hurled overboard. Part of the weather bulwarks were down, the wheel-box and poop skylight had been smashed to pieces, and the saloon and lazarette were full of water. The carpenter, sail-maker, bosun, and cook, who had been asleep in the midship house, had narrowly escaped death; for when the wave struck it, one side of the house was knocked flat. Clad as they were, in their pants and singlets, the 'idlers' rushed out on deck just as the watch below, similarly attired, emerged from the fo'c'sle. Cursing, swearing, and calling the Captain everything they could lay their tongues to, the whole crowd made their way through the riot of water towards the poop.

Meanwhile it had been ascertained that a young first-voyage apprentice, aged fifteen, had been lost overboard. The two sailors who had been aloft loosing the topsail reported that they had seen him go. Instantly the crew's anger towards the Captain swept away their concern for themselves.

'You're a blasted boy-killer!' shouted one man, furiously shaking his fist.

'You ought to be strung up by your neck to the yardarm!' bawled another, shaking a trembling finger towards the forest of masts and spars above his head.

'Maybe you will be, one of these days!' raved another.

'Enough!' thundered the skipper, whose eyes shone like red-hot coals. 'Save your breath for the oars, you scum! I'm going to heave her to now. Then we'll launch one of the remaining boats.'

This announcement instantly struck the men dumb. An exclamation broke from the mate, as he swung round towards the Captain.

'You're not in earnest?' he said. 'You can't be! The poor boy's gone, and that's the end of him. It would be lunacy – murder – to turn her round in this sea, let alone to launch a boat!'

'I mean to, for all that,' rasped Captain X; and having compelled the sailors to brace-up the yards, he swung the ship athwart the thundering combers into the wind.

By a stroke of wonderful good luck she came round without swamping. Directly she was breasting the enormous, hissing ridges of water he called for volunteers to man the boat. Receiving no response he broke into an ironical laugh.

'You haven't got so much to say for yourselves now,' he taunted. 'I'll record your cowardice in the official log. It'll make interesting reading. "Hove ship to and called for volunteers to man the boat. No response." Your pals ashore will think you're a damn fine lot. Dismiss!'

The ship was kept hove-to until the weather moderated; then, after temporary repairs had been made, she was run off before the dying gale. She reached Melbourne without further mishap on the 13th May – 80 days from Flushing.

This was certainly a very smart passage, but the Captain received no praise for it in the Australian Press or from the Australian public. The latter, who always had a warm spot in their hearts for young 'brass-bounders' visiting their shores, were greatly incensed that a mere child should have been needlessly exposed to such great risks; and the Captain was made to know it.

The *Star of Russia* went over to Williamstown – across the bay from Port Melbourne – to discharge her cargo; and when returning to her one night the skipper was set upon by

Circular Quay, Sydney, where the clipper *Candida* is loading wool.

half a dozen furious youths and received a good thrashing, which he richly deserved. During the rest of the time his ship was in port he never went ashore after dark.

Everyone predicted that he would get the sack as soon as he got back to England, but somehow he managed to bluff his employers that the drowning of the apprentice lad and the severe damage to his ship was solely the result of exceptionally stormy weather. Ashore he had a plausible tongue, and the fact that in point of time the *Star of Russia* invariably made good passages was in his favour. He was permitted to hold his job, but – from all accounts – definitely given to understand that he would be dismissed if there was any more unnecessary trouble in the ship.

The *Star of Russia* left London for Sydney, NSW, on the 30th May 1890 on her next voyage. So far as I have been able to ascertain, this passage passed off quietly enough. At

Sydney the ship loaded a cargo of coals for 'Frisco, and once again the passage passed off comparatively peacefully. But at 'Frisco the Captain suddenly jumped into the limelight afresh by running foul of the boarding-house masters.

Having arranged to dispose of his crew to a notorious boarding-house master named Browne, he refused to let any of the remainder of the fraternity come aboard. Some of the sailors, wishing to please themselves in the matter, attempted to defy him and climb down into the forbidden boats. But pulling out a heavy revolver the Captain ordered them back and warned the crimps to clear out. What exactly his arrangement with Browne was, I am unable to say. However, one may fairly assume that this had to do with 'blood-money'. The rest of the boarding-house masters were so incensed over his action that they banded together to prevent him from getting a crew when he was ready to go to sea again. His shady conspirator, Browne, attempted to step into the breach, by finding him some men; and for his trouble the rascal was set upon by his erstwhile colleagues and had to go to hospital. The other boarding-house masters had the matter in their own hands after that and several weeks elapsed before the *Star of Russia* was able to scrape together a crew of sorts to take her to sea.

This was the last straw so far as her owners were concerned. Captain X was summarily dismissed when at length he brought the ship home. He subsequently went out to Cape Town and obtained a post as skipper of a water-boat. Some time later his eyesight began to fail; and one dark night, either accidentally or purposely – no one will ever know which – he stepped off his craft into the water and was drowned.

6 Mutiny in the 'Veronica'

The barque *Veronica* – From the Gulf of Mexico to the River Plate – Malcontents –
Beginning of the mutiny – How Captain Shaw was killed – *Veronica* burned and
abandoned – Mutineers land in the island of Cajueira – Taken off by the SS *Brunswick* –
Suspicion – 'King's evidence' – British Consul acts – Survivors arrested – Lord
Birkenhead prosecutes – '. . . That ghastly ship . . .' – A fitting end.

OF all the tales of murder on the high seas, few are so gruesome as the story of the
mutiny in the *Veronica*. The Captain, mate, second mate, and four other
members of that vessel's crew were killed in cold blood, in revolting circumstances. In the majority of cases of mutiny at sea, ill-treatment of the crew has invariably
been the prime reason for the trouble. But there was no ill-treatment of the men on board
the *Veronica*. Captain Alexander Shaw, her master, was a singularly mild-mannered man,
and in handling the sailors Mr McLeod (the mate) and Mr Abrahamson (the second mate)
appear to have taken their cue from him.

The only reason for the crime seems to have been petty jealousy. Aboard the *Veronica*
was a man named Patrick Doran, who was one of those heaven-sent sailormen who could
always be relied on to make a first-class job of anything he was told off to do. Paddy was a
great favourite with the Captain and officers in consequence. This was the beginning of the
trouble, which culminated in mutiny, an orgy of murder, and arson.

The *Veronica* was a three-masted, wooden barque of 1093 net registered tons, owned by
Messrs Robert Thomson & Company, of St John's, New Brunswick. She was 186 feet in
length, and had been built in 1879. Captain Shaw, who was a Canadian, joined her in 1901,
at Rosano. On 6th October 1902 she set out from Ship Island, in the Gulf of Mexico, on
her last, ill-fated voyage. She was laden with timber, and bound for Montevideo.

Her crew, which was made up of mixed nationalities, numbered twelve hands, all told.
In the fo'c'sle, in addition to Paddy Doran, were three Germans, a Dutchman, a Swede
named Gustav Johannson, a Hindu coolie named Alec Bravo, and a man from Prince
Edward Island whose name was Julius Parsons. The twelfth member of the crew was the
cook – a negro belonging to Virginia, aged twenty-four, whose name was Moses Thomas.

Moses Thomas; the Dutchman, named William Smith; and the three Germans, named
Otto Ernst Monsson, Harry Flohr, and Gustav Rau, were the only survivors left to tell the
dreadful tale – a tale so horrible that it shocked the world.

Monsson and Flohr were eighteen years of age; Smith, the Dutchman, was thirty; and Gustav Rau, who was the ringleader of the mutiny, was twenty-eight.

The first two or three weeks of the passage passed off uneventfully. The ship experienced a succession of calms, but with the help of the Gulf Stream she worked her way slowly down the Gulf of Mexico and through the Florida Strait, out into the Atlantic. On 24th October 1902, in latitude 29 degrees north, longitude 79 degrees west – approximately 100 miles off the Florida coast – she was spoken 'All well'. That was the last time any other ship set eyes on her.

From this latter position to the Equator she continued to experience adverse weather conditions. Calms and head winds persisted, and her progress to the south-east, along the line of the West India islands, was painfully slow.

Disputes broke out on board as a natural consequence. Had the men been all of one nationality, these would probably never have got beyond the healthy argument stage. Being so mixed, however, in race, religion, and temperament, the forecastle hands were soon at loggerheads and split up into different groups.

The three Germans and the Dutchman formed a clique of their own, seizing every opportunity to vent their sullen anger on the remainder of the crew. The fact that Paddy Doran, with whom Julius Parsons and Gustav Johannson remained on friendly terms, was given the best sailorising jobs was their principal bone of contention. They seemed to forget that, all in all, they were very mediocre seamen themselves.

Paddy accepted their unreasonable hostility with complete indifference. 'So long as they keep their thoughts to themselves, I don't give a damn,' he confided to Julius Parsons. 'But I'll plug the bunch, if they start opening their mouths too wide.'

He was big and strong enough to carry out this threat.

As the voyage progressed, the malcontents discussed their imaginary grievance, brooded over it, and generally worked themselves up to such a pitch of hot resentment towards the after-guard and their fellow-shipmates that things really began to look very ugly.

Rau told his companions that the officers intended to throw the 'Dutchmen' overboard, and suggested that the latter had better get busy first and throw the officers over the side.

This was his first hint that he was contemplating violence towards the after-guard, but as the voyage continued he became bolder, and expressed his murderous designs more clearly.

'We have two revolvers, and there are plenty of belaying-pins,' he reminded his companions. Some talk about killing the officers ensued, and Rau suggested that Smith and Flohr should stick a knife into Paddy's throat, while he attended to Julius Parsons. Then they would go aft and kill the Captain and officers.

Young Flohr expressed his horror of murder, and the subject was allowed to drop. But three days later, following an argument with the Irishman, Rau returned to it.

He suggested that the crew should be picked off one by one that night, during the middle watch, while the mate was in charge of the deck and Paddy was on the lookout. Monsson and Smith acquiesced, but young Flohr cried out: 'I cannot bear to see a pig killed, so how can I kill a man?'

Veronica was a three-masted barque, the most common type of ocean-going carrier in the middle of the nineteenth century.

'Shut up, you fool!' Rau retorted. 'Do you want to give the game away? If you don't do as you're told, we'll chuck *you* overboard! See?'

Flohr was overawed, and joined them. Paddy was selected to be the first man to die. About three o'clock the following morning the horrible work began. Paddy was on the lookout, and Flohr was instructed to kill him with an iron belaying-pin. The lad shrank from the task, however, and so Rau decided to do the job himself.

'Can you see the North Star to-night, Paddy?' he asked, in a genial tone. It was quite a natural question, because they were approaching the Equator and expecting shortly to lose sight of that Northern Hemisphere star.

Paddy bent down to glance under the foot of the foresail, and Rau struck him. Smith and Flohr carried the limp body down on to the main deck, and threw it into the paint-locker. The commotion attracted the mate's attention, and Mr McLeod came forward to investigate the matter.

'What's happened to the lookout-man?' he asked; and Rau and Smith, each armed with a belaying-pin, sprang out of the darkness and felled him with a shower of wicked blows. Smith sustained a severe scalp wound in the encounter, being accidentally struck on the head by his fellow-murderer. Without waiting to ascertain whether the officer was dead, Rau and Smith dragged the body to the rail and threw it overboard.

Then, armed with their revolvers, they went aft in search of the Captain and second mate. Thinking that it was one bell, and that he was being called to go on watch, the second mate very obligingly lighted his lamp, and Rau fired at him as he lay propped on one elbow in his bunk. Jumping out on to the floor, he ran into the saloon, crying out: 'Captain, I've been shot!'

Rau and Smith went up on to the poop, and the former told Flohr to kill Johannson, who was at the wheel. The young German could not bring himself to use an iron belaying-pin, but he did take a wooden one and aimed a blow at the terrified Swede, who let go of the wheel and ran forward. At Rau's direction Flohr followed him, but half-way along the deck the latter turned and went back to the poop, to take the helm.

He reached the wheel, to find the Captain standing there. Captain Shaw, who was a very deaf man, seemed dazed and bewildered, as well he might be. 'Where's the mate? Why have they shot the second mate?' he cried.

'Ah! I've been looking for you, Captain!' sang out Rau, striding across the poop. He held an iron belaying-pin in one hand and a revolver in the other. He threw the belaying-pin at the master, who ducked, and then fired at him. The bullet found its mark, and clapping his hand to his side the Captain staggered down the companionway into the saloon.

Rau and Smith next went in search of Julius Parsons, who had locked himself in the sail-locker amidships. Hearing the mutineers trying to break open the door, he attempted to climb out of the port-hole. He was a large man, however, with the result that, having got his head and shoulders through the port-hole, he stuck. Rau came across him in that helpless position, and promptly battered out his brains.

Paddy Doran, in a dying condition in the paint-locker, cried out for a drink of water, and Rau replied: 'Sure! I'll give you a b——y good drink!' With that he killed him. His body was thrown overboard.

Now mad with blood-lust, Rau began to hunt for the cook, who had barricaded himself in his cabin. The negro was told to come out on deck, but he refused to do so, pleading frantically for his life.

'Don't kill the poor cook,' Smith said. 'He hasn't done any harm to us. Besides, who will cook for us, if you kill him?'

Rau agreed that they must have someone to do the cooking. He told the negro to go to the galley and make some coffee, and he might be spared.

'But don't in any circumstances go aft,' he warned. 'And don't ask any questions.'

The cook went to the galley and made the coffee, Rau standing over him with a revolver the while. He was made to taste the coffee before anyone else touched it; and the same precaution was taken with everything else he cooked, in case he might be trying to poison them.

After breakfast on that fatal day boards were nailed up over the ports in the chartroom, to prevent the Captain and second mate from firing through them, or getting out on deck themselves. The officers were kept prisoners in the saloon for forty-eight hours, without any food or water being given to them. On the third day Rau opened the skylight an inch or two, and sang out for a chart and a pair of parallel rulers. The second mate answered, saying the Captain was too badly wounded to move.

'Tell him to move, quick and lively, or I'll empty my revolver into him,' Rau retorted, flourishing the weapon. The Captain crawled to the skylight, and cried out for mercy.

'What have I done?' was his piteous appeal. 'I have a wife and children. Spare my life! Give me a drink of water!'

Rau told him to hand up the chart and parallel rulers first, and when the second mate had done this, a can of water was lowered down through the skylight to them.

The mutineers agreed that it would not be safe to leave the Captain and second mate alive, and three days later they decided to kill them. Having ranged his men on the poop, Rau ordered the prisoners up from below. The second mate came first, and was confronted by the killers. Rau, Smith, and Monsson were armed with revolvers; Flohr with a belaying-pin. Hitherto there had only been two revolvers; the third one evidently had been stolen from one of the officers' cabins. Realising what was coming to him, Abrahamson began to run along the starboard side of the poop; whereupon Smith levelled his revolver and shot him in the shoulder. With a cry of despair the second mate tottered to the rail and dived overboard. He swam with all the energy and strength of desperation, but Rau sang out: 'About ship! He must not get away alive!'

The black cook, Johannson, and Alec Bravo hauled round the yards, while Rau, Smith, and Monsson fired at the man in the water, who suddenly disappeared.

The Captain was next ordered to come out on deck. He refused, and the Hindu was ordered to chase him out of the saloon with an axe. As the wretched master came slowly up the companionway, holding his hands in front of his face, Rau told Flohr to take Monsson's revolver and kill him. No doubt the arch-fiend wished to implicate Flohr, who had not so far done any actual killing. The young German took the gun and fired three shots, but none took effect. Then Rau stepped close up to the Captain and shot him dead. His body was thrown overboard.

Rau afterwards dressed in the Captain's clothes and used the Captain's whistle, which revealed a cheap conceit in his character. He decided to set fire to the ship and destroy all evidence of their crime. In collaboration with Smith and Monsson he made up a story for them to tell, in the event of their being picked up.

This was to the effect that one man had died, another been killed by the fall of a tackle-block, during the voyage; and that after the ship caught fire the remainder took to the lifeboats, but what had become of the second boat they did not know.

'Johannson was ordered out on to the jib-boom'. This photograph, taken on the four-masted barque, *Port Jackson*, shows the deck looking aft.

Rau set his shipmates to learn this story. They rehearsed it day by day, and night by night, for a week. But Alec Bravo and Johannson, who were dull-witted fellows, could not commit the story to memory. That sealed their fate. Realising that they would undoubtedly let the cat out of the bag, Rau decided to kill them.

Johannson was ordered out on to the jib-boom to furl the flying-jib, and while he was doing this Rau fired at him, hitting him in the stomach. The Swede struggled back on to the fo'c'sle head and ran aft, crying: 'Don't kill me! Don't kill me! I've done youse no harm.'

Smith came up to him and, catching hold of him with one hand, shot him through the head.

Flohr was told off to dispatch the Hindu, and following him when he went to haul down the main tack the timid young German fired three shots at him. Bravo jumped overboard and began to swim away from the ship, but Rau and Smith opened fire at him and he sank.

One of the lifeboats had been recaulked a day or two previously, and this was now provisioned and made ready. Bloodstained clothing was piled in a heap, saturated with kerosene, and set fire to. The cabins, store-rooms, and timber on deck were treated in like manner, Stockholm tar being mixed with the kerosene to make a good blaze.

When the ship was well alight, fore and aft, the lifeboat was launched; and Rau, who had been in the German navy and knew something about handling a boat, took charge. That was on 20th December 1902. They hoisted the lugsail and sailed south-east. Five days later (on Christmas Day) they sighted the north-east coast of Brazil. The boat had been well stocked with bread, biscuits, tinned-beef, oysters, condensed milk, beans, and two five-gallon beakers of fresh water. But as soon as land was sighted, on Rau's instructions, most of this was thrown overboard, as well as some of their clothing, to give the impression that they had been obliged to abandon the ship in a hurry.

They landed on the island of Cajueira, owned by Messrs Hugh, Evans & Company, Liverpool merchants, which lies off Tutoia, in latitude 20° 42' south, longitude 42° 16' west. This island was uninhabited except when steamers called there for sugar and cotton, which were brought down from the interior. Rau and his companions subsequently had good reason to regret their hasty decision to throw away their food. They were in a destitute and starving condition when the SS *Brunswick*, belonging to, and bound for, Liverpool, arrived at the island several days later.

Rau and the cook went off in their boat to the steamer and pitched their carefully rehearsed story to Captain Browne, her master, who believed it and took the five men aboard. They attacked the food placed before them with the voracity of wild animals, thus unconsciously adding greater credence to their story. A wealthy South American merchant, who had come aboard to see his goods safely shipped, was so moved to pity by the castaways' plight that he offered, there and then, to take the whole bunch back with him to his estate, clothe them, and give them jobs. For some reason Rau declined this offer, and so strong was his domination over his shipmates that, despite their better judgment, they also declined it. If they had done otherwise, the true story of the loss of the *Veronica* might never have been told.

In turning his back on this road to safety Rau made his second big mistake. His first one had been to spare the cook's life. He had not done this with any humane motive, to be sure, but simply to have someone to prepare meals and order around. He continued to bully and vent his sullen temper on the cook after they had embarked in the *Brunswick*. This was an additional mistake, for Moses Thomas promptly asked to be berthed apart from his former shipmates.

'The black cook says he's afraid of you chaps,' the *Brunswick*'s mate subsequently remarked to Rau. 'Why is he?'

Rau turned the question aside with a gruff laugh. 'He's always afraid of something or somebody, sir,' he replied derisively. 'Don't take any notice of him.'

Another strange fact that attracted attention was that Smith and the three Germans studiously avoided the *Brunswick*'s crew. They would remain for hours at a time talking among themselves in one part of the deck. Then the *Brunswick*'s bosun noticed that the caulking in their lifeboat was comparatively new. This was not consistent with the story they had told of abandoning the ship in a hurry. Nor was the fact that Smith wore his shore suit, instead of his working clothes. The survivors had said that the *Veronica*'s crew were fighting the fire for several hours, and when at last it got the better of them they barely had time to launch the boats and scramble into them. Yet here was evidence that one man had calmly gone to the fo'c'sle and changed into his shore rig. Obviously something was wrong with the story somewhere.

Rau had unwittingly mentioned the many different nationalities aboard the *Veronica*, and one day he was asked how it came that four out of the five survivors were Germans or Dutchmen. Rau accounted for this by explaining that they were all in the same watch, but the seed of suspicion had been sown.

Ten days out from Tutoia there was a sensational development. Moses Thomas intimated that he wished to speak with the Captain privately. Captain Browne acceded to his request, and Thomas told him that the story about one man dying and another being killed accidentally, and Captain Shaw and the rest of the crew putting off in a second boat, was all a fabrication. He thereupon related the actual facts. The horrified shipmaster got out his log-book and made the black cook relate the story again, while he wrote it down. Thomas signed this confession, and his signature was duly witnessed.

Captain Browne reported the matter to the British Consul at Lisbon, and on his advice brought the men to Liverpool. The *Brunswick* arrived in the Mersey on 28th January, and that evening some of the newspapers, believing that it was the right one, published the false story, which had been gleaned from the men on board.

Meanwhile the Liverpool police, acting on instructions from Scotland Yard and the Home Office, had arrested the whole of the survivors. The three Germans and Smith were placed in custody, while the cook was kept under close police observation. All four of the mutineers made long statements, which were inconsistent with, and contradictory to, their previous story. Briefly, these suggested that there was ill-feeling between the men and the officers; that one night trouble arose and the chief mate jumped overboard; and that afterwards the Captain and second mate were murdered by the black cook. The mutineers asserted, in fact, that Moses Thomas was the ringleader of the whole affair.

A few hours after making his statement, however, Flohr voluntarily made another, which corroborated in all main essentials the story told by the cook. The prosecution regarded this as a matter of supreme importance, because Flohr had no notion whatever of what the cook had said. The Crown resolved in consequence to withdraw the charge of murder against Flohr. It was pointed out at the preliminary proceedings that he was a young man who might well have been dominated by minds stronger than his own, and that in a case involving the extreme penalty it would not be right to ask the jury to make their decision on the evidence of one man.

Rau, Smith, and Monsson were committed for trial, and on 13th May they were brought before Mr Justice Lawrence at the Liverpool Assizes. Mr Tobin and Lord Birkenhead prosecuted for the Crown, and each of the prisoners, all three of whom pleaded 'Not Guilty', was defended by counsel.

The charge proceeded with was that of the wilful murder of Captain Shaw. A prominent object in the well of the court was a model to scale of the *Veronica*, all complete with masts, yards, sails, and rigging. The trial occupied three days, and during the proceedings the prisoners' statements were read out. Smith's was a very lengthy one, consisting of fifty pages of foolscap, which took the clerk of assize over an hour to wade through. Monsson's statement, which no one could make head or tail of, concluded with the following remarkable passage:

'We have done nothing wrong, for we fought for our lives. If the gentlemen who go to distant lands, where one lives every day in insecurity, read this story they will be able to say if it is wrong or right. If the story the cook has told is true, then he should be put in bonds. I accept whatever punishment may be allotted to me.'

In their evidence the prisoners all swore that the cook was the instigator of the mutiny, and that Flohr (who had turned 'King's Evidence') was his principal lieutenant. Rau declared that Flohr was always making trouble; that Paddy Doran was his (Rau's) friend; that it was the cook who shot the Captain and two officers, and afterwards set fire to the ship; and that it was the cook who made up the original story they told.

'Did you determine to give up the wicked cook when you got ashore?' he was asked.

'If we came to some wild people, we would not give him up,' he answered. 'But if we came to some people who were not wild, we would.'

Smith, who backed up Rau's story, was asked why he did not tell the truth when he went aboard the *Brunswick*. 'Because they had trouble enough of their own,' he replied.

He admitted under cross-examination that when the Captain and second mate came up out of the cabin, Rau, Monsson, and himself were standing by with revolvers in their hands.

'What for?' demanded the judge sternly.

'To defend ourselves,' Smith replied. 'We had orders to do that.'

'From whom?' demanded the judge.

'The cook,' replied Smith, amid laughter.

In his summing-up, which lasted an hour and ten minutes, the judge referred to the *Veronica* as 'that ghastly ship', and reminded the jury of the 'horrible part in a most horrible story' the prisoners had played – 'standing round the cabin with revolvers or belaying-pins in their hands, while the Captain and second mate came up like rats out of a cage.'

The jury, who were out for an hour and a quarter, brought in a verdict of 'Guilty' against all the prisoners. They, however, recommended Monsson to mercy, owing to his youth and previous good character.

Before passing sentence of death on them the judge addressed the prisoners. He said:

'Gustav Rau, Otto Ernst Theodore Monsson, and William Smith, the jury have found you guilty on evidence which has satisfied them, and satisfied everyone who has heard this case. I am sure of your guilt. They have found you guilty of the wilful murder of Captain Shaw. A more brutal murder – we are dealing only with his murder now – there never was. Not satisfied with killing the three officers, you proceeded to kill a number – four or five – of your fellow-sailors aboard that ship. Nothing remains for me but to pass upon you the sentence which the law imposes upon me. I may say to you, Monsson, that the recommendation of the jury will be forwarded to the proper quarter. That is all I can say with regard to that recommendation, in which I agree.'

Rau and Smith, maintaining their stolid, sullen demeanour to the end, were executed at Walton Jail, on 2nd June 1903. Monsson's death sentence was commuted to penal servitude for life.

7 A Shipwreck to Remember

The message of disaster – Port Philip Bay – One Saturday in May 1891 – The four-masted barque *Craigburn* – The tow-rope breaks – Swept on to the rocks – Lifeboat and tugs to the rescue – The price of safety – Captain *versus* Pilot – Taking to the boats – Hurricane squalls – Pounding heavily – The rescue party – The rocket apparatus – To safety or death.

ONE Saturday in May 1891 a message was flashed from Sorrento, a popular seaside resort in Port Philip Bay, near Melbourne, Australia, to the effect that a large sailing ship was in distress outside the Heads.

The message ran:

'A four-masted barque lies in a very dangerous position half a mile off the breakers between Point Nepean and Cape Schanck. The wind is increasing to gale force and a high sea is running. At intervals the ship is completely hidden by spray. She has both anchors down, but unless the weather improves it is doubtful whether they will prevent her from driving ashore. A tug has been in attendance on her all morning, but was obliged at midday to go for help.'

This message, which excited much interest and speculation, was shortly followed by one from the signal station at Cape Schanck, which read:

'A four-masted barque lying to her anchors close to the breakers about ten miles from here has signalled as follows: "Dragging. Can veer no more cable and have no more anchors to let go. My tug has left."'

The latter, named the *Rescue*, reached Queenscliff a little later, and her master reported that the four-masted barque in distress was the *Craigburn*, which he had towed out through the Heads earlier in the day. Her tow-line had in some way become detached, and finding that she could not beat her way seaward under canvas, the *Craigburn* had anchored. She was holding on well at the moment, the tugmaster stated, but was in a very perilous position. He was of the opinion that if the weather did not moderate before nightfall she would have to be towed away from the shore, and to do this would mean the employment of more than one tug.

The *Eagle*, a very powerful tug, happened to be in the vicinity, and was immediately ordered to proceed with the *Rescue* to the barque's assistance. These two tugs arrived on the scene in ample time to do all that was required of them; consequently this story should end with the dramatic snatching of a fine vessel from the rocks. Actually, however, it ends with disaster, tragedy, and death; and all because of contradictory orders and dissension aboard the barque, bungling, and the loss of valuable time in haggling over the price which was to be paid for towing her to safety.

Laden with 900 tons of ballast, the *Craigburn*, a fine Clyde-built vessel of 1997 tons register, left her anchorage off Port Melbourne, for Wellington, New Zealand, at eleven o'clock on Friday night, the 8th of May 1891. She carried a crew of thirty hands all told, and was commanded by Captain Kerr, a shipmaster of about sixty years of age, who had been her Captain since her maiden voyage, in 1884. At Wellington she was to load a general cargo for London, and it was expected that the passage to the New Zealand capital would occupy about a week. Mr Blanchard, of the Melbourne Pilotage Service – than which there is no finer pilotage service in the world – was in charge, and the *Craigburn* was in tow of the tug *Rescue*.

On the way down the forty miles' stretch of harbour the barque's fore and aft sails were set. Being dead ahead, and fresh, the wind made her progress slow, with the result that the Heads were not reached until six-thirty on Saturday morning. Shortly before this Captain Kerr had conferred with the pilot as to the advisability of anchoring off Sorrento, within the Heads, until the wind came westerly. They decided, however, that it would be quite safe to carry on provided the tug towed the ship well up to windward, beyond Point Lonsdale, before letting go of her. This would give the *Craigburn* a good offing, from which, on the starboard tack, she would have little difficulty in weathering Cape Schanck. The tug-boat was told what would be required of her, and with a wave of his hand her skipper signified that he understood.

All went well until the *Rescue* and her tow were nearly through the 'Rip', as the tide-race between the two headlands (Point Nepean and Point Lonsdale) is called; then suddenly, without any warning whatever, the tow-rope slipped off the bitts on the *Craigburn's* fo'c'sle head, and went careering over the side.

That such a thing should have happened simply proved that the *Craigburn's* chief mate had neglected his duty in not making sure that the rope had been properly secured. However, there was no time for recriminations, with the ship in imminent danger of being swept on to the rocks at one side of the harbour entrance or the other. The tug could do nothing to help until she had got the tow-line hove-in; and that would take a quarter of an hour at least. The only thing for it, in the circumstances, was to get more canvas on to the *Craigburn*, and the sailors were ordered to loose the topsails and the foresail.

Had they been the worse for liquor, as sailing-ship crews frequently were on leaving port, it is doubtful whether they would have got this job done in time to avert an immediate disaster. Fortunately every one of them was perfectly sober. On this occasion it was the after-guard, and not the fo'c'sle hands, who were the worse for drink, the pilot and the second mate excepted.

The *Craigburn* had drifted to within a stone's throw of Point Nepean by the time the topsails were sheeted home; but under their driving-power she quickly forged ahead, out of danger for the time being.

The four-masted barque *Tamara* under tow in September 1924.

For an hour she stood down the coast towards Cape Schanck, close-hauled on the starboard tack. It became increasingly more evident, however, that she would have difficulty in clearing the headland. Had she been in deep trim she might have been able to claw her way to windward; but drawing only thirteen or fourteen feet of water, with the greater part of her side exposed to the wind, she went to leeward like a crab. By the time she was abeam of Rye, another popular seaside resort, it was perfectly clear that she would not weather Cape Schanck; and the pilot suggested wearing her round on to the port tack.

The Captain agreed, and this manœuvre was executed. The *Craigburn* lost a mile in coming round; but this could not be helped, as it would have been useless to try to tack her under such a small amount of canvas, with the wind rapidly developing into a gale and a high sea running.

On the port tack the *Craigburn* fared little better than on the starboard tack. It soon became evident that she would not weather Point Nepean, beyond which lay the entrance to the harbour and safety. In sailor language she was on a 'dead lee-shore', and rapidly drawing closer to it. Five miles more sea-room would have made all the difference, but the slipping of the tow-rope, through the mate's incompetence, or neglect, had robbed her of this, and incidentally lost the pilot his chance of getting back to the pilot-cutter.

Three miles from Point Nepean the *Craigburn* was put back on to the starboard tack. Another mile was lost in wearing round, but the immediate danger – that of piling up on Point Nepean – had been averted. If at this stage the wind had shifted a couple of points more to the westward the barque would still have stood a good chance of extricating herself from her unenviable position. But with diabolical obstinacy it held steadily from the south-west, driving her closer, and still closer, towards the shore.

About nine o'clock – two and a half hours after the tow-rope had slipped – the pilot expressed the opinion that they would have to anchor, and Captain Kerr gave his consent. The *Craigburn* was then midway between Sorrento and Rye, in fifteen fathoms of water, about a mile and a quarter from what is known locally as the 'back beach'.

The canvas having been stripped off the barque, both anchors were let go with their full scope of chain. It was an anxious moment, but coming slowly head to wind, with her cables bar-taut and the windlass groaning under their weight, the *Craigburn* held.

The tug *Rescue* had not apparently appreciated the barque's danger while the latter was under canvas. The letting-go of the anchors evidently brought this home to her, for she immediately steamed towards and stood by the *Craigburn*. Finding that her services were not needed for the time being, however, she steamed away to obtain help, realising that sooner or later her services would be required.

It was now twelve o'clock. A little later, during an exceptionally hard squall, the *Craigburn* began to drag. She instantly hoisted signals of distress, and the authorities at Queenscliff were informed of this.

Their first act upon receipt of this intelligence was to notify the superintendent of the lifeboat stationed there. Then they ordered the *Eagle* to proceed with the *Rescue* to the barque's assistance. A little later they dispatched the tug *Racer* as well.

Whatever hopes might have been entertained that the weather would improve were dissipated by three o'clock in the afternoon, at which hour the *Eagle* and the *Rescue* reached the *Craigburn*. By then the wind had increased to a whole gale, and a high, breaking sea was beating on the coast. Fierce squalls drove over the barque and the two tugs, sweeping them with rain and hail. The *Craigburn*'s topsails and foresail had been left hanging in their gear, but to save the thrashing canvas from being blown to ribbons the order was given to furl them. During the three hours the *Rescue* had been away from the barque the latter had dragged half a mile closer to the shore. Only three-quarters of a mile now separated her from the thundering breakers, which were studded with black pinnacles and flat ledges of rock.

Alive to the fact that there was no time to lose, the skipper of the *Eagle* backed his craft as close as he dared to the *Craigburn*, and one of his men threw a line to her. This fell short, but floated down to the barque, being secured by some men on her fo'c'sle head. Pilot Blanchard, who was among the latter, promptly bent the end of the heaving line to the eye of the *Craigburn*'s hawser, and sang out to those aboard the tug to haul it in.

They were doing this when Captain Kerr rushed up on to the fo'c'sle head.

''Vast paying out that hawser,' he ordered; and then, cupping his hands, he bawled: 'How much do you want for pulling me off this lee shore?'

That he should be asked such a question at such a time evidently took the tug's skipper aback, for he made no reply for several moments. This clearly being a case of salvage, it would have been more customary to leave the question of payment to an arbitration court to settle. Captain Kerr was determined, however, to settle it there and then.

'How much?' he again demanded, keeping one hand on the tow-line to prevent its being paid out.

This time the tug skipper found his voice.

'Five hundred pounds, sir,' he answered.

'I'll give you fifty pounds,' Kerr shouted.

The tug skipper shook his head, and Kerr put his offer up to a hundred pounds. But the former still refused to accept such a comparatively small sum.

'Let's leave it to the people ashore to settle, sir,' he shouted. 'Come on; pay out your line and let me get it on my hook.'

'I'll be damned if I will,' retorted Kerr, whose tone and manner filled his crew and the pilot with apprehension. 'If you're not prepared to tow me clear for a hundred pounds, let go of my hawser and clear out.'

With that he moved over to the other side of the fo'c'sle head and began to haggle with the skipper of the tug *Rescue*, who also refused his price.

In justice to the tugmaster it must be pointed out that if, in order to get hold of his line, they had accepted Kerr's offer, they would have placed themselves outside the jurisdiction of the arbitration court; for a definite contract, no matter how disadvantageous to their owners, would have been made. No one could reasonably expect them to do that. A good deal of unfair criticism was subsequently levelled at them. In one quarter it was suggested that they had held a pistol at Kerr's head, while his ship and crew were in peril. It might have been more accurate to say that he had held a pistol at their heads, in trying to shame them into towing his ship to safety without regard to a fair and reasonable salvage award.

He continued to haggle with the master of the *Rescue* until, exasperated beyond measure, the pilot told the sailors to pay out the tow-rope, and shouted to the *Eagle's* crowd to haul it in.

This act roused Captain Kerr to fury, and rushing across the deck he struck the pilot.

'You're exceeding your authority!' he shouted. 'Get off the fo'c'sle head, or I'll have you thrown off it.'

Pilot Blanchard turned and appealed to the bewildered sailors.

'As you can see for yourselves, men, the Captain is drunk,' he said. 'I therefore advise you, if you wish to save the ship and your lives, to take him aft and lock him up.'

Half a dozen men instantly closed round Kerr, and began to hustle him towards one of the ladders. He argued with and threatened them, but finally submitted to their demand that the pilot should be allowed to assume command. Two sailors accompanied him aft, and upon his giving them his assurance that he would not interfere with the work they left him at liberty in the saloon, instead of locking him up.

Meanwhile the tow-rope had been placed on the *Eagle*'s hook, without any further discussion as to payment. The tug took the weight of the ship, and the pilot told the *Craigburn*'s crew to heave up the anchors. Steam had been kept on the donkey-boiler; but the windlass refused to budge when its valve was opened, having broken under the tremendous strain on it. The only alternative was to slip the cables, and the pilot told the carpenter to do this. He refused, saying he would take orders from no one but the Captain or the chief mate. The second mate seized a top-maul and endeavoured to knock out one of the pins; but it was 'frozen' in its shackle, and the rest of the shackle-pins were in a similar condition. As a last resort the tug endeavoured to tow the ship seaward while the latter's anchors were still down, and this resulted in the bitts on which the tow-line was made fast being torn out of the *Craigburn*'s deck.

The *Racer* now arrived on the scene. She and the *Rescue* backed in towards the *Craigburn* and managed to get their tow-lines aboard her. For some inexplicable reason, however, the *Racer*'s rope was not made fast by the barque's crew, and when the tug went ahead she pulled the whole of it into the water. The rope fouled her propellers, and while it was being hacked clear she very nearly drifted on to the rocks. The *Rescue* made a valiant effort on her own to tow the barque clear, but the latter's anchors with their long scope of chain defeated her; and before the *Eagle* could come to her assistance night had fallen.

The *Craigburn* was now left to her own resources, and such help as those on shore might be able to offer, since further effort on the part of the tugs was out of the question until daylight next morning. To ease the strain on the windlass, wire lashings were placed on the cables. Pilot Blanchard then returned aft, to find the vessel's stern almost in the first line of breakers. Beyond the breakers, about five hundred yards from the *Craigburn*'s poop, reared the barren and rocky cliffs which stretch from Point Nepean to Cape Schanck and rise almost abruptly out of the sea.

As the result of the unavoidable disturbance of her anchors, the *Craigburn* had dragged half a mile closer to the shore. She was holding on well at the moment, but realising that she might start to drag again at any time the pilot went below to consult the Captain.

Much to his surprise, Captain Kerr was asleep on the settee in his cabin. Having awakened him, the pilot said:

'We're very near the breakers, Captain. Our position is about as bad as it could be.'

'Thanks to you,' sneered Kerr. 'If you hadn't let those blasted tugs pull the anchors all over the place the ship wouldn't have dragged a second time.'

'If the shackles had been workable we'd have slipped the cables and been inside the Heads by now,' retorted the pilot. 'Still, it's no use talking about that. The question is, what are we going to do?'

'I'm going to have a good night's sleep,' said Kerr, whose obstinate refusal to admit his ship's peril was one of the most extraordinary features of this disaster. 'It will be time enough to talk about what we're going to do when daylight comes.'

The two men were still arguing, when suddenly there was a jarring motion underfoot, as if the vessel had grounded. Half a dozen sailors rushed down into the saloon a moment later and announced that she was among the breakers. The pilot ran up on deck, to find her almost surrounded by white, broken water, with rocks on both sides of her.

'Well, we'll have to take to the boats,' he told the sailors, who were assembled on the poop. Captain Kerr appeared at that instant and began to criticise this suggestion.

'Take to the boats by all means, if you wish to be drowned,' he said. 'But if you take my advice, you'll remain by the ship until daylight.'

'There won't be any daylight for us, unless we get out of the ship now,' retorted the pilot excitedly. 'The ship'll go to pieces in no time when she gets on the rocks; and it won't be long before she does that.'

'A lifeboat'll go to pieces a darn sight quicker than the ship on the rocks,' said Kerr, addressing the crowd. 'However, it's up to you men to make your choice. You've heard the pilot's views, and I've given you mine. I can do no more.'

The sailors conferred among themselves for a few moments, while the wind roared overhead and the ship sheered about wildly. Finally one of them spoke.

'We're in favour of taking to the boats, as the pilot suggests, sir,' he said.

'Very well,' replied Kerr. 'But please don't say it was my suggestion.'

The lifeboats, which had already been provisioned and prepared, were hanging ready in their davits. The pilot said he would take the starboard boat, and the second mate said he would go with him. Lifebelts were served out, and it was arranged that thirteen of the crew should accompany the pilot and the second mate, and that the remainder should go in the port boat. The pilot's crew took their places, and their shipmates lowered the boat into the water. For a few seconds it bumped heavily against the ship's side, and those on deck thought it would be stove in. However, its crew managed to thrust it off and row ahead of the ship. A moment later it was lost to view in a wilderness of torrential rain and crashing seas.

Sixteen men, including the Captain and the mate, were left aboard the ship. The majority of these wanted to take to the port boat at once, but the Captain persuaded them to wait. Blue lights were burned and rockets were sent up, but there was no response from the shore.

About ten o'clock the gale culminated in a burst of hurricane wind, and a few minutes later the ship dragged on to the rocks. She instantly listed to starboard and began to pound heavily. Captain Kerr, whose personal courage had never been in question, again urged the men to stand fast; but, seized by panic, the bosun and eleven hands lowered the port boat and scrambled into it.

Hardly had they succeeded in unhooking its tackles than the boat capsized, losing all its gear and three of its occupants, who were swept away and drowned. A wave righted the boat, and nine of its original complement of twelve scrambled back into it. Without oars, or even a sea-anchor, they were, however, completely at the mercy of the waves. Swept against a pinnacle of rock, the boat capsized a second time. Two more of its crew were drowned on this occasion, but the boat righted again and the rest of the men scrambled back into it. They were still clinging to its thwarts when it was flung, battered and waterlogged, on to a narrow strip of sandy beach at the foot of the cliffs.

Four men now remained aboard the doomed barque. These were the Captain, the chief

The rocket apparatus in use at the site of the beaching of the full-rigged ship *Orient*. She ran ashore after a hawser broke when she was being towed into East London with a cargo of wheat in 1907.

mate, the carpenter, and a young Scots sailor named Mackenzie. Kerr had refused to abandon the ship because he believed that it was safer aboard her than in the boats. The mate might have been willing to go, if someone had dumped him into a boat. But as no one had taken the trouble to do this he just remained where he was, an object of neither use nor ornament. Anything the Captain said was generally good enough for the carpenter, which accounted for his remaining behind. Mackenzie's reason is best given in his own words. 'I did not go in either boat because I did not care for the crowd,' he subsequently told his rescuers.

Lying athwart the incoming rollers the ship continued to pound heavily on the rocks. About two in the morning the carpenter crawled down into the 'tween decks and found the lower hold half-full of water. The weather bulwarks collapsed a little later, and thereafter the seas swept more easily over the ship. From their precarious position on the poop the

Captain, the carpenter, and Mackenzie continued to send up rockets; and presently half a dozen bonfires began to glow ashore, telling that friends were at hand.

Carrying lanterns, and led by a constable who was a local man, the rescue-party had come from Sorrento. Their journey had not been an easy one, for they had been compelled to strike across five miles of dense bush, by means of bridle-tracks, with the wind and rain beating in their faces. A faint cry reached them when they came to the edge of the cliff, above the wreck, and having made their way down to the beach, they stumbled across the shattered lifeboat and its seven survivors.

The latter, who were very exhausted, were helped or carried up a narrow pathway to the top of the cliff, and then to some quarrymen's huts a mile away, where they were given food and dry clothing. Two of the sailors were badly injured, and after one of the quarrymen's horses had been harnessed to a dray they were placed in this on bundles of sacks and conveyed to Sorrento.

Meanwhile the Queenscliff lifeboat had picked up the rocket apparatus kept at Point Nepean and brought it on to Sorrento. The arrival there of the horse and dray provided a convenient means of transport, and just as dawn was breaking the apparatus arrived with its crew at the scene of shipwreck.

Three men could be seen on the barque's fo'c'sle head, and it was subsequently learnt that these were the Captain, the carpenter, and Mackenzie. The chief mate, who had been at the ship's spirits during the night, had refused to leave his cabin. The jiggermast had fallen, and the yards on the other masts swung violently to and fro as the ship rocked from side to side, a plaything of the waves. There was a big rent in her side amidships, through which water poured in and out, and from the way she sagged in the middle and stuck up at the bow and stern, it was abundantly clear that her back was broken.

The life-savers lost no time in dragging their apparatus into action. Its gun exploded and a rocket with a thin line attached zoomed over the breakers and fell across the wreck. The carpenter and Mackenzie seized and hauled on the line, and presently a tail-block, with an endless rope-fall rove through it, was swaying across the maelstrom of jagged rocks and thundering surf. The tail-block was secured to the foot of the fore topmast, whereupon the people ashore hauled over the end of the hawser, which was made fast just above the tail-block. A cradle followed, jolting and jerking along the hawser from which it was suspended. All this can be told quickly, but actually it took three hours to establish communication with the *Craigburn*.

The carpenter was the first of the four men to leave the stricken ship. While he was being hauled to safety the Captain went aft to persuade the mate to come forward and save his life. The latter declined to do so, saying that the ship would last until nightfall. The Captain argued with him, but it was no use. Finally Kerr returned forward alone and got into the cradle. The mizzen topmast fell while they were hauling him ashore.

After the Captain's departure, Mackenzie went aft to try to get the mate to come forward. He still refused to leave his cabin, but the tenacious Scot refused to take 'No' for an answer.

'You'll come forward with me, if I have to knock you doon and carry you,' he said, and thus roused out of his drunken stupor the mate followed him out on deck.

The two men did not reach the fore rigging a moment too soon, for suddenly the scream of torn and twisted steel rang out; a moment later the ship broke clean across the middle, her stern slewing almost at right angles to her bow.

Reaching the fore top, Mackenzie peered over its rim and urged the mate to hurry. The cradle was within his arm's reach, and it was his intention to get the mate safely ashore in it before leaving the ship himself. At that moment, however, the hawser, which had been chafing against the rigging, carried away, and the cradle fell on to the fo'c'sle head.

To reach the shore now the two seamen would have to let themselves be hauled through the surf, which was infested with rocks. There was no alternative, and directly they got down on to the fo'c'sle head the Scotsman urged his companion to get into the cradle and take the chance. The mate refused.

'What would be the use?' he cried, pointing a trembling finger at the boiling maelstrom.

Mackenzie argued with him, but it was of no avail. He might have carried out his threat – knocked the mate down and bundled him into the cradle – but that would simply have been making sure of his death, for an unconscious man would have stood no chance at all in that raging surf.

A shout from the shore attracting his attention, the Scotsman glanced aloft, just as the fore and main topmasts with all their impedimenta came down with a blinding crash. Realising that the end was near he shook the mate roughly by the arm.

'Say what you're going to do,' he demanded. 'I'm only giving you one more chance. Are you going to get into the cradle?'

'No,' answered the mate.

'Pull yourself together, and take a chance, man,' urged Mackenzie; but the mate merely shook his head.

No one could have done any more for the wretched fellow, and climbing into the cradle Mackenzie signalled the rescuers to haul him ashore.

He was in a pitiful condition when they lifted him out of the cradle. His clothes had been torn off him. His face, arms, body, and legs were terribly lacerated, and he could not stand or speak. After a lengthy spell in hospital he happily recovered, to enjoy the hero-worship his pluck had earned for him.

An account of the final break-up of the ship was given to me many years ago by an eyewitness.

'Hardly had the cheering which greeted Mackenzie's safe arrival ashore died away,' he said, 'than with a loud crack the main lowermast broke off and fell into the sea. The mizzen lowermast followed it a moment later; and then a big roller toppled the stern portion of the vessel over on to its side, so that the poop deck stood up almost vertically out of the sea. The middle portion had by now entirely disappeared, and the forward portion was gradually upending and becoming submerged.

'From his position near the bows the mate had been watching Mackenzie's perilous journey ashore. When the main and mizzen lowermasts fell he climbed slowly up along the side of the fo'c'sle head and ascended a few ratlines of the fore rigging. We could not haul out the cradle again as one part of its double endless fall had chafed through in the surf. A single part of the fall still stretched between the ship and the shore, however, and we shouted to the mate to haul out the cradle himself. He made no attempt to do so.

'Presently he descended the rigging and dragged himself in the same dispirited fashion back to his former position in the bows, where he crouched with the sprays breaking over him. He did not remain there long, but got up and made his way back to the rigging. The thin line was still rove through the tail-block. Having unrove it, the mate made its severed end fast round his body and then clambered back once more into the bows. The sprays continued to lash him unmercifully, and suddenly the fore lowermast and foreyard came down. Almost at the same instant a big wave broke over the fo'c'sle head, washing the wretched mate into the sea.

'We hauled on the line quickly, and his head appeared once or twice above the swirl of white water; then it disappeared for good. When we hauled in the whole of the line there was nothing on its end. By nightfall the *Craigburn* had entirely disappeared.'

Hoping to find some trace of the missing lifeboat, the rescuers searched the coast for several miles in the vicinity of the wreck, but without avail. It was concluded that this boat had sunk with its crew of fifteen, including the pilot and the second mate. Much to everyone's surprise, however, it was picked up close to the Heads later in the day. Its crew had a stirring story of hardship and suffering to tell.

Time and again the boat had narrowly escaped being dashed against the rocks while struggling to get clear of the *Craigburn*. Finally it got away and the pilot headed it out to sea. The sailors, who were unaccustomed to rowing, soon got tired; but they were kept at it until the boat was five or six miles off shore. A sea-anchor was then put out and the boat was allowed to drift. A lighted globe-lamp had been brought away from the barque, and one of the sailors nursed this all through the night. It was bitterly cold. The sky was inky black and rain beat down incessantly, drenching the crew through and through. Two men kept baling, for seas constantly broke into the boat. The steward, who was one of the crew, had wisely brought along a couple of bottles of rum, which did more than anything else to keep the men's souls in their bodies. At dawn a schooner was sighted steering towards the Heads, but although the sailors waved and shouted, she failed to see them. Once again the oars were shipped, and when the boat had regained a sufficiently good offing the pilot headed it for the harbour. The tug *Eagle* picked it up.

A Marine Board of Inquiry into the disaster was subsequently held. It came to the conclusion that the loss of the vessel was occasioned by the default of Captain Kerr. The pilot was exonerated from all blame. The Court considered that he was justified in taking the ship to sea when he did, and that but for the slipping of the tow-line, through the chief mate's negligence, she would probably have got away safely. It had no fault to find with the tugs, which were given credit for doing their work in a thoroughly efficient manner.

'The master of the *Craigburn* was not justified in refusing their assistance,' said the President of the Court. 'He should immediately have availed himself of any opportunity that offered that would enable him to vacate the dangerous position in which the ship was placed.'

Captain Kerr's excuse was that he was confident that the ship would weather the gale, even in the dangerous position into which she had been forced. But the Court held that this was a gross error of judgment on his part.

A disciplinary court was later convened to investigate the matter in the light of the charges of default and drunkenness that had been made against Captain Kerr. Both charges were sustained, and his certificate of competency was cancelled. In addition, he was ordered to pay part of the expenses of the investigation.

Thus, professionally, he was ruined. Matters might have been even more serious for him if he had been found directly responsible for the loss of life which occurred. But the Board held that those of the crew who took to the boats, and were subsequently lost, acted, not merely of their own free will, but against Kerr's advice; for he urged them repeatedly to stand by the ship until daylight. This seems to have been about the only time that he displayed good sound judgment.

The lifeboat people came in for a good deal of criticism for remaining inside the Heads, instead of proceeding to the scene of shipwreck. Their excuse was that the land station telegraphists had not kept them sufficiently advised as to how matters with the *Craigburn* were progressing. The telegraphists indignantly repudiated this allegation, and the respective departments held an investigation into the matter. Still further criticism was aroused by the fact that each department exonerated its own officials and blamed the others!

In his address to the Court at the conclusion of the Marine Board Inquiry, one of the counsel said:

'No one who has heard the evidence before this Court will forget the extraordinary and tragic story of this disaster – a story all the more tragic because the disaster could easily have been avoided.'

8 The Anchor's Weighed – 1859

Maritime achievements of England – Barque *Flying Fish* – A ship's boy – 'Anchor's a-weigh, 1859' – An Irish Master and a Geordie Mate – Fo'c'sle life in the 'sixties – Channel gales – Hovellers of the Downs – A lookout with horn and bell – A curious assault – Work aloft – Hungry days – The *Flying Fish* runs aground – Up the Berbice river – Georgetown in the 'sixties – Mud ballast – Barbados – Screw-jacking hogsheads of sugar – Fever – A North Atlantic gale – Huge rollers on the west coast of Ireland – Walking home.

THE sea has spelled romance to the people of these islands for untold years, and how many boys have yielded to its lure can only be estimated from the maritime achievements of England through the centuries. Up to what, I suppose, may still be termed comparatively recent times, the 'seventies and the 'eighties of last century, there were sea families – the aristocracy of sail – who, in large measure, comprised the oversea adventurers, the pioneers of trade and Empire, and the creators of Britain's sea-power.

Yet I know of no ancestry from whom might have come my sea-fever; and all these things so apparent now did not occur to me, however, when, as a boy of fourteen, I arrived with my father at Tilbury on the bitterly cold and grey afternoon of 17th January 1859 to go aboard the barque *Flying Fish*, 221 tons register, W Davis, master.

We heard that she was lying below Gravesend, and so took a boat, with two old men to row, and soon discovered the smart little barque – it was her maiden voyage – in the Hope, off the 'Ship and Lobster', a solitary old inn. I said good-bye; not very gaily, however, as I knew my father would have to pay about ten shillings for the boat, which he could then ill afford. Somehow I clambered on to the deck; a rope was lowered to the men in the boat, and up came the small chest containing all my new dunnage. Before I could realise what was happening, the boat had almost disappeared into the winter haze.

EDITOR'S NOTE
The author of the next four chapters, Harry Hine, RI, gives a series of personal reminiscences of life at sea, and of places, countries and peoples as they appeared in the days of the East Indiaman, the Tea clipper, and the old Square-rigger of the 'sixties – three-quarters of a century ago. These memoirs must surely be unique, as they are the work of one who served in the fo'c'sle in 1859, rose to the rank of mate within a few years, observed and recorded at the time much that he experienced, achieved fame in later years as an artist, and is happily alive to-day to tell the story – probably the last that will ever be recorded at first hand – of life afloat and ashore in the halcyon days of sail.

The four-masted ship *Francesco Giuseppe*, ex-*Falls of Afton*, lying in the Thames, 'a waterway',
wrote Conrad, 'leading to the uttermost ends of the earth'.

'Get hold of the capstan, boy!' The words came brusquely from a small, dark, fierce-
looking man with coal-black hair, and eyes that seemed to be all iris and no pupil.

Thus jerked back to reality from such a mixture of tumultuous thoughts and feelings as
could scarcely be described, although still clear in memory, I seized what I knew to be a
capstan.

Some of the hands, who, to my surprise, were at work on the poop in their Sunday or
go-ashore rig, laughed at my mistake. 'Sit on the deck, get a hold of the fall, and surge
handsomely,' I was told.

By a vague hint and good luck I got hold of the fall, and certainly sat on deck, but, as the
rest of the order was meaningless to me, I failed to *surge handsomely*. The result was that I
slacked up the fall too late, the men at the capstan bars pitched suddenly forward, and I was

not complimented, but called a little —––, for my first work aboard the *Flying Fish*.

As the ebb tide was running fast, the barque was quickly got under way. First we went to the windlass brakes, working them up and down, setting the pawls clanking loudly. To my astonishment, a big Swede suddenly let out a roar in a rough bass, with frequent breaks in it, giving a yodelling effect, the other hands joining in the chorus:

> 'Oh – I wish't I was ole stormy's son,
> With a yea – you – storm along!
> Oh – I'd give my sailors plenty of rum!
> Aye! aye! aye! Mister – storm along.'

'Anchor a-weigh, sir!' suddenly shouted the carpenter, who also acted as second mate, when many verses of the chanty had been sung, accompanied by the rattle of the incoming chain and the click of the pawls.

'Run up the jib and hoist the fore tops'l,' ordered the mate. One of the men, who had loosed the sail, came down from aloft swinging about on the fall of the tops'l halyards, adding his weight to that of other members of the crew hauling from the deck.

'Belay! Belay there!' called the skipper from the break of the poop. 'Well the halyards, sheet home.'

I thought he meant to warn the hand who was swinging on the halyards, as it seemed to me then much too dangerous. Oh, how quickly was I to learn better!

Having dropped down under easy sail to the mouth of the river, we anchored for the night. The crew was mustered, the watches chosen, and the men were then sent below for supper. This consisted of what was called 'bread', really large and very hard ship's biscuits, and tea, in hooked pots and brightly polished tin pannikins. There was no butter or milk, both of which I missed sadly, and only coarse brown sugar. The men lit their clay pipes, and the almost black plug tobacco, in the airless and confined space, caused me to choke. About three bells the anchor watch was set – one man and myself.

Captain Davis was a tall and rather severe-looking Irishman; the first mate was the small, dark, and fierce-looking little man who had greeted me so roughly on arrival – he was a 'Geordie'. In later years I saw many like him in the North of England, and I think they must be the descendants of the old Picts. Curiously enough, his name was 'Fear'.

There was a passenger in the cabin, a young man, said to be rather given to drink. As I never heard of anything but water on board, it seemed to me that he had a good slant to get cured. The second mate was also the carpenter, of whom the Captain seemed to think very poorly. The cook and steward (one man) possessed a head far too large for his thin body, and his light mahogany-coloured face, with a fringe of dark hair all round, was cross-wrinkled beyond belief. By the more favoured members of the crew he was called 'Slushy', others gave him the usual title of 'Doctor'. As my meals were taken in the galley, I was with him a good deal.

The eight hands also included Old Bill, who was really only thirty-seven and wore great silver rings through his ears, and whose hands were like shiny pieces of horn; the big Swede,

Manning the capstan on the *Grace Harwar*, the full-rigged ship.

who was the chanty man; Nelson, swarthy and earringed; McClane, a lively Irishman; Cousin Jagger, a nice West Countryman; Ike Brittain, another man who was somewhat of a bully; and my very small self.

Not being on the ship's books, I received no wages and was not entitled to what Jack in those long-ago days called *his* 'Act of Parliament' – a menu that would startle the seaman of to-day. I was allowed three biscuits, tea, and a piece of salt meat, generally at dinner-time. They seemed to think that more meat would be bad for me!

The eight hands and myself were berthed in a deck house forward of the mainmast. There were four bunks on either side and two athwart-ships at the fore end. The chests, called 'kistry boxes', or 'donkeys', were placed round this fo'c'sle, and there was just sufficient room left for all the legs, with not much to spare, when the bread-barge and beef-kid were down on the deck at mealtimes. The tin pannikins were deep enough to hold the pea-soup – Mondays, Wednesdays, and Fridays – and for the salt 'horse' and other unappetising solid foods we used our sheath-knives, with the iron or horn gibby.

With a slant of wind from the eastward, we hove up the anchor at daybreak and got under way; soon, however, the wind chopped round to the west and began to blow. That settled – or rather unsettled – me. She knocked about so much that I could not keep on my legs, and felt very bad. Still I kept about, but was ignored, and felt utterly miserable.

Tired of clinging and staggering in the darkness and bitter cold on the spray-swept deck, feeling sea-sick and useless, I crept into the fo'c'sle and lay down on my chest. Before long, however, I heard Mr Fear singing out: 'Where's that little brat?' Then a hand gripped my very thick hair, hauled me out on deck, and gave me a kick to get me up straight. I don't think there was any ill-feeling. It was simply the Geordie way of starting a boy right. This happened several times during the succeeding days, but somehow I felt too ill, too helpless, and too much at a loss as to what to do, to care very much. Nevertheless, I tried to do what I was told, and for the rest, well, I was simply ignored, being useless.

It blew harder and harder. The old man at last grew tired of useless thrashing against the heavy westerly gale, making but little on either tack. In order to save wear and tear of sail and gear he 'upstick' and ran back to the Downs. Twice we got away, only to be forced back by the wind, and during all this time I only nibbled a piece of biscuit. Never was I actually sick, but no doubt felt worse on that account. In some ways, however, there was an improvement. Now I could stand and begin to remember the names of things and understand their uses.

Lying with scores of other sailing craft in the Downs, where there were no steamers, we had visits from the crews of the Hovelling boats, or Deal luggers, who put to sea only in bad weather, with spare anchors and cables, as well as men, to help vessels short-handed or in any difficulty. A hardy lot, without fear or any particular conscience, as appeared when one, who noticed a pale, sea-sick boy, as I was then, thought he would use my misery to aid his own purpose.

'Look ye, boy, would ye like to go ashore? I'll put ye there quick if ye gives me three pounds and ye chest of clothes!'

But I had no intention of giving up, although so far I had realised none of my expectations and hopes, derived from reading *Robinson Crusoe* and other sea romances. I told the wrinkled cook, who said: 'Don't 'ee, boy; don't 'ee. Th' shark!' I had not got even threepence; and as for my very small chest of clothes – bought at Jackson's, on Leadenhall Street, then a little old shop with double-bowed windows of small panes and a door in the middle – the whole kit cost only five pounds.

At long last there came a favourable easterly wind, then, with the music of the windlass pawls clanking and the crews chantying at the brakes, or singing out as they hauled, the whole crowd of ships got under way, spreading their white wings together and squaring away down Channel.

Bowling along we got far beyond the Wight before the wind hauled again to the west, and we were 'jammed on a bow-line'. Tack, tack, day after day, with little gained, except

Deal luggers hauled up on the beach with the crowded anchorage of the Downs in the background.

hard, cold work. I took my spell as lookout on the topgallant fo'c'sle, although not at the helm. I had to blow a horn at short intervals when the vessel was on the starboard tack, and ring a bell when she was on the port tack.

It was an anxious time for me, as I often mistook the phosphorescent gleam on a wave for a ship's light. Having got down as far as Torbay, the old man, sick of the slow progress, ran her in there, where we lay in welcome quiet for three days, feeding on insipid ray, brought aboard from the Brixham trawlers.

The breeze then came easterly, allowing us at last to slip out of the Channel and into blue water. Soon the keen edge of the wind disappeared, and the grey pall of scudding clouds, which had seemed almost to touch the masts, rolled away, and each day the sea glittered and the warm sun shone, making me feel entirely different.

The first moment that I realised this very pleasant change came one morning when I was sent below to feed some fowls that were being carried on top of the cargo in the wake of the main hatch. Quite firm on my legs, and swaying gently with the long roll, I felt warm and comfortable for the first time. The crooning of the hens seemed quite homey. And so the days passed. I had learned to go aloft a bit, and the men now took some notice of me. One said: 'Here, boy, there's cherries up there in the fore top!' I didn't believe it, but thought it a good idea to go up and have a look. Climbing the weather fore rigging, I went over the cat harpins and not through the lubber's hole, which pleased the men, who had been keeping an eye on me unseen. Then I started up the topmast rigging, and eventually stood up in the crosstrees, finding the motion of the ship quite pleasant.

At five o'clock each morning a drain of coffee and a piece of biscuit were served out to all hands. This unauthorised meal all good sea-cooks managed to squeeze out of the allowance of half an ounce of coffee a day for each man. It was always very welcome in this, the 'gravy eye', a term used by square-rigger men to denote the curious half-light before turn-to at three bells.

To help when the decks were being washed down, I had to stand on the top rail with the canvas draw-bucket, cast it deftly into the sea and catch it full, hoisting it up with a swing and emptying it into the wash-deck tub standing near. In order to prevent myself being dragged overboard I curved my leg round the standing part of the fore brace.

Once or twice a day the carpenter and I had to pump the ship out, and it was my duty to get a bucket half-full of water with which to fetch the pump. One day, as I poured the water in, 'Chips' suddenly banged his fist in my face, making my nose bleed. I could never understand why he did it. Going to the side, to let my nose bleed into the sea, the Captain saw me.

'Boy, what's made your nose bleed?' he asked sternly.

When I told him that I had run into something, he grunted and strode across the deck to the fo'c'sle door. 'If that boy wants correcting, I'll do it, and if one of you lay a hand on him I'll break your back and chuck you overboard!' he hissed angrily. To this there was no reply, and no reference was ever made to the subject. 'Chips' and I were on normal terms afterwards.

A spell of fine weather came with the north-east trades, and we bowled along amid the little foam-topped, china-blue seas across the North Atlantic. Until the coming of the fine weather I had scarcely given a thought to our destination, which was Georgetown, British Guiana, or Berbice, as it was then called, and now I longed to see the tropical lands and islands of the old Spanish Main.

In the steady winds and sunlit seas of the trades I gained confidence in going aloft, and was told that it was a boy's work to furl the gaff topsail and the royals. I soon tackled the former, but found it not so easy as it had appeared when watching from below. I gathered in the sail, but could not pass the gasket before the wind blew it out like a balloon. Again and again I tried, losing my temper at last. Thumping and kicking it, I cried with vexation; then, glancing down, I saw through the booby hatch, which was open, the Captain lying on the settee smoking his long churchwarden pipe, and looking up at the half-stowed sail. Shame seized me, and at the same moment a voice from forward gave me the hint so sorely needed: 'Get your legs round it, ride it down, and pass the gasket.'

With an effort, and a certain amount of nervousness lest the sail should throw me into space, I mastered it, and was grateful for the rough voice from the deck. Being now allowed to take an occasional spell at the wheel, I soon learned to steer, within the limits of my strength. Needless to say, on my restricted diet, I was always hungry. One or two of the older men, who did not eat all their bread allowance (one pound of biscuits a day), saved

A young apprentice at the wheel of an unidentified barque.

the rest in a canvas bag kept at the head of their bunk, and they often gave me a piece or two at night. It was a long time to go without food from supper at six in the evening to breakfast at seven-thirty or eight on the following morning. I was, however, quite well, active and strong for my size. One day Old Bill grabbed me by my jumper, held me out at arm's-length, and said: 'You're as wide across the shoulders as a skeeter is between the eyes.'

There came a time when the colour of the sea changed from blue to a muddy green, showing that we were nearing the banks that form at the mouths of all the great South American rivers, which bring huge quantities of mud and silt down in their course of hundreds or thousands of miles to the sea.

The night fell very dark and hot, with almost constant thunder and lightning. There was a damp wind and we smelt the land. The mate went into the main chains and hove the lead, singing out in a high falsetto: 'And a half four – by the deep four – and a half three – quarter legs three!' The Captain became very anxious, troubled by the decrease in the depth of water. Suddenly he roared out: 'Stop that damned noise and let's know what water you've got!'

'Two fathoms!' shouted the mate, and stopped heaving; so did the barque, softly embedded in the mud!

Nothing much could be done till daylight, and all hands turned in. I alone did not, being too full of curiosity. Soon grey dawn came, and muddy water was eddying all round the vessel. As the light increased I could see a blur on the horizon, meaning land, with here and there little points, like palm-trees. The dinghy was under the counter, so, towing it round to the gangway, I jumped in, curious to know what were the queer things I saw afloat.

They proved to be the lilac-coloured sails of Medusas, or Portuguese men-o'-war, as the sailors called them. Not until full daylight did the hands come on deck. Then, as we were having our biscuit and coffee, a large schooner came bowling along on our starboard hand, reeling over to a stiff breeze, the weather rail manned by what I thought were Christy Minstrels, the whites of their eyes and teeth, in their black faces, flashing in a line above the dirty white side.

The schooner luffed, coming close aboard, and her black skipper shouted to our Captain, giving him the position, course, and distance to Georgetown. But the *Flying Fish* was fast on the bank, and although the water sued a bit she did not move. The main hatch was stripped of its tarpaulin, the battens knocked out, and all hands set to unloading and jettisoning some of the cargo. Stock and patent bricks, green cases filled with Geneva gin in square bottles, known the world over to seamen as 'squarey-facey', all went splashing overboard. Not then feeling the loss of this liquor, it amused me to watch the pained look on the faces of the men as each case plonked into the muddy water. One man gave such a violent shake to a case that the gin ran out at one corner, to which his mouth went at once. With beautiful self-denial, however, he let all the others have a go. As the vessel was lightened, and the tide rose, she floated again. Soon we got the canvas on her and arrived at Georgetown, Berbice.

We made fast to a wooden quay and discharged some cargo, but not much, as the bulk of what was left consisted of bricks consigned to a Portuguese, whose plantation was situated a long way inland. Our job now was to take them up the Berbice river against an almost constant ebb. We sailed, when possible, in a dodging kind of way. The almost constant wind would be fair in one reach and foul in the next. The river also varied in breadth; and we would tack across, jam her nose right into the forest, which shut in the river on both banks, then back out and take a stern board out of her (go stern first, all aback).

When the wind fell light we lowered a boat and towed her till the breeze freshened. At times it was necessary to take a light hawser ashore, make fast to a tree, and warp the barque up to it. For many days, in fact, we just got along as best we could, each night making fast to a forest giant to get rest and food.

That which astonished me most about the Guiana jungle was the chorus by creatures of many kinds that made sleep very difficult. Although I never saw a single one, it was said that much of the din was made by frogs. It began at dusk, and as far as I know it continued until daylight. What was so intensely irritating was the peculiar and unchanging rhythm. A few appeared to start with a whop! whop! whop! Then more and more of the creatures would take up the same cry, louder and louder, up the scale, higher and higher, till it became one united scream. 'Hold on to the top note', some creature seemed to order. A few seconds later the noise suddenly ceased, and only the tweet and buzz of innumerable insects could be heard – and often felt. Then the eternal whop! whop! whop! would start again.

I cannot describe the appearance of the forest with any hope of success. As Old Bill said: 'You couldn't see it for trees.' It was so thick that darkness closed every glimpse between the boles and undergrowth. The trees were laced together with huge creepers. One day I caught sight of an armadillo and a kind of porcupine, on another occasion a huge scarlet flower hung down from a lofty creeper. There seems no need to mention the clouds of mosquitoes and other insects, one takes them for granted with a swampy forest close aboard all the time.

At last we reached a clearing in the jungle. There was a crude jetty made of tree trunks, and to this we tied up, put out a staging, and commenced to unload the bricks. One day I went ashore after coconuts. I saw a fine palm, about forty or fifty feet high, that leaned over at an angle just sufficient to enable me to climb it without much trouble. One of the hands tackled another palm with the aid of 'fleeting strops', a method that was too slow for me.

When I stood up among the fronds I saw many square yards of beautiful grey lace. I gazed, lost in wonder, until it dawned on me that it was a mass of desiccated fronds and leaves, piled up many feet deep on the crown of the palm. Having thrown down a number of nuts I began to descend, sliding and hugging the bole, arriving on the ground with the loss of much skin off my chest and covered with insects. These I got rid of by getting into the river, just deep enough to wash them off, as I could not swim.

We did not see many people in this forest-clearing. There were a few brown-coloured Portuguese, some negroes, and a larger number of East Indian coolies, there to work on the apprentice system – a ten years' spell, I believe. Having finished unloading the bricks, we were not long in dropping with the current down to Georgetown again. What interested

Opposite: Dry decks and a fair wind, a welcome respite from harsher conditions.

me most at this place, as I was often ashore, were the sugar works, then very primitive. They consisted of large open sheds, covering a series of bricked basins, four or five feet in diameter. The first of these was situated below the great rollers which crushed the canes, and into it ran the juice. Underneath there was a fire; and two tall negroes, whose clothes cost nothing, were continually stirring the boiling liquid. From this basin the stiffened juice ran into a lower receptacle and was again stirred, by two more naked ebony giants, and so on until it appeared like treacle.

The *Flying Fish* now being light, and bound for Barbados to load sugar for Dublin, we took aboard some ballast. In later voyages I ballasted with stone, and many other things, but only this once with mud! There was nothing else available, or so cheap, for it cost only the labour of two negroes, armed with iron scoops having handles at least fifteen to eighteen feet long. They stood in the waist of the ship and scooped blue clay up from the bottom of the river. Much water went into the hold with the mud, and during the passage to Barbados, as we pumped this out, the vessel became so top-heavy and cranky that we were compelled to shorten sail, and finally to single-reef the topsails to prevent her turning turtle.

Luckily we had only a nice sailing breeze, and anchored in Carlisle Bay, opposite Bridgetown – so close in that I could see a number of nigger boys, all alike and in invisible suits, sitting in a row on the edge of the quay, all gnawing at the same long piece of sugar-cane. In the evening many crude boats came out, with nets set like sails, between two masts, and a lamp in the centre. The flying-fish jumped towards the light, struck the net, and fell conveniently into baskets arranged in the bottom of the boat.

After several days of misery unloading the blue clay and cleaning the hold, our cargo of sugar began to arrive, and was stowed by big negro stevedores, under one who gave all his orders and directions in the form of a song. The hogsheads were of some tough and new wood which allowed them to be screw-jacked into odd shapes to fit closely in the hold. All this work was done to song in the major key, with words something like this: 'Gif me lef hand, boys, lef hand more, then the screw-jack, two iron handles – Roll a rolly, leo, roll leo, roll 'im up to de winder, oh roll oh!'

McClane, one of the fo'c'sle hands, became friendly with a negro stevedore, who invited him to his house, and I went also. It was a large hut, and some kind of meal was served, mostly fruit and yams, which I liked. There were several in this family, and all were quiet and well behaved. Mac had several tots of rum, but I was not allowed even to taste it, and when we came out into the soft tropical night, amid the palms and hibiscus, with the trade wind caressing the long dark fronds that stood out black against the starry sky, he became very lively as we rolled down the old bay road.

We had two cases of fever, one of which we left in the hospital, and, in consequence, the Captain tried to obtain another hand. The old man, I know, did not think much of 'Chips' as second mate to take the Captain's watch. This led to his shipping a West Countryman, about thirty years of age, as second mate. He turned out to be a good sailor, quiet and able. After taking aboard some stores, and repairing the decks where they had been forced up by the heavy screwing of the hogsheads, we sailed away for Dublin.

The voyage was uneventful until, in a North Atlantic gale, we got away off the north-west coast of Ireland, giving me a sight I shall never forget. The cliffs were 2000 feet high, against which the ocean rollers broke, rushing very slowly up the cliffs and spreading out like lace. Gradually they faded from sight, *invisibly* the waters returned to the sea. These huge rollers, the aftermath of a storm, gather their might and their height during a 2000-miles journey across the Atlantic, and break like this in fine, calm weather. They are huge undulations, and often have little forward motion.

In Dublin, the evil smell of the Liffey, the rats that walked out to us on our mooring-ropes at night, and the visits from beggars, who besought in the name of the sacred ones for alms, were the things that impressed me most. For my services afloat, during this first voyage, I was given a ten-shilling ticket to take me in a small coasting steamer back to the Port of London. No provision was made for my food, and being entirely without money I had a thin time during the five days' passage. At each place we called at I went ashore with two of the ship's boys and bathed. I slept on deck and got what food I could. One Sunday afternoon I found myself at East Smithfield, than which I have never seen a less inviting place. After a walk of six or seven miles I reached home, and found that my father had gone somewhere else to meet me, having been misdirected. My people were shocked at my appearance, being burned brown, and having no boots on.

9 Bound for Algoa Bay

The carronades of the *Tudor* – East India Dock Road, 1860 – 'Andrew' (the Royal Navy)
– Apprentices ashore in Whitechapel – The Standard Theatre – Differences in 'donkeys'
breakfasts' – The *Tudor* sails for South Africa – Life on board an emigrant ship – The
lady 'constable' – Lights o' Brighton in the 'sixties – Irish 'biddies' and sailormen –
Discontent – Mutiny – Desertion – Cape Mounted Rifles – Port Elizabeth in 1860 –
Across the Indian Ocean – India just after the Mutiny – The corpse-laden Hooghly –
Mauritius and a tropical storm – Reeftopsail Valley – Ascension.

MY second voyage was in the East Indiaman *Tudor*. She was a full-rigged ship of
1100 tons, teak-built and bell-bowed, with quarter galleries, stern windows, and
carried fourteen carronades on the main deck. There were stands of arms in the
saloon, cutlasses, pistols, and muskets, the two latter with flint-locks, but a few with caps.
She had, until a year or so before, been one of the ships of the navy of the Honourable the
East India Company, but was now privately owned.

Her figurehead was a large white bust of Henry VIII; and there were spacious quarters
on either side of the stem. She was lying in the East India Dock, at Blackwall, on the dark
and snowy afternoon in December 1860, when six of us lads placed our sea-chests under the
t'gallant fo'c'sle, slung our hammocks – for everything on board was done as in 'Andrew',
the nickname by which the Royal Navy was known – and then, on looking round,
discovered that she did not sail until the following morning.

Finding that there was no food available, and that we should not be allowed to have any
light, we pooled our few shillings and swung off up that long East India Dock Road to the
Standard Theatre in Whitechapel. We went into the sixpenny gallery, and saw a crude and
coarse burlesque called *Virginius the Rum'n*. The story was based on the Virginius who
sacrificed his daughter, but no student of ancient Rome would have recognised any
similarity between life in the once capital of the world and the scenes we saw in the
Whitechapel Theatre of the 'sixties. Although I was only just over fifteen years of age,
months in the fo'c'sle of the *Flying Fish* had made me far older in thought than in years.

About eleven-thirty we turned out for the long and cold tramp back to our ship. It was
dark, and sleet was falling, which did not trouble us, but we were also very hungry. In those
days only a few public-houses – or gin-palaces – were open so late, but by good luck, or if
you are of a pious disposition you will, perhaps, say by 'special Providence', we overhauled
a baked-potato man with some of his wares all hot, singing out, after his vulgar kind: 'Baked

A forest of masts in London Docks.

taters! Baked taters! Fill yer belly and warm yer 'ands!'

A big floury potato cut open, and with a lump of butter dabbed into the cut, made our view of life quite different. We had been allowed to draw a month's advance-pay before sailing. This was called the 'dead horse', which had to be worked off before we began to feel the benefit of our sea labours. This sum was at once cashed by the outfitters around the docks, or 'slop-chest merchants' as they were more often called. Careless youngsters, such as the one who stood in my boots, would, after enjoying a day or two of doubtful pleasures, rush off at the last minute, as an afterthought, and expend one shilling and sixpence on a 'donkey's breakfast', or hay mattress. If funds were good it might even be 'carpenter's feathers', or wood-shavings. On the other hand, with only a shilling to spare, there was no alternative to a mattress stuffed with dried seaweed, but this was not a favourite on account of its being a weather-glass. I generally preferred the bare deck, with a coil of rope for a pillow – lovely smell, Stockholm tar!

The *Tudor* was bound for Algoa Bay – Port Elizabeth, South Africa, as it is called to-day – with two hundred emigrants, mostly Irish, and a few saloon passengers. The emigrants were berthed in the 'tween decks, which had been specially fitted for the purpose. Single men were accommodated forward, married folk amidships, and single women aft – under a huge matron. They were all divided into messes, with one of their number, called 'the constable', in charge of each. They had their own galley, with two cooks and two cook's mates. The Irish were nearly all fine-built men and women, mostly bare-legged, and but few could speak any English.

The crew, twenty able-bodied and four ordinary seamen, were berthed under the topgallant fo'c'sle. We lads had our berths under the break of it, abaft the windlass, and the bosun, carpenter, and sailmaker occupied similar quarters on the opposite or starboard side. Captain Armstrong was a smallish man, with a florid complexion, blue eyes, and rather more than sufficient nose. He was a good sailor and plucky, as subsequent events proved. The chief officer looked very immaculate in his brass-bound uniform; the second was a Scotsman; the third an Englishman, of medium build but with only one eye, the other having been plucked out by a 'booby' (sea-bird); and the fourth was a young man with a big head and discontented-looking face, rather lame in one hip, who never went aloft.

Owing to the *Tudor*'s former position in the navy of 'John Company' almost everything was done man-o'-war fashion. The bosun, a navy man of the old school, used his pipe to direct us, but we often pulled and hauled merchant-ship fashion, singing out as we did so.

The morning was bright and frosty when we left the East India Dock, near to the exit of which was a small public-house, well known and beloved by all outward-bound sailors, as it was here they could, and did, get the last drink for many long months. It was then quite a common occurrence for several members of the crew to leave just sufficient time for a pier-head jump as the vessel passed; and in the *Tudor* many of the crew not being quite sober as we passed down the river, with the tug ahead, led to odd scenes.

I saw one AB going up the fore rigging in a top hat, a double-breasted frock-coat, a gaudy coloured waistcoat, and a heavy 'gold' fob. He went up to overhaul the fore tops'l bunt-lines, which had got foul. We did not laugh or think it strange, knowing that he had come from the shore with no time to shift rig. But the cook had a bottle of rum, and as many as possible squeezed into the galley to have a tot. One man, in order to make room for those clamouring outside, sat on the stove top, but quickly got off when it was brought to his notice that the fire had been lighted. What he said was sincere, and so was the roar of laughter.

After rounding the South Foreland we had to reef-down, as it blew a gale. One could not help understanding the contrast in people's lives as the lights of Brighton came into view, although, like most of the seamen of those days, I had already commenced to feel the safety and comfort of being on board ship again after a spell ashore. The poor folks on the 'tween decks were, however, nearly all terribly sea-sick and alarmed as the ship knocked about in the choppy little Channel sea.

For several days the wind remained foul, and we had to go below to lend a hand with the sick emigrants. Some of the men washed and dressed the children of couples who were too ill to even help themselves. During this blow we shipped a heavy sea in the waist. It hit me and over I went, rolling across the deck with the surging flood. By curious ill-luck I struck the chief officer at the back of his knees, and down he went into the waters on top of me.

It was not my fault, but that I never had a nice word from him throughout the voyage was not easy to explain, except that he could not forget.

One night, after having fought our way out of the Channel into blue water, I was on watch on the lee side of the poop when a figure came up the weather ladder, from the quarter-deck. 'Hullo, what do you want?' asked the second officer sharply, as it was quite against all sea rules to come up on the weather side. 'Sure, sir, the ship's full of water, and we can hear the iron floating about in the hold', the man complained earnestly.

Now the officer, knowing all about it, did not give himself airs on the strength of his knowledge, but kindly explained to the man that the iron was stowed so that it could not shift at all, but might just rattle, and the water was nothing more than the usual accumulation in the bilge.

Once or twice we played tricks on these big Irishmen, which they enjoyed as much as ourselves. One day, when the ship was rolling in a heavy swell, an outsize in handspikes, which we called 'Big Ben', was thrust down a scupper-hole. By pretending great alarm several of them were induced to hang on to it in order to keep the ship from going over. Encouraged by us they put their great strength on the bar every time the vessel rolled. After a while we let them off, on some absurd pretext.

When we got into fine weather they often had a very sober dance on deck. The young women and men stood in rows opposite to each other, and only a few feet apart. One man

An early photograph showing the East Indiaman *Tudor* in Calcutta in 1861.

played the flute, whilst the two rows stood and moved their feet slightly, each dancer looking at the person opposite – only very occasionally with a smile. One man would give a little 'Hough!' And that was all. They would keep it up for an hour or two sometimes. The old 'biddies' would come on deck in the morning, after breakfast, with a clean apron, a white frilled cap tied under the chin, smoking 'Black Jack' in large stone pipes, with tin covers to keep off the wind. Sometimes strapping young women would get behind the poop ladder, up and down which we lads had to go, and pinch our bare legs so hard that we avoided the passage as often as we could by running along the top of the nettings, out of their reach.

The north-east trades took us down almost to the Line, which we were insistent that all who wished should see – through a carefully prepared telescope, as none could see it with the naked eye. Then Father Neptune came on board, and was taken as *bona fide* by many, who were duly shaved and ducked in the bath, improvised from a sail tied at the corners and partly filled with sea-water.

When voyages were much longer, old stories and beliefs were held as possible, and life was much slower, simpler, and many think more enjoyable. The positive and comparative were good enough, unlike the present age when nothing but the superlative will suffice. For good or evil those days, however, with their happy limitations, have passed away.

Discipline on board the *Tudor* was rather lax, perhaps the reason was the presence of so many emigrants of both sexes. Some of the men on watch could mix with them and escape notice. Also, there was a lot of card-playing in the fo'c'sle, not for money, which seemed to lose value on long voyages, but for tobacco, or other prized possessions. The games went on from watch to watch, even all night, as the players by arrangement among themselves could see that the proper supply of men for the wheel and lookout should be always ready.

Much of this unusual state of affairs was due to some half a dozen men from Glasgow, rough blackguards and insubordinate. At last things came to a head. There was acute discontent, either real or fostered, leading to a refusal of duty by some of the crew, among whom were these Glasgow beauties. With much noise and bluster they came aft on to the quarter-deck, demanding all kinds of impossibilities.

The Captain, from the break of the poop, high above the heads of the mutineers, told them to go forward and make any complaint properly, in the usual way. This did not suit them, as it was clear that they wanted to make trouble. In a minute there were preparations to storm the poop deck. Leading the mutinous seamen was a big, red-headed Glasgow man, Alick Braid. He mounted the weather ladder and defied the Captain, who had a double-barrelled gun, which he pointed at the man's chest.

Two or three of the men passengers in the saloon appeared on deck with loaded pistols, which they fired over the heads of the mutineers. At this critical moment the captains of the messes, a fine body of men, who had been summoned by the officer of the watch, together with the bosun and his mates, came up on to the poop. This accession of armed strength, as the old weapons had been snatched from their cases, cowed the mutinous section of the crew, who were overpowered after a struggle, and placed in irons. We were all glad to be done with fustian heroics.

Fine weather and a fair breeze from astern allowed us to set the stun's'ls – or, as they were

Durban Harbour, northeast of Port Elizabeth, with its ramshackle quays and jumbled
foreshore. (*David MacGregor Collection*)

called in the Queen's ships, the 'studding sails' – and with these wind-bags aloft we
shouldered a way over the Cape rollers. Our bluff bows plunged into the creaming sea, and
the sunlight of those summer days in the Southern Hemisphere tinged the vast expanse of
white canvas with golden light. In our pride of ship we hoped for an admiring passer-by on
this lonely expanse of rolling blue and emerald ocean.

One evening, just as the sun disappeared behind the land, we anchored in Algoa Bay, off
Port Elizabeth, a small collection of wooden houses, unmade roads, and, if I remember
aright, no proper landing-place, except the surf-washed and, in places, rocky beach. After
the anchor watch had been set, and the others had turned in, the Doctor, whom we carried
on account of the Government emigrants on board, informed the Captain that he had heard
a boat being lowered.

Suspecting desertions, the old man quietly replied: 'All right, I'll get them in the morning.' After breakfast we manned the gig and pulled ashore through the heavy surf. Being one of the crew, I was left with others in charge of the boat while the Captain went to the port authority to complain of the men's desertion. That person, whoever he was, offered to send Cape Mounted Rifles after them, and expressed the opinion that they had gone off to Grahamstown, about twenty miles distant, with mostly sandy desert between.

And so it was. We heard afterwards that the Cape Mounties had come up with the fugitives, covered them with their rifles, and called upon them to halt and surrender. This they were not at all sorry to do, as, being hungry, tired, and hot, they had already regretted leaving the ship. They told us later that their only request was that each of the troopers should take one of their number behind on his horse. On arriving back in Port Elizabeth they were given a good meal and were then locked up.

The following morning we again took the Captain ashore in his gig, and it was discovered that the prisoners had chummed up with their guards, broken out of prison, and that all had got so drunk that they had been found, early in the morning, lying about on the ground. In due course they were tried, and our Captain was given the choice of having them back on board or of paying their fines. He refused point-blank to do either, and this was the last ever heard of them. In consequence the ship became a happy one, although she seemed very empty and dull without the emigrants, who had provided us with much merriment.

It was quite amusing to see many of the seamen going about their work glum, silent, and with no more expression in their faces than a sea-boot. A few sought a sad relief in hunting for souvenirs of the dear departed, finding trifles, some very odd indeed.

Algoa Bay is exposed to the south-east, so, when it came on to blow hard from that quarter, we had to let go our best bower anchor, and in the end to pay out one hundred and twenty fathoms of cable, in addition to the ninety fathoms fast to the other big anchor. Even then she dragged for some distance, as the bottom was foul, the rocks affording no good holding-ground. Luckily we brought up at last with rocks awash in the boiling sea just astern.

During this south-easterly 'buster', as it was called locally, we could seldom approach the forecastle. Each time she dived into a huge sea the water and heavy spray reached half-way up the foremast! Several ships went ashore and broke up in the surf. One foundered at her anchor, but, although both difficult and dangerous in the steep-breaking seas, we managed to save the men on board her.

It was an ill wind for shipowners, but a harvest for the beachcombers. When the wind and sea abated, many fine ships were high and dry amid the sand and jagged rocks of this notoriously treacherous bay. When the time came to leave Port Elizabeth not a soul on board expressed regret, although there were still sad hearts as she ploughed her way across the Indian Ocean through the tail-end of the monsoon.

At long last we worked our way up the Bay of Bengal, made the Sandheads, the Sunderbunds, Saugor Island, and took a pilot off the Brig. The call of 'Stand by a rope for the boat!' is a rather thrilling sound after the long unbroken solitude of an ocean voyage in sail. There is no throb of engines, no certainty of when or where a landfall will be made, and only seldom the sight of another ship. In the days when wind was master, each ship that set

Garden Reach, on the river Hooghly, just downstream of Calcutta.

forth ploughed a lonely furrow; there were no 'shipping lanes'; each was an oasis of life surrounded for weeks or months by the seemingly immeasurable deserts of the sea.

Although the ship was still heeling to a breeze, and moving rapidly through the water, a native boat from Kedgeree came off to us, bringing a welcome change of diet – fresh fish. There were many men in this big native boat, which had a great sheer and was pointed at both stem and stern. The native crew brought her alongside, struggling wildly for the coil of rope which fell from our side about their heads and shoulders. With no clothing except a tiny loin-cloth, and with a mop of hair, lots of quick jabber, courage, and ability, they passed their gleaming catch aboard, and were soon astern.

Onwards we sailed with all our yards squared to a quarter breeze, past Diamond Harbour, the perilous James-and-Mary's – the treacherous nature of which I was to experience in a later voyage – and then Garden Reach, the King of Oudh's palace, and, finally, our moorings near Prinsep's Ghaut.

This was my first visit to India – the India which but a year and a half before had been in the throes of the great Mutiny. Being very young, knowing but little of affairs beyond my immediate ken, and having been isolated for so long from all contact with the great world beyond the everlasting horizon of the sea, no doubt accounted for my lack of observation of those remnants of the great upheaval which doubtless the Calcutta of those days had to show.

Curiously enough, I hated this great and teeming city of India from the first day I saw it until the last, many years after. Even now I can smell the corpse-laden muddy water of the Hooghly, having also tasted it. Although in my accounts of later voyages I have said all that this 'Kali Ghautta' deserves, it was perhaps when we went into dry dock at Howrah, opposite to Calcutta, that its more objectionable features first impressed themselves on my memory.

We lay, waiting to go into dock, for some considerable time right to leeward of the Gentoos burning ghaut. Operations ashore started in the evening, when the bodies were placed on the funeral pyres. The heavy fumes tried us sorely. We smoked strong tobacco until 'quite crisp about the gills', as Mark Twain said. The curious smell was wafted across to us every night, and remained in our mouths, noses, food, and clothing. Nothing seemed to get rid of it. We tied rags steeped in vinegar and water across our faces when it became extra strong. Whether it was a rich or a poor person being burned we knew by the height of the flames, caused by the number of pots of ghee left by the deceased. We could hear what was said to be corpses, popping and frizzling like sausages in a frying-pan. It was ourselves, doing anchor watch, who were the real victims.

At last we left the muddy, evil-smelling Hooghly, homeward bound for Old England. There were passengers aboard, some of whom had been long in India, having but recently passed safely through the Mutiny. All seemed to bear marks of their ordeal, and none of them were happy-looking. There was a Captain Muriel, his wife, and a boy of six or seven, with a male nurse, not an ayah. The first two were sallow, thin, and wrinkled, though barely middle-aged. The child was puny and querulous. A Major White I remember well, because he was tattooed in red and blue more than any sailor I had ever seen. At wash-deck time these men would sit on deck naked, whilst we poured buckets of sea-water over their heads.

The *Tudor* was now doing from seven to nine knots across the Indian Ocean. When we passed through the widespread Maldive Archipelago a beam wind carried the scent of these spice islands far out to sea. These odours of the land, so apparent to everyone aboard a sailing ship, and noted in almost every record of life at sea in the days of sail, do not appear to be so noticeable in a steamer, which always carries with it an aroma peculiar to itself, or its never-varying cargo, whether it be a tanker, a smoky, oily tramp, or a freshly painted food-filled liner.

To pick up fresh water and some medical stores we called at Port Louis, Mauritius. As a boy I had seen woodcuts of this place, showing the wonderful conical mountain with its huge cap of rock apparently hanging right over the town. It had been climbed long ago by a man named Pete Botte, since when it had borne his name. We lay anchored well up in the bay for several days, the Captain going ashore each day in his gig, I being one of the crew.

The people ashore told us, among other things, that the ravages of the white ant were so bad that they had to stand all wooden furniture with its legs in water, held in cups with sides that battered outwards, up which the ants could not climb. The few that succeeded fell into the water. Without this precaution there would be no furniture left within a few months.

All went well until the night of our departure, when, it being someone's birthday in the saloon, healths were drunk – and soon were the drinkers also. We had a French pilot aboard to take us out clear of the rocks, and he was 'half-sprung' too. This, combined with his natural volubility, caused him to rattle off his orders like a piece of poetry, and long before each movement or evolution could possibly be carried out. It began with an outburst: 'Leggo main top, leggo fore top, haul down jib, brail up spanker, leggo anchor! Ah! *sacre nom d'un chien,* never have I see such *matelots!*'

Having banged into all or most of the other craft in the harbour, fouled their anchors, and carried away their spars, we managed to get away to sea at last, but with someone's jib-boom lying athwart our poop deck and other acquired pieces of wreckage lying about the fore part of the ship. Luckily it was fine weather, so we set to work and cleared away the stuff that we had no right to, as well as some of our own battle honours, such as the fore topgallant mast and yard, and with it the royal mast and yard.

Nothing worth recording occurred until we reached the Agulhas Bank, off the Cape of Good Hope. Owing to the shallow water hereabouts and to the meeting of the cold Atlantic eastward-bound current with the warm stream from the Indian Ocean, fogs were frequent. It also blows very hard there at times. While we were trying to avoid running down a Dutch brig that was too close to our course, the wind came in a series of terrific gusts, each gaining in both strength and duration.

The Captain snugged the ship down at once to double-reefed topsails, reefed foresail, storm jib, and he also 'scandalised the spanker'. The wind continued to increase, black clouds rolled up, and as night came on the thunder and lightning were worse than I have ever experienced since. Despite the howling gale the air seemed hot and stuffy, with a strong sulphurous smell.

I record these facts, but do not pretend to be able to account for them. At four bells (2 AM) all hands were called to close-reef the fore and main topsails and to furl the mizzen topsail. There were four of us wrestling with the sail on the latter yard, when we saw a fire-ball coming straight on to the ship. It rushed rapidly down from the blackness above, looking about the size of a dinner-plate, with a long streamer of fire behind it. Suddenly it struck, with a sharp metallic ring, and sparks flew in every direction. It seemed to me that it must have hit the iron band on the end of the main trysail gaff.

The carpenter was ordered to sound the well, but found only the usual amount of water there. The Captain seemed puzzled because no damage to the ship or rigging could be discovered, but the mate told us all that it was only a fire-ball, and that he had seen many of them when in the 'Harches', which was Jack's name for the Grecian Archipelago. We found nothing on deck, but as it was being swept by frequent seas, which came aboard without hindrance as the bulwarks on both sides had been broken away by the gigantic waves, leaving only the timbers standing, anything there might have been would have gone overboard at once.

As nothing more could be done, the Captain gave us a tot of grog and sent the watch below, with orders to stand by for a call, as the weather seemed to be getting worse. We lit our pipes, wrung out our wet gear, and turned in 'all standing'. By next morning we found ourselves well round the Cape, so squared away for St Helena with a ten-knot breeze on our starboard quarter. With this favourable wind we bowled along merrily for many days.

About the time we expected to make the island it was my 'gravy eye', or lookout, from four to six in the morning. About four bells (6 AM) we saw the loom of the land, soon making out those features familiar to several members of the watch, such as 'Reeftopsail Valley', so called because sailing ships invariably got a strong puff when abreast of it, then Ladder Hill, up which there is one of the longest flights of steps in the world. The curious thing was that, although doing a full nine knots, we seemed to get no nearer. Everyone appeared to be too surprised, including the officer of the watch, to pay any attention to routine; and I was stuck at the wheel. The breeze freshened and yet we did not come up with the land. Then, to our discomfiture, the outline became fainter, and eventually disappeared altogether.

I was then relieved from the helm, it being four bells in the first watch (10 AM). Puzzled, and sore put to it, the Captain hauled the ship to the wind and made long legs to the east and then to the west, all day, hoping to pick up the island. Seeing nothing, however, he gave it up, and squared away for Ascension, about seven hundred miles to the north-west of St Helena. It was generally believed that we were a good bit out on our longitude and what we took for St Helena must have been a mirage, which is more often observed at sea than recorded. One of the most frequent forms is seeing, quite distinctly, the land raised a few degrees above the horizon and showing the sky beneath it.

Ascension, which we made without difficulty, appeared to be just a bare rock. Instead of turning in, I remained in the boat we had lowered to take the Captain ashore. I hung my head over the gunwale, lost in admiration of the golden sand and the many fish of marvellous colours that could be seen through the clear water.

It may not be out of place to record here the old-time way of calling the watch by the two boatswain's mates. The call formed a rhyme:

'Oh, you Starbolins, sleep no more in sin,
For if you do we'll cut your clew, and let Larbolins in.'

Then came the shout of 'Rouse out here, bullies! Show a leg!'

Having obtained what we required at Ascension, we sailed away north, with nothing unusual to record until, at the end of a voyage which had lasted one year, five months, and twelve days we picked up a pilot off Dover and arrived safely in the London river.

Once in the narrow waters of the English Channel pilots and, for the larger vessels, tugs were the first contacts that ships might have had for months. Here, off the South Foreland, the Finnish four-masted barque *Passat* is towed up Channel on arrival from Australia in September 1933.

10 Bound for the East in the 'Tippoo Sahib'

A 'St John's Spruce Box' – An apprentice at last! – London to Liverpool in 1862 –
Alsopp's Waxworks – Salt House Dock and the *Tippoo Sahib* – We are eight – A
starving ship in the North Atlantic – A 'drogher' breaks up – In the 'doldrums' –
Waterspouts – Sea-cuts and Stockholm tar – Coming of the west wind – Greybeards –
Effect of moonlight on falling snow – The Hooghly – Old-time dangers of the James-
and-Mary quicksands – Calcutta in the 'sixties – 'Strong-backs' – Native bazaar, Fort
William – Apprentices ashore in Calcutta – *Baboos* and *Bunniars* – A link with
Napoleon – A Christmas pudding.

M Y third voyage was in the *Tippoo Sahib*, a full-rigged ship of 1000 tons. She was
one of the 'St John's Spruce Boxes', which it was said were built in this New
Brunswick port by the mile and afterwards cut off in lengths as required. Square
in the stern and also in the bow, but running fine downwards from the rail, they were good
sea-boats, with a limit of about ten knots sailing a point or two free.

The *Tippoo Sahib* belonged to a Liverpool firm, to which I was bound as an apprentice
for four years in return for the sum of thirty-five pounds, which was to be paid back to me
each year at the rate of six, seven, ten, and, finally, twelve pounds. Little enough for a boy
of sixteen and a half who was in knowledge and experience an AB – able to *hand*, *reef*, *steer*,
and *splice* – and who had already made two long voyages.

The railway journey from London to Liverpool in 1862 occupied eleven hours. The
third-class was then called 'Parliamentary', a name which, I believe, was due to an Act
whereby railway companies were compelled to run two third-class trains a day in the
interests of the general public, whom these companies had not yet recognised as their best
customers – in bulk.

I was met at Lime Street Station, Liverpool, by a man who told me his name was Coward,
and that he was to conduct me to a small temperance hotel in Islington Flags, where I was
to stay until the ship sailed. I felt rather grand, but very lonely. As we passed a public-house
in Lime Street, a big Irishwoman came out of the door, and, seeing me, exclaimed: 'Ah,
sure, here's a little dear!'

Picking me up like a baby, she rushed across the street and dropped me in Alsopp's
Waxworks, among the crowd. Of course I fled out, greatly indignant, and joined my

The port of Calcutta.

conductor, who stood on the pavement helpless with laughter. Early one morning I went to the Salt House Dock and there joined the *Tippoo Sahib*, which was loading salt in bulk for Calcutta. There were seven other apprentices who had recently come on board. They were still in shore clothes, and *none* of them had been to sea before. With two long voyages to my credit, I was rather deferred to, although there were several who were bigger than myself.

We soon got on good terms with each other and settled down in the half-deck, which contained eight bunks. It was situated under the poop deck, on the fore side of the cabin. During the days before the ship sailed we worked hard on board, getting our meals and sleeping ashore. There was a nice-looking boy, Tom Llewellyn, who soon became known as 'Loo'; John Davids, another apprentice, came from a small Welsh town which we looked up in a gazetteer, where it was described as having 'a blacksmith's shop and a gin mill'. He was, of course, chipped about this for many a long day. There were also Dick Johns, a Manx boy, who knew a song in which the word 'optimy' occurred several times, but he did not know either its meaning or how it was spelt; tall and thin Charlie Stephenson, who, because of his sedate and old-fashioned ways, we called 'Fifty'; Sam Wilson; and two cousins, Hugh Nish and Ned Beggs, from Wigtownshire, who had gained some sea experience in Scottish fishing craft.

After leaving Liverpool we had an ordinary passage for some days, but, when well away into the North Atlantic, we fell in with a small barque showing signals of distress. Getting within hail, we learned that she was Italian, and her skipper came aboard from a dinghy. As no one on the *Tippoo Sahib* could talk Italian, and the skipper of the barque knew no English, it was with difficulty we found out that, after a long and bad passage from the River Plate, they were without food or water. The skipper, a dark and rather handsome young man, showed us his pigskin boots, pieces of which had been cut off and chewed.

We gave them both food and water, and they were very grateful and happy. One man showed us his tongue, which was dry and almost black from thirst. Our Captain received a bill on the barque's owners at Genoa for what was supplied. Soon after leaving this Italian ship we sighted floating baulks of timber. The Captain was afraid we might strike one end-on, and damage our stem post or bow port, so one hand was stationed in the fore topmast crosstrees with orders to keep a sharp lookout. Every few minutes he sang out: 'Log-O!' From the poop came the usual: 'Where away?' Then the voice from aloft gave: 'Two points on the port bow, a cable's-length ahead', or other similar direction.

There could be no doubt that it was the remains of a timber 'drogher', which, in spite of windmill-worked pumps and chain cables passed round the vessel's waist, had broken up. Old ships were often sent to sea like this, loaded, both below and on deck, with heavy, rough-cut timber. Their owners knew they could not sink, although they might break up. In those days, when wireless was unknown, there was no searching for ships thought to be in distress, nor for the lifeboats from what might be just another sea disaster.

In a fine spell, with the orderly everyday work of the ship, one day is very like another. This 'flying-fish' weather generally occurs in the trades, when the running gear can be triced to the shrouds, and everyone, except the Captain and the mate, paints, scrapes, varnishes, splices, mends sails, overhauls the chafing-gear, and does other necessary repair work on deck and aloft. In the *Tippoo Sahib* we were on watch-and-watch, and this gave us all a chance to do washing and mending instead of turning in. With one hand at the wheel, one on the forecastle head as lookout, and the officers on the poop, the watch on deck during 'Jack's holiday', which is the name by which the region of the trade winds became known, were able to 'caulk' on deck or lay on the spare spars. There was, of course, the possibility of a sudden squall, but one soon learned to be sound asleep one minute and wide awake the next in a sailing ship of those days.

This slackness was never allowed in rough or squally weather. If the vessel was shipping much water we stood under the lee of the weather bulwarks, or, if at all possible, under the break of the forecastle, to keep as dry as possible, until a whistle from the poop called us to action on the exposed deck or aloft.

The north-east trades are usually carried to near the Line; then come the doldrums. In this heart-breaking region of calms and cat's-paws anything from a few days to a few weeks may be spent. When we approached the Equator there was a flat and glass-like sea. Some shavings thrown overboard one morning were floating in exactly the same position on the following day. This continued for over a week, then came heavy rain squalls, with puffs of wind, lightning, thunder, and finally waterspouts. I counted twenty in sight at once, forming or falling. One came up from astern with a breeze, and when startlingly close the Captain fired a light brass signal gun we had on the poop, and the spout broke before it reached us.

I was at the wheel, and the rain poured over my face so that I could not see the binnacle, let alone the compass card. To get out of this region we had to keep box-hauling the yards, turning to every puff. This continued for hours, and we all became weary and sick of it. The constant hauling of the braces, soaked with a mixture of fresh and salt water, caused the thick skin on the palms of our hands and the inside of our fingers to open into what are called 'sea-cuts'. These became very painful when one could not leave off hauling on sodden ropes. Each sea-cut was filled with worsted soaked in our usual and general remedy, Stockholm tar.

At last came a swell, which often foretells a breeze, but before the wind reached us we spent several uncomfortable hours rolling very heavily, the yardarms often touching the water, first on one side and then on the other, with the sails slatting heavily against the masts. Soon afterwards, however, we picked up the south-east trades, and bowled merrily along over a sparkling sea for glorious and carefree days.

Several times we sighted the coast of South America while working aloft preparing for the gales and heavy seas of the Southern Ocean. Soon the trade wind eased a little, and in the night watches the atmosphere became damp and cold. I glanced one day at the chart and noticed what little land there is in the whole world below the fiftieth parallel of south latitude. For this reason it is not strange that within this belt is found the biggest, the longest in drift, and the most regular sea in the world.

Leaving the south-east trades, and getting as far south as forty degrees, the sky became overcast, and after a day of calm, with light and variable winds, there came at sunset one evening a rush of bitterly cold air from the glaring yellow streak of light which stretched across the western horizon. It was the arrival of the great west wind that carried the sailing ship round the world. Each day the sea mounted higher, and became streaked with foam. It changed in colour also, from the sparkling blue of the trades to the grey-green of low latitudes. An occasional albatross floated majestically astern; and the thick storm-canvas aloft, which had replaced the old and patched light sails of the tropics, stretched to the gathering force of the wind.

It came with a wild, piercing shriek during the second night watch; and dawn saw every man and boy still aloft, clawing at stiff, wet canvas, that broke away from bleeding fingers before the gaskets could be passed to secure it. Sail after sail was slowly taken in during that

'The great west wind that carried the sailing ship around the world.'

first wild night of the almost perpetual gales, that sweep unchecked by any land across those thousands of miles of ocean. With the wind came also the long regular seas. The drift between each foaming crest is difficult to guess. By some it is estimated to be anything up to two miles, and, although I think this is excessive, it certainly does appear to be considerable.

The great seas of the far south provide a grand, inspiring, and, at times, a threatening sight; so much was this realised that it led to devices for preventing the helmsman from seeing aft, such as the erection of a canvas screen, or, more generally and effectively, by the construction of a wheel-house with an arched roof, but these things were not approved by the best steersmen of my day, who much preferred to have a clear view astern. Being able to see what was coming, they actually steered by the overtaking rollers, and were ready to check the yaws by giving as little helm as possible *at the right moment*. A few spokes to meet her as she came to, or fell off, was all that was necessary. Young and inexperienced helmsmen might, however, be relieved not to see what would undoubtedly appear to them to be mountains of hissing water spelling inevitable destruction.

As a boy, I was glad to have this explained to me by older men, and was able to put their advice into practice when it was my trick at the wheel. In fact, aboard the *Tippoo Sahib*, it became an exciting pleasure to look aft at the huge, mounting, swelling rollers rushing forward, with curling crests and immense, slowly swelling bosoms of a dull greenish blue, delicately laced with foam in intricate and lovely patterns. But their slow, awe-inspiring advance seemed suddenly to quicken, then to hit the ship under the counter, or, if not running quite true, on the quarter. Racing and roaring along the side, mounting up and going ever faster, they suddenly crashed aboard. Perhaps a hundred or more tons of water deluged on to the deck, catching some unlucky beggar and smothering him feet-deep in icy swirling foam.

Away went spare spars, harness casks, seven-pounder carronades, and anything not securely lashed. These heavy deck fittings struck and smashed the bulwarks between the stanchions. As the vessel rolled her yardarms under, some of these things went overboard. This, however, only happened when a roller seemed to break away from the line, and with ever-increasing speed and volume came charging aboard. Faulty steering often had the same result. The forward impulse of these tall and regular seas was as much as two or two and a half knots, at least, so I have seen it logged.

An albatross brought on deck and displayed for the camera.

As constant as the waves were the sea-birds that followed the ship. Sometimes they passed ahead and then wheeled back to over the ship's wake. The attraction may have been the very little food thrown overboard from a sailing ship, possibly a desire for company, or perhaps mere curiosity; but there they were, day after day for weeks; the question of when they fed and where they slept, as far as I know, remains a mystery. Albatross were the most numerous, and one that we caught without injury measured eleven feet four inches from tip to tip of wing. Then there were the frigate-birds, mollyhawks, bosun-birds, Cape pigeons, and others I could not distinguish.

The *Tippoo Sahib* boomed along before a strong gale for many days; and when about forty-five degrees south we had snow squalls. One night the order came to lay aloft and pass the gasket round the main t'gallantsail, which was blown adrift. Being handy, I skipped up to do the job, and, while on the yard, saw a fine and unusual sight. A stiff snow squall struck the ship aft and passed quickly ahead. The moon, bright in the west, shone full on the black squall-clouds, while the snow, looking like a white wall, served as a screen on which was displayed a huge, perfect lunar circle, brown to purple in colour.

When sufficient easting had been obtained we hauled round on to the port tack and ran north-east towards the tropics. Soon the weather showed signs of improvement, and then, as each day passed, the sun at noon mounted higher in the heavens, and the heat steadily increased as we drew up towards the Equator.

Nothing worth recording occurred during this part of the voyage. On arriving off the Sandheads, about three hundred miles south of Calcutta, we obtained from the cutter stationed there a British pilot, who brought on board with him a Eurasian leadsman, a poor, skinny specimen of humanity, who required one of us to haul in the lead after a cast. About here, when looking west, we could just see the Car of Juggernaut. During the annual festival, when this holy vehicle is dragged by long ropes through the streets, it was, in those days, no uncommon occurrence for religious fanatics to throw themselves in front of it and be crushed, one after another, beneath its enormous wheels. Years later, however, this form of religious frenzy and suicide was rendered of very rare occurrence by a threat to stop the festival unless it was discontinued.

Suagor Island soon appeared away to the east. Its swampy forest was then infested by tigers. After a picnic party had been attacked and eaten, however, a safe refuge was built. Off the village of Kedgeree the usual native boat came alongside with fresh fish; and how we all enjoyed the change of food after living for months on salt beef and salt pork. I believe the Indian dish of rice and fish called 'kedgeree' received its name from the fact that a fishing boat always put off from this village to the sailing ships of olden days.

After being taken in tow by a steam-tugboat, flat land appeared right ahead, with a few trees sticking up here and there, although the River Hooghly still remained very wide. Close to the dangerous quicksands of the 'James-and-Mary' a boat was stationed to show pilots the exact soundings on the bar before taking ships across it. If once a sailing vessel hung on these sands, the rolling became so great that invariably she turned right over. In the old days ships often were lost on these sands, but with the coming of more powerful tugs disasters were greatly reduced; and now, I suppose, steamers run little if any risk at all.

Calcutta after the great cyclone of 1864 when a huge tidal wave, accompanying the storm, threw ships into tangled masses of wrecked and battered hulks.

When the *Tippoo Sahib* approached this bar the station boat signalled less water by many inches than we drew forward, but our pilot risked it. He stood on the t'gallant fo'c'sle urging the little paddle-wheel tug to pull harder. In his anxiety he jumped up and down, waving his arms frantically. He was short and fat, and wore a pith helmet like a large basin, and his antics made us laugh uproariously, although our laughter was cut suddenly short when the ship hung on the treacherous sands.

Almost at once the *Tippoo Sahib* began a quick, violent roll. The carpenter stood by the towing-hawser with an axe, ready to cut it if she did not get off. We all seized hold of chicken-coops, ladders, and anything that would float, knowing that even a powerful swimmer would have no chance amid the down-sucking eddies. After hanging on the bar for a few minutes, with the roll steadily increasing, she slid clear; but we saw an American ship on her beam ends and nearly sucked down in the quicksand.

There appeared to be no docks in the Calcutta of the 'sixties, and we lay in tiers moored to buoys about half a cable's length from the muddy banks. The work of mooring was carried out by boats called 'strongbacks'. They had crews of stalwart natives under a *serang*. One man, a diver, would place a piece of flat wood against his nostrils, then go down and shackle our cable to the anchor below the mark buoy. I think the depth was about five or six fathoms. We lay in comfort not far from Prinsep's Ghaut. Two native boats were hired, one for the afterguard and one for the crew. Every night, and whenever we obtained day leave, our boat was ready to take us ashore. The craft was of the usual native type, pointed at both ends, with no keel, but having a little shelter of matting amidships. She had a great sheer, was rowed by two men with flat round-shaped paddles, and was steered by a larger paddle fastened on the quarter to one thole-pin by a strong twisted withe.

Calcutta was a primitive place in those days. We had, for instance, to use the river water for both cooking and drinking. As the Hooghly is a branch of the sacred Ganges, the natives throw their dead as well as their deceased animals into its waters; for this reason we kept a sharp lookout before dipping a bucket from which to drink. The water was very muddy, and certainly tasted of *something*.

The carrion-birds, which seemed very numerous, were a great asset to the health of a place like Calcutta as it was then. Crows, brahminy kites, vultures, and the adjutant-birds, five or more feet in height, who stalked about the streets, gobbled up every kind of offal. Not only did they carry on the work of scavenging unmolested, but were protected by law. The crows and kites were continually hovering above the river, or were perched in numbers on the floating corpses, which often went seawards with the ebb and returned again on the flood, until one or more became quite familiar to us.

There was, in fact, one old man whose corpulence afforded a *pied-à-terre* to several big birds for some time, and when finally he failed to reappear after passing down-stream, we apprentices noticed the fact. The bodies of animals, horses, buffaloes, and occasionally an elephant, would pass and repass. A kite or vulture would get hold of an intestine and fly with it into the air, hauling away on it until it broke. The long-snouted pigs, which no one eats, browsed on those bodies that floated ashore.

In the native streets of Calcutta there were open drains, or ditches, on both sides of the roadway, which were crossed here and there by a plank of wood. To supplement the usual food on board, I was often sent to an open-fronted shop in which sat a native butcher, half-dozing in the great heat, with a fly-whisk motionless in his hand, having given up trying to cope with the million flies that literally blackened the meat.

The sight always sickened me, and I was seldom able, although hungry, to eat any of the purchases made for the half-deck mess. In another street there seemed always to be a row of *bheesti wallahs*, with waterskins on the backs of donkeys or sheep, squirting water on to the dusty road. Frequently I saw two or three tiny brown babies asleep in a round flat basket, laid on the edge of the sidewalk and apparently left unattended. Three men were making a hole in which to place a post, but they did not use spades. One sat on the ground to guide the point of an iron drifter to the right spot, and the other two lifted the heavy bar up and down with as little exertion as possible. After a few strokes they all sat on their heels and passed round the *hubble-bubble*, or native water-pipe.

The *dhobis* washing clothes in a public water-tank always interested me as a youngster, with my own things to wash every Sunday morning at sea. It all seemed so simple to these people of the old Calcutta. They sat on their heels and expertly flicked twenty or thirty yards of light cotton material straight up into the air. It fell back on to the same spot all creased up, and this took the place of rubbing. When a line of *dhobis* were at work, the thin columns of light material against the sky gave a very pretty effect. Laughter, smoking, and chatter, with every movement a labour-saving device, seemed to be the sum-total of existence for these Indian washers of seventy years ago.

We apprentices would go ashore to the bazaar held by the natives in Fort William, where we could get a light meal of sorts, and cheap. It consisted of tea and a kind of cream, with *rooti* and *mukeen*, or bread-and-butter and fruit. Then we hired a *gharri*, or four-wheeler, with no glass at all, and the horse rigged with rope attached to a straw collar. Closing the dust-covered shutters across the windows, we lit our pipes and cheap Indian cigars. The first of the six or seven boys inside the vehicle who choked and gave in had to pay for the hire of the vehicle.

On other occasions we would go to the *Maidan*, a large plain, and, if the night was dark, lie down and scream and howl to entice the packs of jackals that were always prowling around. If they came close enough, we gave chase, but never succeeded in catching one. Failing the jackals, we would chase a passing native, but only once did we succeed in catching one, because, like the jackals, they were too fleet of foot. This one we held down and smacked, just in fun, and afterwards sent him off laughing with a few annas in his hand.

On board no lights were allowed in the half-deck, so we were forced to go ashore in the evenings, and, with little or no money between us, we had to make our own amusement – in which we succeeded so well that each night's escapade remains with me as a vivid memory. Once, when given day leave, I walked out into the country to where I heard a rich native kept wild animals loose in the grounds of his home. The story proved to be quite true, and directly I arrived a hippopotamus came blundering up to me with his mouth a yard or so open. I felt like bolting, but remembered that I had read that 'These amphibious beasts are not carnivorous', and after tentatively offering a leafy branch I walked away, just a little 'crisp about the gills', as Mark Twain would have said.

A bore on the River Hooghly used to occur at full and change of the moon. I suppose it still takes place, but is probably less noticeable. The strong ebb delays the flood, which at last overruns it and races up the river in the form of at least two waves. Although it varies in strength, the height of the first wave used to be about fifteen feet. Once it lifted the ships moored off the muddy bank, tore the buoys away from their anchorages, and over a dozen big vessels were adrift and fouling one another. The 'strongbacks' came to the rescue, and after hours of labour the work of re-mooring was completed.

My first experience of the Hooghly bore occurred during my time on board the *Tippoo Sahib*. Seated amidships in a native dinghy, the two paddlers turned her bow-on as the wall of water came towards us at a speed that seemed greater than it really was. The first wave cocked her nose up until, for a second or so, we hung almost vertical, and, clinging to the thwart, it appeared certain that we should all have to swim for it. Then came a second and third wave, but the crew kept her straight.

It was after this experience that I determined to learn to swim properly, although in those days many seamen were against learning. Once overboard from a sailing ship, especially if it was one of the new tea clippers moving fast through the water under a great press of canvas, there was little hope of rescue. Many captains refused to jeopardise the lives of all on board by backing the yards to stop the ship and lower a boat if the wind was piping high. And so many an old-time sailor refused to prolong the agony of drowning, if by some mischance, or act of God, he fell from aloft, perhaps clad in oilskins and sea-boots.

During the hot weather in the Calcutta of those days many people, both white and tinted, rode or drove up and down the river-side between four and six in the early morning. This struck me as curious, for although there was seldom any sun at this time of the day a rank mist hung over both land and water. In the stillness it seemed that one was breathing the stale air of the previous day. After nine or ten, however, it became much fresher, and there were often faint zephyrs, which dispelled the odours of the river.

What a rum-looking lot many of these people were, especially the tinted ones. 'Snuff and butter jelly bellies', with the slack of their tummies rippling down over their knees, seen through the thin muslins. *Baboos* and *Bunniars*, we supposed. Although true, this is perhaps a rather crude and rude description of what we saw and the manner in which we discussed it.

Every evening they appeared again, but in a different rig. Along the miles of that river-road, which I learned to know so well, there was much to be seen and heard, mostly the latter. Any time after dusk, packs of jackals, crying and screaming like children in pain, tore along like the wind; or, far off, one heard the squealing and grunting of the long trains of home-made, bamboo-built, and buffalo-drawn carts. For miles before they hove in sight these cranky vehicles could be heard.

The wheels of these craft were never round, the spokes were of bamboo, the felloes of wood, but roughly shaped and put together, seldom near a true circle, all very archaic and, to me, romantic, but always making a beastly row in the few hours of darkness during which sleep was possible.

I learned to swim in the dirty, corpsey Hooghly. Before that we youngsters would hang on to a rope over the side, two or three at a time. One evening Old Smoky, the cook, slacked away on the line until we were really half-drowned. I was below two other boys, one of whom had his legs round my neck, so I felt very frightened. The old wretch belayed, however, and let us struggle up on to the deck. There and then I decided to learn to swim, and was encouraged by an old shell-back, who said he himself had mastered the art as a boy on board the *Bellerophon*, when that ship had taken 'Boney' to St Helena.

All the water required for drinking and cooking we drew from over the side; but the next time I was in Calcutta a newly appointed Medical Officer came aboard, and filter-boats supplied water to the ships. Even then it was not clear, and rather 'tasty'. The carrion-birds were bold and aggressive. They dashed into the galley for the grub being cooked. One actually seized a lump of meat out of a boiling copper. That was more than Smoky would stand, and he let fly with a quart hooked-pot, killing the crow instantly. He then came out on to the deck and tied the dead bird to a backstay.

Soon there was a terrible commotion in the air. All the crows in the world (or those handy) circled high above the ship, singing out in a rough chorus. Their rage was great, and went on for hours, until the corpse was flung overboard. Even as it floated away down-stream, they kept on whirling round above it.

Having other ships close aboard there was much ship-visiting in the evening, when we would have a sing-song and, perhaps, Geneva – or 'squarey-facey'. This drink we obtained through the bumboat man, who came alongside each morning between six-thirty and seven.

We were allowed to deal with this man, who booked whatever we bought against us, our skipper paying before the ship sailed and debiting our wages. No drink was, however, allowed, so it had to appear as clothes, food, or curios. Of course this was not 'Johnnick', but few are perfect!

After we had sailed from Calcutta and the *Tippoo Sahib* was down south in cold weather, so many of us wanted slops from the chest that the Captain asked one young AB what he had done with all the clothes obtained from the bumboat.

'We drank 'em, sir,' was the answer.

'Ah,' said the old man thoughtfully. 'Well, there's plenty of coal tar in the fore peak, and you can paint your sterns with that.'

We did not leave Calcutta until after Christmas, however; and one day the Captain sent the steward to say that he would give us all geese and plum-duff on Christmas Day, and to ask how many geese we could eat.

'One each?' asked the steward.

Looking modestly at one another, we tentatively suggested that perhaps one between two of us would be sufficient.

The cook was also to have as much flour and raisins as he could cram into the copper.

'That's all very well, but what am I going to boil it in?' he questioned, looking at each of us. 'There's no cloth big enough.'

All sorts of useless suggestions were made, until a chubby apprentice, rather diffident and shy, remarked awkwardly: 'I've got a pair of canvas pants – quite new – eh?'

'Bully for you!' shouted the cook quickly. 'Why, that'll be a fair do – a leg for each watch.'

There were some rough jokes when the long sausage-shaped puddings were hoisted out of the copper – but it *was* a fair do.

11 Sail in the 'Sixties

Liverpool in the 'sixties – An old-time pantomime in the eyes of Victorian youth – A bedroom in sailortown – Armed men common on the water-fronts – Boarding the *Fulwood* – Battened down and hove-to – Jib-boom and fore topgallantmast carried away by a waterspout – In the 'rain area' of the South Atlantic – Drafting a piece – Heavy shocks caused by whales or earthquakes – Ashore in Aden – Replacing chain plates in Rangoon – Privations – The Kinsale pilot comes aboard – Home.

WE came out of the theatre, one of several in the Liverpool of the early 'sixties, into the cold drizzle of a December night. In the comparative warmth and gas glow, amid the dirt, the bare benches, and sawdusted floor, my shipmate and I had spent three hours in the ecstatic enjoyment of an old-time pantomime, culminating, as was then usual, in a glorious 'Transformation Scene', full of light and colour, depicting the change of the seasons from snowy, sparkling winter to soft but radiant summer, until the climax was reached by what we thought were the most beautiful girls in the world posing in fairy-like ways. All equally lovely when seen from the gallery by eyes of youth accustomed only to lean, unkempt men and empty, restless seas for months at a time.

Harry Mason, a bright-faced Cumberland lad, shipmate of a coming voyage, pulled his blue cloth cap with flag-badge over his eyes and gazed out for several minutes into the dismal murk of the ill-lit street.

'How they get all those lovely girls in theatres beats me!' he suddenly burst out. 'One never sees them anywhere else – I suppose——' And the emphasis changed to a sigh.

It may have been that I was less susceptible, or, more likely, was brought back to reality by the leaking black void above.

'No,' I answered, assuming a cheerfulness that was not felt, for we were sailing the next day. 'But it's no use talking about them here. It's past midnight – I heard St Nicholas' strike a while ago. We can't knock up Mother Williams, and I don't think she would let us in if we did. Neither do we want to walk about all night in this drizzle. Let's go down to the Goree Piazza; I think we can find a dry spot to caulk in.'

On our way, however, we passed through Paradise Street, the heart of sailortown in those days; but all the dismal-looking houses were closed and silent, except where a streak of light fell across the roadway. It came from the unguarded gas-jets in the window of a cook-shop, to which we made.

'Have you got a bed?' I asked.

The crew of the *Fulwood* photographed in 1864.

'Yes. Ninepence each. Up that ladder,' and the big flabby shopkeeper pointed to where a well-worn ladder led through a square hole in the ceiling.

We paid our ninepence each and, climbing through the lubber's hole, found ourselves in a low-pitched attic, the roof sloping down each way. On the left side it formed a kind of alcove in which a big, rather handsome man, with curly dark hair and large gold earrings, was lying on top of a bed, seemingly drunk, with only his coat and vest off.

To our 'Hello, mate!' he gave only a grunt, and slewed himself over, apparently going to sleep without even a glance in our direction. We noticed, however, that lying beside him was a belt, a sheath-knife, and a small pistol.

This miniature armoury was not so uncommon seventy years ago in the boarding-houses of the water-fronts as it would be in the sailors' homes of to-day. Taking no further notice of it, therefore, we gladly turned in to another bed under the other portion of the sloping roof. I had the inside berth, the ceiling being a few inches only above my nose. Dog-tired, we slept until roused out at grey dawn.

No supper the previous night and now no breakfast – for our entire capital had been expended on the price of a bed – we walked out into the raw air, called at Mother Williams' for my donkey, or sea-chest, and began the search for our ship, which was not in the dock we had expected, but over in the great float on the Birkenhead side.

'Gone over to load coal,' we were told by some river-side loafers. The problem of how to get aboard before she sailed on the tide now became serious. There was no ferry boat at this

The full-rigged ship *Fulwood*, the sistership of the *Wavertree*.
The latter is now preserved as a museum ship at South Street Seaport.

early hour of the morning, and I had my donkey to carry. Making our way down to the landing-stage – and there was only the one, called St George's, in those days – we found a twelve-foot boat, with two oars, tied to a ring high up in the piling. Jumping in as quickly as possible, thinking the owner might be near by, we pulled hard across the river, as we could now see the *Fulwood* – the only ship in the float – loosing her fore topsail.

Arriving at the Birkenhead side we jumped out, and seeing an old waterman near by asked him if he would return the boat to its owner.

'I know. She belongs to old Joe Barlege. All right, mate, I'll see she's safe.'

I shouldered my donkey and off we went. Mason's chest was on board, and for him, therefore, the mile run along two sides of the float was not so bad. We could see the ship sailing slowly towards the narrow entrance under fore topsail and jib. It was hard going, and as we turned the corner I felt we were done. She was forging ahead, even under her small canvas.

'Run, Mason!' I shouted breathlessly. 'I'm nearly done, and shall lose my passage, but you can just do it.'

His reply was to come behind and take a part of the weight off my back.

'Drop it and run, you fool,' I almost hissed at him, as I saw his chance to board her at the waist.

He did so, and jumped, scrambling over the rail just abaft the main rigging. Two men on the dock side, seeing my plight, caught hold of my chest and hove it on board, whilst I made a rather risky leap from the quay into the mizzen rigging.

I slipped quickly down to the half-deck, where we apprentices were berthed, and changed into working kit. All hands were kept busy now, some aloft bending sails, others with chain hooks flaking the cable in case we had to let go the anchor. The whole deck and everything on it was more or less covered with coal-dust. Even the beef kid, or barrel, from which we two hungry young sailors obtained and devoured some salt beef, was coated with the black dust, which seemed to work its way into everything.

We were soon outside the Rock Light, and, as it was blowing hard, the old man reefed her down. The seas coming aboard washed the dust off everything, as well as some fifty tons or more of coal still on deck. We soon had the hatches battened down; but for some reason that I never knew we had sailed before the canvas and running gear were in proper order. Seeing this, the pilot hove-to under the lee of the Isle of Man for the night, which gave us time to get things in working order, muster the crew – some of whom were still feeling the effects of the last glass – pick the watches, and see all hands properly berthed.

Next day the weather moderated; and then came a favourable slant of wind, which carried us clear of the Irish Sea, and out into blue water, where we soon overhauled other south-of-Spainers, or 'lime-juicers', as all British ships bound for long voyages were then called. Owing, however, to light winds and an unusual easterly current, we crossed the Line farther east than was the general rule among sailing ships.

This brought us into a very strange and carefully avoided area of the South Atlantic, called by old sailors 'The Rains'. It is a region on the edge of the Gulf Stream with light and variable airs, shifting continually. Now and then come furious gusts and water spouts, all of which we had in succession.

One spout crossed our bows at great speed, snapping off our jib-boom and bringing down with it our fore topgallantmast, owing to the sudden drag on the fore and aft stays. I was in the waist of the ship, on the starboard side, at the time, so had a good view of the whirling spout as it came down on us from the port hand. The dark column of water whizzed across our bows, with a huge flurry of misty rain scurrying around a shallow depression in the sea, which was trimmed with a fringe on its outer edge of rips and squirts of water.

The ship's speed carried her rapidly ahead, and almost immediately the wind fell light, then calm. Little puffs of air from different directions kept us all box-hauling the yards about. The only way of getting out of this curious and depressing region was to take advantage of every puff that would help the ship on her course.

'All aback forrard!' someone shouted. 'Fore brace!' yelled the bosun. Then, when there came a strong puff, 'All aback aft!' was the cry. The ship wallowed about, and the sails slatted against the masts and rigging with the noise of gunfire. The spanker boom took charge with a shuddering and flapping; and all the time we sweated in the damp heat bracing the yards to use even the lightest air that ruffled the glass-like surface of the sea with long thin ripples.

One trifling but unpleasant feature was that our hands, rain-soaked for many hours, cracked and bled. Our constant remedy for these sea-cuts was Stockholm tar. During one watch, when it was my trick at the wheel, the rain poured down over my face like a cataract, veiling the binnacle so that it was impossible for me to see the compass. During this downpour I noticed the strange effect produced by a pall of grey cloud over the whole sky, except for a strip about ten or fifteen degrees above the horizon, which gave out a sickly yellow light nearly all round and was edged with waterspouts. At one time I counted thirty in various stages of formation.

'How's her head?' suddenly roared the Captain, his voice rising above the staccato drumming of the tropical deluge.

As it was impossible for me to see the compass I could not reply, but hastened to give a lusty shout: 'Waterspout coming up astern with the breeze, sir!' And there, true enough, it was. When looking round at the circle of queer yellow light I had seen it approaching less than a minute before, but there were so many within vision, moving in circles, that it had then seemed useless to report its presence.

Becalmed as we were, the huge column, sizzling and ill-defined, bore down on us with the coming wind; but without steerage way on the ship nothing could be done to avoid it.

'Run out that signal gun over the taffrail,' ordered the old man, when it really seemed that the spout would pass along the ship from stern to stem.

The little brass four-pounder was soon loaded and pointed astern. The mate had taken my place at the wheel, and with two other men of the watch on deck I waited for the near approach of the spout before firing. Some sixty or seventy feet away it burst. There was another deluge of water from the skies, a strong puff of wind, and that was all.

How glad we were at last to get breeze enough to clear out of that dismal spot! A fair westerly wind, gentle at first, soon became a steady eight-knot one, while the weather gradually cleared, enabling us to start work on the ship's gear, to trice the running to the standing rigging, scrape, paint, and varnish.

We passed rapidly into the trades and enjoyed a peaceful time. At two bells came the usual 'Turn-to' from the second mate or the bosun. Then it was: 'Jack, you and Tom go up forrard, overhaul all the beckets on the jackstays, make up the gaskets, rig in the stun'sl boom and, before you *lay* down, grease the parrels. Sim, you help the sailmaker to fid out those cringles on the leech of the new mainsail. Bill, get those two blocks out of the bosun's locker and strop them with two-inch manilla, worm, parcel, and serve – and a throat seizing of marline. You, boy, get a bolt and chip the rust off the stock of the big kedge. You, Dick, take a strand, get a bucket of tar out of that barrel in the fore peak——' And so the day's work of each watch was apportioned, and the *Fulwood* settled down to easy trade-wind routine.

And here I may remark that these quiet halcyon days are a fair example of the best that fell to the lot of a sailor in those days. We had some fun, too, at times. A paint-box and a sketch-book had been given me by my father, who was an artist. When passing the rocky Desertas Islands, near Madeira, I made a fairly accurate drawing of them. The steward brought me a message one day from a lady passenger who wished to see it. I was surprised, and somewhat diffident, as I did not think much of the sketch, for I knew more than I could carry out. However, I let him take it, and within an hour or so he returned with the message that the lady would like to have it, and would I prefer pots of jam or bottles of stout?

As money was quite forgotten during the long voyages of sailing ships, except when some of the crew amused themselves by beating out a Mexican dollar, made of pure silver, and fashioning it into a ring or some ornament, such as a ferrule to splice the stem of a favourite 'Burns' cutty', I put the choice of jam or stout to the vote of the half-deck. The result was stout, and half a dozen bottles were soon drunk amidst cheers.

As I have said, my father was an artist, and before sailing he gave me the colour-box and sketch-book, saying: 'You may like to try to sketch what you are interested in.' Everyone forrard of the poop credited me with his ability, and this led them to approach me in a rather furtive manner, half shy and half ashamed. One would come sidling along, looking rather sheepish, like a fellow stalking a man for half a crown.

'I want you to make me a draft of my piece,' he would say, with a curious mixture of pleading and defiance in his tone. This meant that he desired a sketch of his sweetheart.

'Well, what's she like?' I would invariably ask, knowing quite well that he could not explain. 'Fair or middling? What's the colour of her eyes? Fresh or pale skin?'

Shifting uneasily from one foot to another, the reply of the boy, or man, would always be the same, although the words took a long time to come from his lips:

'Well, er-er-er-I really can't say – but she's good-looking, she is!'

'Oh, of course,' I replied, as mildly as possible, as the last of his words conveyed a challenge. 'Better leave it to me and I'll do my best.'

Then I would look up the types of beauty which appeared in *The London Journal*, of which we mostly had a lot on board, it being one of the few papers then containing woodcuts. Selecting one, I drew and coloured it to the best of my ability. On showing it, very privately, to its future owner he would exclaim:

'Well, I never, that's the very spit of her!' And it generally gave entire satisfaction to both parties, for my pay was a plug of baccy, or he would wash and mend some clothes for me.

Nothing much happened as we rounded the Cape of Good Hope and bore away northerly through the Mozambique Channel, except two nasty bumps. The first was a peculiar, shaky jar, causing most of us on deck to fall down, but there was only one shock. The old man backed the main topsail, and when the ship lost way we took a cast of the deep-sea lead, weighing twenty-eight pounds. As this method of sounding is a thing of the past it is worth describing.

One hand took the lead out on to the jib-boom, while others stood in the chains, each holding a few flakes of the line, the last in order being the mate, standing well aft on the quarter. When the ship had lost way enough, the Captain shouted: 'Heave!'

The hand on the jib-boom swung the lead as far out ahead as he could, and called: 'Watch, there ! Watch!' As the line came aft, each hand dropped his portion and repeated the warning cry. Finally, the Captain and mate noted when the line was vertical, and the mark on it, at the water's edge. The line was then hauled in and the arming of grease in the cavity at the bottom of the lead examined to see if it had picked up anything from the sea-bed. In this case, however, there was nothing, as we got no bottom at a hundred fathoms.

The bump that had shaken the *Fulwood*, we all believed, had been caused by an earthquake. The other shock, experienced farther up the coast, was not so severe, and was the result of a blow from a sperm whale – at least we thought so, because a couple of them had been seen earlier in the day blowing quite close to the ship.

Soon after passing the island of Socotra we anchored off Aden, in about ten fathoms of clear water, through which could be seen the white coral sea-bed. A gang of black-skinned and fierce-looking Abyssinians, together with a few brown and laughing Somalis, came on board to unload the coal, which we heard was intended for the recently installed condenser engines, converting sea-water into fresh. In Aden there was little or no ordinary fresh water, except the dirty-looking liquid we saw in 'The Tanks', said to have been built in the time of the Queen of Sheba.

During our day of liberty ashore we of the port watch mounted rather small but strong

A view of Aden from the sea.

donkeys for a ride up to the top of 'The Tanks'. There was no real road, only tracks, that varied in width, roughness, and incline. Sitting well aft on our game little beasts, the long-legged among us helping them along with our toes, which would otherwise have dragged along the ground, we climbed up past the six or seven tanks, one above the other, until we came to the uppermost.

This was about twenty or thirty feet in diameter, and the mountains sloped down to its edge. Steep too, the sides were scored with rugged gullies, nine to twelve feet deep, made by rain during vague and vast periods of time, and there was several feet of water in this highest tank.

The surface was covered with a green scum, as was the case with the water in two of the lower tanks. It has been said that rain never falls in Aden, but for what purpose were the tanks constructed by great labour, and how about those rugged water-worn slopes we saw?

Coming down the track, much of which was only a yard wide, with a wall of rock on one side and a precipice on the other, and along the very edge of which our donkeys insisted upon walking, Tom Barr, the bosun's mate, remarked with emphasis: 'I'd b——y well rather be out at the lee earring, reefing topsails on a dirty night – and chance the baccy juice a'cummin down from the chaps to windward.' And we all thought the same.

The black men working the cargo were berthed between the foremast and the break of the forecastle, our men reserving the latter for themselves. One day an Abyssinian trespassed up there and was promptly knocked off on to the deck below, with some slight injuries. There was, of course, a hell of a row, but having no language in common the matter was soon settled by their boss, or *serang*, who knew a little English and managed to pacify the crowd – big strong fellows, who, when working, chanted a rather mournful dirge. Naked and black, yet after work they would stand on the heaps in the lighters and scrub themselves all over with big lumps of coal. They slept ashore on the pale, ivory-coloured sand, hiding themselves under big rush-mats. It was amusing to see their black arms and legs emerging from cover at gunfire in the early morning. Here, on the sand, they did their cooking as well as their sleeping, so, like their clothes and their coal-washes, it cost them nothing.

The little black boys of Aden came off from the shore to offer to dive for small coins thrown into the sea. It began with the usual invitation to trade: 'Changey for changey, black dog for white monkey. Me black dog, you white monkey.' I have heard this in many foreign ports, or, in the sailor parlance of those far-off years, in 'The country'.

The heat of Aden was great, and some nights we lay on the bare deck nearly bare ourselves. We youngsters were troubled with an eruption on parts of our skin, of which I got clear first, with the aid of flowers of sulphur and cream of tartar from the medicine chest, taking so much that it came through my skin in the form of a dry powder that I could brush off.

We were not sorry to leave for the open sea once again, to return to our salt pork, beef, and biscuit, which had, at all events, far more flavour than the skinny so-called mutton supplied to the ship while in Aden. I saw the steward, a big man, carrying four or five carcasses on the fingers of one hand. He held them aloft and said with disgust: 'Just a candle inside and there you have a good lantern.'

Decks awash on the four-masted barque *Pommern*.

As we were in ballast – pieces of rock which Aden was able to spare – we could not carry much sail: courses, topsails, staysails, and jibs being as much as she could stand, except in the lightest of airs, when the topgallantsails were hoisted. We were bound for Calcutta and Rangoon. Nothing of special interest occurred, however, until we left the former port.

During the passage across the Bay of Bengal the *Fulwood* encountered a series of heavy squalls, which came on very suddenly. These seemed to strain our chain plates, on which ultimately depended the safety of the shrouds and masts. At Rangoon these plates were replaced by Chinese ironworkers, who, after a considerable delay, brought on board what appeared to be excellent replicas of the old ones. These were bolted to the ship's sides. When homeward bound across the Western Ocean we met with a succession of strong gales. One after another these plates gave way. On examination they were found to be only a number of pieces of sheet iron artfully made to look like a solid block.

Rigging preventers with the ship rolling and pitching and the wind blowing a full gale proved a tough job. In addition to this, some of the planks had been badly strained, compelling us to pump almost continuously instead of only twice a day. The *Fulwood* was not a good sea-boat, shipping a lot of heavy water, especially midships. The galley was so often swamped that it became impossible to keep a fire going; and in the bitter cold of midwinter in the Atlantic with little to eat, for provisions were running short, and no hot food or drinks, the hardships were indeed great.

The water penetrated into our berths and all our clothes were wet. Going into the deck house, we peeled off sodden clothes and thick woollen sea-boot stockings, wrung them out, and hung them on a line. When called on deck, however, either to shorten sail or to go on watch, we turned out of our damp bunks, steaming like boiled potatoes, and had to dress in wet and half-frozen gear to face the icy wind for four hours at the wheel, lookout, or up aloft. It left me with a lasting impression of sheer discomfort such as I had not felt before – or since.

The worst came to me when, going into the bosun's locker to get a strop, I found it flooded with about ten inches of water. Hearing a plaintive moan I found that it came from our pet, an Indian bear, of whom we were all fond. He died as soon as I put my hand on his head to see if he was cold. I don't mind admitting that I cried. The privation and discomfort we could stand, but the loss of our little bear left us with a feeling that we did not care if the leaky old tub went to the bottom. This was, of course, temporary, but it was very acute and real at the time.

All things considered, we were a good-hearted and jolly lot of youngsters. One night, in the middle watch, we shipped a particularly heavy sea. It either broke or forced open a port in the half-deck house and came pouring into my berth. I knew lots of songs and often started one appropriate to the moment. As the water swished over me I tumbled out singing: 'The lark now leaves his watery nest.' But it fell on arid soil. One of the apprentices said: 'I don't see any lark in it. Look at my suffering pants, all wet again, and it's my turn at the wheel.'

We were bound for Queenstown for orders, and at last got a slant of wind that carried us up the Irish Sea with a nine-knot breeze on our port quarter. Everyone started the old chanty:

'A good sea running with a curling crest,
And the Tuskar bears about West-sou'-west,
So heave, my lads, and do your best,
    And Jimmy, get the Hoe cakes done.
        Jamboree, Jamboree, etc., etc.

'And now we are inside of the Rock
With our hammocks all lashed and our chests all locked,
Hoo ray! me boys, for the Albert Dock,
    So Jimmy, get the Hoe cakes done.
        Jamboree, Jamboree, etc., etc.'

Off the Old Head of Kinsale a hooker with a pilot on board ran under our stern and the crew shouted for a rope. We hove one to them with a bowline at the end, and a hardy old pilot placed the bowline under his arms, jumped overboard into the sea and shouted: 'Haul away, ye ugly divils, and bad scran t'ye!'

When the *Fulwood* finally docked in Liverpool we went ashore as soon as she was made fast, this being the custom in the halcyon days of sail. The solid ground felt very different

Fulwood at anchor in the early part of the last century. In 1919 she was lost on a voyage from Buenos Aires to Korsør, Denmark.

from the unyielding and ever-varying surface of the deck. Among the mobs of people, all strangers, the men appeared to be always fat and the women all delicate-looking and beautiful. This was how it struck those who for long months, often *years*, had seen only the same spare forms and brown weather-beaten faces of their shipmates.

Going ashore full of hope, expectation, and with a sense of being of interest – asking for a welcome from all and sundry – we had to awaken to the dry fact that no one cared a jot about us or our voyage, leaving us all to drift off in various ways, according to chance, to spend like *asses* the money we were said to have worked for like *hosses*.

12 An Adventurous Voyage

Every voyage in sail an adventure – The full-rigged ship *Cleomene* – Outward bound
from Leith, 1892 – Apprentice falls from aloft – A meeting years later and then
torpedoed – 'The Sleeping Genius of Brazil' – Fired at by the Rio de Janeiro forts – Civil
war – Five months of war and 'Yellow Jack' – Apprentice blown to pieces – A dago runs
amok – Rounding Cape Horn – Loading manganese ore at Coquimbo – Ship rolls like a
pendulum – Setting up loose rigging in a heavy sea – Waist and neck deep in icy seas –
A blizzard off Cape Hatteras – Refitting in the island of St Thomas, West Indies – A
difficulty about a mate – Eleven days of fog.

IN the days of sail, which seem but a short time ago, even to those of us who are only
middle-aged, every voyage was an adventure, some more than others, but invariably
each brought its quota of peril and hardship. When the full-rigged ship *Cleomene* left
Leith one breezy spring morning in the year 1892 not one of us aboard her could have
foreseen the strange and even tragic events of the coming months. We sailed away to the
usual accompaniment of sea-chanties – so characteristic of the carefree disposition of the
seamen of those times – despite the knowledge that in the hold beneath our feet were
thousands of tons of that most dangerous cargo when on a long voyage, anthracite coal.

We were bound for Rio de Janeiro, and in order to avoid the prevailing westerlies in the
Channel we shaped a course into the Atlantic round the north coast of Scotland. The gale
that met us almost as soon as the open sea was reached was the cause of the first unhappy
event. The watch on deck were sent aloft just before midnight to make the mainsail fast. A
first-voyage apprentice and myself reached the weather main yardarm. Although stormy it
was not very dark, and, sitting on the foot-rope, I passed the gasket up to him. In a moment
of forgetfulness he let go of the jackstay and clutched the rope with both hands.

Luckily I was alongside a stirrup, for the next instant he fell backwards into the darkness,
and had it been impossible to steady myself I should have followed him down.

My shout of 'Man fallen from aloft!' proved unnecessary, for the mate had seen the
accident from the poop. Missing the hand main winch by inches, the boy crashed to the
deck. Some of the watch below were quickly aroused, and he was carried into the saloon
unconscious.

EDITOR'S NOTE
Captain J H Mabey of the full-rigged ship *Cleomene*, and in later years a Suez Canal pilot, describes one of his
most adventurous voyages in sail.

Working aloft on the huge four-masted German barque *Kommodore Johnsen*, ex-*Magdalene Vinnen*. Originally built to carry bulk cargoes between Europe and South America and Australia, she was acquired by the Soviet Union as war reparation in 1946. Renamed *Sedov*, she now has the distinction of being the world's largest training ship.

When his oilskin and clothing had been cut away the Captain and mate found that his arm was broken and a splintered bone had been driven through his shoulder. They managed to pull it back into place and set it before we arrived in Rio, which seemed to us all a remarkable example of medical skill for amateurs. A naval surgeon came on board when we made port, however, and although he congratulated the old man, he nevertheless insisted on the boy being sent home at once, as the broken bones would have to be reset in hospital.

Many years afterwards, when we had both become officers, I met my old shipmate in New York, and he told me that he could never lift his arm above his head. During the War we met again in the Suez Canal, where I was serving as a pilot. Shortly afterwards his ship was torpedoed, with the loss of all hands.

On arriving off Rio we were shown by the Captain a strange sight, which even to-day few people have seen. It is 'The Sleeping Genius of Brazil', formed by the shape of the mountains half-surrounding the city, with the 'Sugar Loaf' for the feet of a reclining giant. On the following afternoon we entered the magnificent harbour, and events both humorous and tragic followed in quick succession.

On the starboard hand there was an old fort with a signal flying from a *small* flagstaff ordering us to stop immediately. Unfortunately the Captain did not see this, and we sailed on with the afternoon breeze astern. This wind is called locally 'The Doctor', and in those days was not inappropriately named. Then a shot was fired which came across our bows, a few seconds afterwards another passed between the fore and main masts, and a third came over between the main and mizzen. Needless to say, we hove-to and anchored like 'One John Smith'. Halyards and sheets were let fly, and no ship could have come to an anchor more quickly. The Captain told us afterwards that a large sum had to be paid by the ship for each shot that was fired for disobeying the signal, which could scarcely be seen.

While lying at anchor we saw some warships in the harbour firing their guns, and immediately the forts on shore also started blazing away. At first we thought they were practising, but on entering the harbour learned that a civil war was in progress. For over five months we were detained in Rio, with war and yellow fever all around us, and could not get away for two reasons.

One reason was that our cargo was intended for the Brazilian Government, and it could not be unloaded. The naval authorities warned the Captain that if the ship attempted to leave the harbour it would be sunk by the guns of the forts. The second reason was that people, both ashore and afloat, were dying like flies from fever, and very soon our crew were nearly all down with the dreaded 'Yellow Jack', twenty-eight out of a total of thirty being transferred to hospital. An ordinary seaman and myself were all that were left aboard for a fortnight. Nine of our crew died, including the second mate and an apprentice.

As the town of Rio was in a state of siege it was not safe to go on shore, although at first we did land in the ship's gig. One day, however, I saw an apprentice from another ship, who was taking shelter close to our boat, blown to pieces by a shell from a small gunboat that was firing on the lower part of the town. After five and a half months we managed to shanghai some men to take the place of our dead and get away from this plague spot. There were, however, about twenty sailing ships still left in Rio Harbour, nearly all their crews having died of yellow fever.

We were now bound for the Horn and the west coast of South America, to take aboard a fresh cargo. The new members of our crew formed a motley crowd of different nationalities. Luckily we were in ballast, otherwise several of them would have been lost overboard, as they knew nothing of sea-life. This made it harder for the apprentices, who were really more capable seamen than a lot of the fo'c'sle hands. Fortunately we had a 'hard-case' third mate, a huge, raw-boned Highlander, who had been promoted from the fo'c'sle when the second mate died in Rio, the former third becoming second officer.

The new steward, a dago, and one of the sailors, a Spaniard, after we had been at sea for several days, suddenly attacked the third mate with knives. He succeeded, however, in knocking them both senseless with his fists, and they were very respectful to him afterwards. For three weeks we were trying to beat round Cape Horn against continuous westerly gales.

Ships lying off Antofagasta, just north of Taltal, another of the major Chilean mining ports.

The *Cleomene* wallowed in the great seas, which swept her fore and aft. Blinding snowstorms and freezing spray soon covered everything with ice. In the half-deck and fo'c'sle nothing was dry, clothes and bedding were continually wet and cold. The wind roared and shrieked, the flying spume made it difficult to look to windward; and all of us suffered severely from the bitter and damp cold following so closely upon the months spent in the tropical heat of Rio de Janeiro.

After seventy-two days we arrived at Taltal, on the Chilean coast, and received orders to proceed to Coquimbo to load a quantity of manganese ore, one of the heaviest and most dangerous cargoes it is possible to carry. From this place we went to Carrizal, to finish loading, and were compelled to handle the cargo ourselves. The heat was now terrible, the work very heavy, and our hands became painfully sore. When eventually we got to sea the ship never ceased rolling.

By the time a latitude sufficiently far south was reached to enable us to square away for rounding the Horn all the lower rigging had become slack, through the severe straining of masts and yards, due to the pendulum-like motion of the ship in the great Pacific rollers with the concentrated weight of the manganese ore in the bottom of the hold.

With the strong west wind came also the immense 'grey-beards' of the Southern Ocean and the penetrating damp-cold characteristic of these sub-Antarctic latitudes. The loose rigging had to be set up while the wind-tormented seas came aboard in tons of green water, and we often plunged waist or neck deep in the swirling flood which crossed the deck with every roll.

Slowly we worked our way north from the region of gales and great flat-topped bergs, or really ice-islands, to the calms and tropical storms of the Line. Nothing eventful occurred again, however, until off Cape Hatteras, where we encountered a blizzard that proved to be one of the worst ever known. Yards came adrift, sails were blown away, and the gale-driven snow made it impossible to effect repairs aloft. The Captain decided to turn and run south before it with only a 'goosewing' main lower topsail, which, luckily, was a new one.

For several days the blizzard raged and we continued to run, finally making the island of St Thomas, in the West Indies. This was a well-known place for lame ducks, as it possessed a large engineering works and a dry dock. Our cargo, which had been stowed pyramid-fashion from forward to aft, had sagged down, and part of it had to be shifted into the 'tween decks and placed in casks. We remained in St Thomas for nearly two and a half months, and when finally ready for sea the mate became ill, and was taken to the hospital on shore.

A new difficulty now arose. The second mate possessed only a second mate's certificate, and it was illegal to proceed to sea under-officered in this way. The Captain tried hard to find another qualified mate. We left the harbour and anchored outside for ten days, when the captain of a Nova Scotian schooner, a lame duck like ourselves, was signed on. This vessel had been sold in the island. He was, however, a 'fore and aft' sailor, and knew little about square-rig. Nevertheless, away we went, bound for Philadelphia.

When about forty-five miles south-east of Cape Hatteras we encountered thick fog, and so dropped our anchor. This lasted for *eleven* days, during which time we never took our clothes off. The boats were swung out ready for us to jump into at any moment, as we were right in the track of shipping. On the eleventh day our bell cracked down the middle, but soon afterwards the fog cleared and we found ships all around us. A small American steamer, the *Bluefields*, came close to us, scenting salvage, and offered a tow, which our Captain declined, as she would not have been able to move us far with our heavy cargo.

Two hours later an American tug came alongside, having been sent out to look for us by the company's agents. I shall never forget how glad we all were when the order to pass the tow-rope was given, and the powerful tug 'walked away' with us to Point Breeze, below Philadelphia, to discharge our cargo and load crude oil in barrels for Dunkirk.

The Captain went home by steamer, and the mate was given command to take the ship across the Atlantic. We were all very sorry to lose the Captain, who was a fine seaman, and, moreover, looked after us aboard and gave us a good time when in port. It took thirty-seven days to make Dunkirk, because the mate was very cautious, and insisted upon reducing sail every night. From here we were towed to Liverpool by the *Jane Joliffe*, one of the famous Joliffe tugs. Off Land's End we encountered a heavy westerly gale, but the tug held on to us, although at times it was impossible to see one ship from the deck of the other. Eventually we arrived at Liverpool, after an adventurous voyage of eighteen months.

13 An Eventful Voyage

Apprenticeship in the *Aspice* – Third mate of the four-masted barque *Inverness-shire* –
Off to Honolulu – Unhappy ship – A battle of fists – Pitcairn island – Plague and fire –
Sailors on night guard – A stay-in strike at sea – *Inverness-shire* adrift – Mutiny.

ONE of the most eventful voyages I ever experienced occurred in the Pacific Ocean, during the year 1900. We called it mutiny in those days – and, because it occurred on the high seas, it would be mutiny at the present time.

I had just completed in the Port of Sydney, NSW, a gruelling four years' apprenticeship in the fine Glasgow full-rigged ship *Aspice*, and I was ordered to take over the third mate's berth in the big four-masted barque *Inverness-shire*, then loading coal for Honolulu. She was a fine ship, but her nondescript crew were a scratch lot of all nationalities, newly combed out from Sydney's water-side dives, and a more useless bunch I never hope to see. Some of them had never been aboard a sailing ship in their lives, and one, at least, was a bricklayer, of all things! The ship was by no means a happy one, and to make matters worse our second mate was a steamboat man, unaccustomed to the handling of a large sailing ship, a point of special grievance with the hands before the mast and also with the Captain.

We eventually put to sea, but as the days went by the crew began to get troublesome, and relations grew strained between the skipper and our unhappy second mate. Somewhere off the southern tip of New Zealand, one night during my watch below, when I was trying to snatch a few hours' sleep, the trouble between these two came to a head. Suddenly I awoke with a start to hear, just outside my door, the Captain bellowing to the second mate in angry tones:

'Mr R——, you're no sailor, and you're certainly not fit to be second mate of my ship. I'm going to disrate you, for I've got a better man to fill your place. I want sailors, not sojers!'

He threw open my door at the same moment and called me, but I 'lay possum' and said nothing. Just then the ship was struck by a sudden squall and heeled over heavily, so the quarrel was temporarily forgotten and the two officers rushed up on deck to regain control of the heavily labouring barque. All hands were called to shorten sail, and we quickly

EDITOR'S NOTE
Captain W W Waddell (and John Anderson), after an apprentiseship in the full-rigged ship *Aspice*, joined the big four-masted barque *Inverness-shire*, and describes one of his most evenful voyages.

A painting of the full-rigged ship *Aspice* which once hung in the offices of her second owners, Thomas Law & Co of Glasgow. She encountered terrible conditions off San Francisco in April 1915 and, her cargo having shifted, was blown ashore off Santa Rosa Island where she was wrecked.

stripped her down to topsails, foresail, and two headsails. Unfortunately, while working on the mizzenmast, the poor bricklayer fell from aloft, striking the rail with his head and cannoning from it into the raging sea.

The ship was now making a steady ten knots, with a strong following wind, and the skipper flatly refused to heave-to and lower a boat. Undoubtedly the man was lifeless before he touched the water, but the Captain's action further embittered most of the men, and one of them, a stalwart Norwegian, openly blamed the second mate for this unfortunate accident.

The Captain happened to overhear this man grousing about the mishap, so one night he invited Mr R—— to his cabin, plied him with whisky, and urged him to tackle 'that damned square-head'. With the fiery spirits coursing through his veins the second mate was nothing loth, so the precious pair sent for the Norwegian, and soon a battle royal with bare fists was raging on the deck. An apprentice hurriedly called me, and I arrived to see the Captain coolly standing by chewing an unlighted cigar and watching the cursing combatants jumping about the deck. Both men were seasoned warriors, and I must say it was the prettiest scrap I ever witnessed in all my years of going to sea. However, it proved to be a ding-dong contest, and, as no decisive result seemed likely, the skipper eventually

Pitcairn islanders, descendants of the
mutineers from HMS *Bounty*.

stopped the struggle and strolled away aft, leaving the two men to patch up their bruises as best they could.

This fight certainly did not improve the strained relations between the crew and the afterguard. However, the voyage dragged on, and one day we sighted that mutineers' paradise, Pitcairn Island, and shaped our course towards it in a very light breeze. Our progress was slow, and by nightfall we were only just in sight of the tiny settlement, so the islanders lit a bonfire to guide us. When we hove-to, three whale-boats put out full of islanders and came alongside to barter fresh fruit and vegetables for anything we could give them, from old clothes to tobacco. When the friendly bartering was over, we squared the foreyard, and our visitors returned to their craft, cheering wildly and treating us to a concert of Moody and Sankey hymns as the big ship slowly got under way and left the boats bobbing astern.

We now had a good spell of the south-east trades and enjoyed most exhilarating sailing weather, the lofty four-master simply romping along, with every sail full and drawing. Arriving at Honolulu, and sailing into the beautiful harbour, we berthed safely and prepared to discharge our cargo. Imagine the horror of every man jack aboard when we learned that a virulent plague was raging in the town and that the inhabitants were dying off like flies! Still, this could not be allowed to interfere with the working of the ship, and discharging began, but the crew worked unwillingly and were a constant source of trouble and worry to us. Both by day and night, Honolulu was indeed a city of the dead, and our only relaxation from work was to visit the other ships in port, mostly 'lime-juicers' and 'down-easters'.

After a week in port we heard that the plague was abating, and the town gradually came to life. One of the last fatal cases occurred in a building in the native quarter, and later the authorities set fire to the structure. Fanned by a stiff breeze, the flames quickly spread to the surrounding houses, so that the entire native quarter was soon ablaze from end to end, and hundreds of natives lost their homes, and barely escaped with their lives. Gradually the fire burned its way to the water-front, and ship after ship cast off and sought anchorage in the bay, where their crews constantly poured buckets of water over the sails to prevent them catching alight. Fortunately our ship was berthed some distance from the line of fire and was therefore in no danger. The whole native quarter was reduced to ashes, and the homeless victims were herded into hastily improvised camps and guarded by sailors from the various ships, who received for this the princely pay of five dollars per night.

Most of our crew snapped up these jobs, with the result that they were quite unfit for the arduous labour of shovelling coal by day; and trouble with a capital 'T' quickly followed. Fights between officers and foremast hands were not unusual, growling was the order of the day, rank mutiny was in the air, and conditions aboard the *Inverness-shire* speedily grew intolerable.

After completing our discharge we received orders to proceed in ballast to Astoria, in the Columbia river, to load for home, but during our last day in Honolulu the trouble aboard came to a head. The crew remained in their bunks and refused to do any work. The 'stay-in strike' had begun, and we could do nothing to prevent it. Early next morning the officers and apprentices had to man the capstan and heave up the anchors; then we towed outside the reef and let go the port anchor in ten fathoms. While all this was going on not one of the crew appeared on deck, and the old man was beside himself with anger. As soon as the anchor splashed overside he went forward to try the effects of gentle persuasion, but the men unanimously consigned him to hell; so he resolved to take them out to sea and there starve or terrorise them into submission.

I then took four apprentices and rowed the Captain ashore in the gig to enable him to clear the ship and get away to sea without delay. Suddenly, while we were awaiting the Captain's return, a furious gust of wind swooped down on the bay from the volcanic mountain overlooking Honolulu, blowing dense clouds of blinding dust before it. When I had cleared my eyes, and looked out to sea, I saw to my horror that the *Inverness-shire* was adrift stern first and moving steadily out into the wide Pacific. I rushed away to the shipping office to inform the skipper of our predicament. He at once enlisted the aid of a stevedore,

The four-masted barque *Inverness-shire*. Dismasted in a storm off Tasmania in 1915, she was towed into Hobart by the *Cartela* (still extant), a small passenger ship, a fraction of the great barque's size.

who hired a fast-sailing pilot cutter with a bunch of Kanakas and, taking the gig in tow, we were soon racing out towards the drifting ship as fast as wind and sail could drive us.

We quickly overhauled and boarded the ship, now drifting steadily before the wind at a speed of three knots, with only the two mates and a few apprentices on deck. After a hurried meal, hastily dished up by the flustered cook, we got to work. Both anchors were trailing in the deeps of the ocean. These had to be hove-up so we at once got down to it, working in four-hour watches. For the first spell the mate and I, with sixteen Kanakas, manned the windlass and began to heave-in the ninety fathoms of cable attached to the port anchor, or at least we attempted to do so. With two men to a bar, we heaved with a will, but not an inch would it move. Then suddenly something went crack inside the head of the capstan, and to my disgust I found one of the gear wheels had dissolved into tiny pieces, rendering the whole windlass absolutely useless. To make matters worse, we had no spares on board, so the pilot put back to Honolulu in his cutter for help; but we never saw him again, and had perforce to rely on our own unaided efforts to extricate ourselves from a very dangerous situation. And still the ship drifted out to sea and the crew refused to do a hand's turn.

For five weary days and monotonous nights we struggled with cumbersome tackles and small deck capstans. By the end of that time only one dripping anchor had been hove up to its hawsehole. All the work was done by the officers, the half-dozen apprentices, and the few Kanakas which the pilot had left with us, and we were all pretty well fagged out. As we were in no condition to tackle another five days of back-breaking toil we slipped the other anchor, and, getting some canvas on the ship, headed back for Honolulu. It took us a further five days to beat back to our anchorage, and as we sailed up the bay every ship in port flew the signal 'Welcome Back' from her masthead.

As soon as we dropped the hook, the Kanakas were paid off and rowed ashore; then the police launch came alongside, and the mutineers were rounded up and taken to the lock-up. The resulting inquiry held us up for another week, and we certainly needed that time to clean up the filth left by the Kanakas, as they had messed up almost every part of the ship from stem to stern, and the forecastle was no drawing-room either.

As a result of the trial, every man of the crew was fined several dollars and spent a month in jail. That was the end of the stay-in strike. Some days later we engaged a new crew, and pulled out for Astoria once more, this time completing the passage in good time and without further mishap.

14 Full Aback

A stormy winter – The four-masted barque *Elginshire* – Across the Western Ocean – A
pyjama race and its sequel – The big barque acts up – Blowing great guns – Dragging
anchors – Fleetwood lifeboat stands by – Christmas Day, 1902 – The *Primrose Hill*
blown ashore on the South Stack – Gale follows gale – A sudden change of wind – Full
aback – Mountainous seas sweep the ship – On her beam ends – Hove-to for a month –
A 600-mile drift.

THE winter of 1900–1901 was one of the hardest and stormiest I can recall in all my
years of going to sea. From October to March a succession of fierce gales followed
close on each other, with only occasional spells between. In February the weather
grew even worse, and that month was simply one long gale, which blew unceasingly day
after day right into the early part of March. Many a good ship was lost during these stormy
months; and many a fine seaman, after the experience of that bitter winter, gave up 'going
to sea and went into steam'. Life in a sailing ship at that time was indeed a hard one.

In November 1902 I was appointed second mate of the fine Glasgow four-masted barque
Elginshire, then discharging wheat from Portland, Oregon, at Barrow-in-Furness, after an
eventful and stormy homeward passage, during which her master died at sea and a baby was
born on board. I joined the ship at Barrow, and found her new master was the well-known
'Shire' skipper, Lachlan MacKay.

After discharging and dry-docking, we took on board stone ballast, as the ship had been
ordered to New York to load case oil for Australia. The crew were signed on, and soon the
old hooker was fit and ready to battle her way across the Western Ocean. The elements,
however, were all against us, and gales outside kept the *Elginshire* tied up in port for nearly
six weeks, which was not to the liking of many of her crew.

Fierce south-west gales blew in all their wild fury week after week, keeping us to our
moorings, and the discontent aboard quickly came to a head. Late one night several of the
men quietly packed up their belongings and slunk ashore. They were seen by the watchman,
however, who at once roused the sleeping mate, and that worthy, clad only in thin pyjamas,
raced down the gang-plank after the deserters, heedless of the bitter wind and rain. Just as

EDITOR'S NOTE
Captain W W Waddell (and John Anderson), when second mate of the fine four-masted barque *Elginshire*, tells
of a stormy voyage during which this famous square-rigger was taken full aback.

A beautiful photograph of the four-masted barque *Elginshire* becalmed on a still and silent sea. She made, however, some remarkable passages and in one, from Santos to Balla Balla in Western Australia, averaged 224 miles for 36 days.

he caught up with the men, and began arguing with them, a policeman came on the scene, attracted by the lurid language, and promptly marched mate and all to the lock-up.

I was hurriedly aroused and, gathering up the mate's clothes, made my way ashore to rescue the chief officer from his unenviable predicament. I found the police station in an uproar, with the wrathful mate surrounded by angry sailors and policemen. Every man seemed to be shouting at the top of his voice. I at once butted into the argument, but, before long, was also arrested, and we all spent the remainder of the night behind bars. Next morning, through the efforts of Captain MacKay, we were released, but the deserters absolutely refused to return to the ship, and, as there were no men available in Barrow, we

The four-masted barque *Primrose Hill*. She was lost in December 1900 on the South Stack, Holyhead, with the loss of all but one crew member.

had to comb out every low dive in Liverpool to fill their places.

However, on 24th December, the tug *Furness* took our tow-rope, and the big barque shook off her port languor and moved majestically seawards. Towards sunset a stiff south-westerly gale sprang up, and it began to blow great guns by nightfall. The tug, though steaming full-speed ahead, could make little or no headway. At length she gave up the unequal contest, and we anchored off the coast for the night, with two hooks and 200 fathoms of chain down in shoal water.

All night long the gale blew with unabating fury, and the ship pitched like a mad thing, her bows swinging round the compass, while all hands remained on deck, hauling the big yards about to relieve the terrific wind-pressure on our spars. The anchors dragged slightly, but the cables nobly stood the test. So dangerous was our position, however, that the Fleetwood lifeboat stood by us all through that fearful night. The motion of the ship was terrible, and we were indeed thankful to see the dawn breaking over the distant hills, ushering in Christmas Day, 1900, with the wind abating slightly.

Later we heard that the sailing ship *Primrose Hill*, outward bound from Liverpool, had snapped her tow-rope and gone ashore during the same night on the South Stack, with the loss of all hands bar one.

We lay at our anchorage for four days; then, on the 29th, we again ventured forth in the wake of the *Furness*, which was to tow us as far as the Tuskar Rock, off the east coast of Ireland. Hardly had we got under way, however, before another gale swooped down, and we were forced to scurry into Holyhead, anchoring in the bay at midnight of the 31st, just as the bells ashore began to peal in the New Year.

After the tug had bunkered, we decided to remain at anchor until the weather moderated, but gale after gale lashed the Irish Sea into wild fury. The wind abated somewhat on 11th January, so we hurriedly put to sea, and early next morning the Tuskar hove in sight. As soon as the rock was abeam, the battered little tug cast off the tow-rope, and, to our amazement, swirled round and dashed off for home at full speed, leaving us without a rag of canvas set and not even helping in the work of getting the big hawser aboard! She certainly had her fill of the good ship *Elginshire.*

All hands began to make sail and get the tow-rope inboard as quickly as possible, but these tasks occupied the best part of four hours. At length, with all sail set to a moderate ESE. wind, the big four-master fairly skimmed along the Irish coast, and we looked forward

The *Elginshire*'s decks awash in a heavy sea.

Elginshire's single topgallants and double topsails just visible over an ocean swell.

to a smart passage across the 'Pond'. The *Elginshire*, in her prime, was a good passage-maker; in fact she once ran from New Caledonia to Glasgow in 88 days, a record which has never yet been surpassed by any sailing ship. However, our hopes for a crack passage were speedily shattered.

Wind and weather, for a wonder, remained fair until the ship passed the Western Isles, seven days out from Holyhead, when we entered the stormy regions of the Gulf Stream, and conditions quickly changed. Gale after gale blew up, and the crew had their hands full making sail and taking it in again; in fact the only sails untouched were the lower topsails and the fore topmast staysail. One day the ship would be bowling along under full sail, then by the next morning she would be staggering against a heavy head wind under lower topsails only, with the yards jammed on the backstays, losing all the advantage gained during the fair weather.

One Saturday night the *Elginshire* was making good headway on the port tack, under topsails, foresail, and two headsails. She was doing a good ten knots and, as it happened to be my watch at the time, I was in charge of the ship. Suddenly the wind veered round without the usual warning lull and caught the barque full aback. Amidst the thunderous crash of madly flapping canvas, and the ominous creaking of masts and spars, all hands tumbled out on deck, in various stages of undress, and raced for the braces, while the ship rapidly gathered sternway, rolling madly all the time.

The strain on the masts and rigging was terrific, but not even a rope yarn split, though I expected the tophamper to go over the side any minute. Heaving with a good will, the crew swung the afteryards round and brought the ship before the wind, no easy task owing to the terrible rolling. We then filled the foreyards, brought the ship up on the starboard tack, and so the danger passed. After the foresail and inner jib were taken in, the old man gave me a proper dressing-down; but I had a good excuse, as an abnormal shift of wind was the cause of the trouble.

All that night the wind gradually increased in force, and towards dawn we had to take in the upper topsails. Some hours later the steward went down to the lazarette and found the carefully stowed barrels and cases of stores smashed and scattered around in chaos, as a result of the rolling of the ship during the night. Flour, sugar, rice, beans, and a hundred-and-one other things were hopelessly mixed together, and, as most of our stores were quite unfit for use from that time, it was a case of short rations for all hands, both fore and aft. Under these circumstances life on the big barque was not exactly a pleasant one.

As the days passed the wind increased to a whole gale and gradually veered round to the south-west, while mountainous seas swept the ship from stem to stern, washing everything movable over the side. Soon we found ourselves in the grip of a North Atlantic hurricane, so the labouring ship was hove-to under lower topsails – a perilous task in the heavy seas. We lay hove-to for a full month, lashed furiously by shrieking winds and surging seas, and a dreary four weeks it was, I assure you. The weather was too bad for any work to be done, so all hands had a month of enforced leisure, except for wheel and lookout; but certainly no one enjoyed it. The officers, however, had to stand their watches, on the lookout for a favourable shift of wind, which seemed as if it would never come.

One day in early March the rain suddenly came down in torrents, adding to our many discomforts, and a howling squall of hurricane force swooped down on us, heaving the labouring ship right over on to her beam ends. For one long anxious hour she lay, helpless and stricken, tons of water surging over the bulwarks, and it seemed certain the 'sticks' would be blown right out of her. To our intense relief, however, the shrieking wind suddenly moderated, and the big ship slowly righted herself, like the fine vessel she undoubtedly was.

How she rolled and tossed in the trough of the angry sea, the aftermath of the hurricane! The officer on watch had to be triced up to the weather rigging of the jigger-mast, and the helmsman was lashed to the wheel grating, so violent was the motion of the ship. Thank God, the ballast was well stowed, and did not shift an inch, or the *Elginshire* would have gone to 'Davy Jones' Locker', and I wouldn't be alive to tell this story.

Some days later the wind moderated considerably, and the sun burst through the storm-clouds at last. We took sights and found the ship had drifted at least 600 miles while hove-to. Hardly waiting for orders, all hands speedily made sail and got the ship under way again. The *Elginshire* seemed determined to show us she was still the 'heeler' we knew her to be, and fairly romped away westward, with every sail drawing well and every rope as stiff as an iron bar. No longer was she tossing madly in a welter of screaming wind and mountainous sea, with a wisp of canvas in her rigging, unable to make an inch of headway. She was at last

An unidentified barque makes sail while being towed out towards Sandy Hook lightship,
stationed to guide ships past the New Jersey Shoal into New York Harbor.

in her element, bravely bowling along with a stiff breeze behind her and all sail set, reeling off the knots like a steamer.

At length the *Elginshire*, battered and rusty, was towed into New York Harbor, over 100 days out from Barrow. As she came alongside her loading wharf every man jack of the crew hopped over the side, even before the ship was made fast.

'Well,' I thought, as I set about mooring the ship, 'I don't blame them.'

In all my forty years of sea-life, before and since this voyage in the *Elginshire*, I never had such an experience. Nevertheless, a few weeks later the old ship put to sea again, bound out for Australia, looking none the worse for her gruelling in the North Atlantic.

Elginshire in ballast, making stately progress.

15 The Nigger of the 'Chelmsford'

The four-masted barque *Chelmsford* – Officers and crew, types in the last days of sail – A night ashore and a gipsy fortune-teller – The nigger and the Swedes – A knife attack – The 'Roaring Forties' – A faulty grommet – Man overboard – A blizzard – A ship and her crew in agony – Nine weeks rounding the Horn – Hate grows – Poisoned – Death of the two remaining Swedes – The nigger is missing – Effect of superstition – Thrown overboard by a capstan bar – Nursing an apprentice.

RUMMAGING in an old sea-chest, inside the lid of which was a crude painting of a ship that had long passed from the realm of things in being, yet might even now form the driftwood on some island, or the lintel of a cottage in a far-off land, William Deal produced a neat package of old photographs and papers – relics of his early life in sail.

There tumbled from the box that had been all over the world with this fine seaman of the old school – and yet not so *old*, for he was a young AB in the 'nineties of last century – those sailorising oddments which speak of long voyages in other days, and by other ways, things which still retained the odour of Stockholm tar. Among them was a picture of the old *Colony*, one of the hungry fleet, in which he had served as a boy; another of the *Mount Stewart*, and there was pride in his voice when he described her as 'one of the last two sailing ships built for the Australian wool trade and one that could show a clean pair of heels to most others of her day'.

Age-yellowed discharge papers from this fine old square-rigger showed that she had left Sydney on 22nd November 1893, and docked in London on 22nd February 1894 – a ninety days' voyage home from New South Wales which, 'we could have done in eighty-five days, but when we were in mid-Channel the tow-boat cut away and we had to lay-to for five days before being picked up again and towed to London. We were paid-off in the old Chain Locker at Tower Hill'.

EDITOR'S NOTE
William Deal, a fine sailor of the old school, describes an amazing voyage as a young AB in the four-masted barque *Chelmsford*.

The four-masted barque *Colony*. She traded right through the First World War until sunk by U-151 ninety miles off the coast of Virginia, in June 1918, bound from Buenos Aires to New York.

Then, finding the faded photograph and water-stained papers for which the search had been instituted, William Deal – who, doubtless, could still goosewing a lower topsail in the 'roaring forties' – told the following authentic story of curious happenings during a voyage from Cardiff to Santa Rosa, Mexico, by way of Cape Horn:

The *Chelmsford* was a four-masted barque, registered at 2196 tons, and was outward bound from Cardiff round the Horn for the Gulf of California with a cargo of coal, patent fuel, and coke. She was on her maiden voyage, and carried a crew of thirty-odd, together with the Captain, who was an Irishman, the first mate, a Norwegian, and the second and third officers, who were both Britishers. The deep-water sailing ship was at this time

The bow of the three-masted wool clipper, the full-rigged ship *Mount Stewart*.
Her figurehead was later replaced with a simpler scroll.

fighting for its life against the steamer, and in consequence of low wages foreigners filled the forecastles of the comparatively few remaining foreign-going British sailing ships. The crew of the *Chelmsford* were mostly Norwegians and Swedes, with a few Italians, a Frenchman, one nigger, and myself the only Britisher in the forecastle.

Now this voyage to Santa Rosa was interesting in many ways, but before relating anything about it I must explain what happened in Cardiff on the night before we sailed. Among the crew was a nigger – not the one in the photograph, who joined later in the voyage, but an older negro from the Southern States – who asked if he might share my company for our last evening ashore. In our wanderings in search of pleasures we, in common with hundreds of other sailors from the ships in port, were attracted by the lights of a near-by fair. After wandering to and fro visiting the various side-shows, and being pretty well oiled and feeling quite happy, we finally found ourselves under the guidance of a gipsy woman, who professed to have read the hands of various crowned heads throughout the

The four-masted barque *Chelmsford* waiting to load.

world. We entered her tent, and the nigger sat down to have his black paw read first. The gipsy woman, whether a fake or not, told him he was going on a long voyage, but if he took her advice he would not, as his going would result in the death of three on the outward-bound journey and two on the homeward.

Finding this fortune-telling little to my liking, I decided against having my own hand read, and paying but slight attention to what the gipsy had said we both left the fair, and arrived aboard the *Chelmsford* considerably the worse for wear.

I awoke in the morning with a blinder of a head, and mucked around doing odd jobs until we were ready to sail, which we did at midday on Thursday, 16th March 1894, and were towed into the Channel, loosened sail, and had a fair wind down. At eight bells in the second dog-watch all hands were called aft, that the watches might be arranged. I was given the port watch, and thereby started the voyage to the Far West.

Among the Swedes in the forecastle there were three brothers, as alike as three sheep, all good seamen, quiet, speaking but little English though understanding it well, reserved, and so little interested in the doings of others that their disinterestedness became almost an offence. Fair of complexion, and each standing over six feet, they were fine specimens of their race.

From the very first these brothers took a strong dislike to the nigger, whether it was because they themselves were expert seamen and he, in contrast, a slacker, I don't know. They were always ready to quarrel with him, however, and treated him as something unclean. One day I asked the oldest of the Swedes what the nigger had done that they should always be 'on to him', or whether it was that they did not like his colour. To this question the great blond giant replied that it wasn't his black skin that they objected to, but that, 'By Yesus Crist he was yust no damn good'.

There can be no doubt, after reviewing subsequent events, that the nigger *was* a slacker, and that when it came to hard work the Swedes were right in saying that he was no damn good as a sailor either, but he was cheerful company, and many is the time I have been stretched out on the bunk with the fo'c'sle floor awash listening to him sing his plantation songs. Somehow it seemed to lessen the discomforts of a wet 'donkey's breakfast', aching limbs and hunger, and to allow my mind to wander to happier scenes; so he had his uses.

We had a good voyage to the so'th'ard and reached the Line in about twenty-eight days;

The officers and crew of the *Chelmsford*. The captain is standing at the bottom of the ladder and the author of this piece is standing second from right.

then, running into the doldrums, we also ran into hard work. With every breath of wind the mate would cry: 'Weather fore brace!' And in acknowledgment the crew answered: 'Weather fore brace, sir!' Then the mate would slack the lee brace and the crew haul in the weather, taking in the topsail and t'gallant as well. This, lasting for eight or nine days, and being terribly hard work in the great heat, began to tell on the tempers of the crew, so that before long everybody's nerves, including the officers', were thoroughly on edge, and fights became numerous.

It was during the seventh or eighth day of doldrum weather, I forget which, that I began arguing with a dago about something or other and said a few things which got under his skin, and the little skunk came at me with a knife. Fortunately he was only half my size, so I banged his head against an iron bunk and laid him up for a day or so.

On the ninth day we picked up the south-east trades and set every sail that would draw. The work soon became easier, and, our sleep being less disturbed, tempers became more normal, and life went along very smoothly. The trades held for five weeks, until nearing the River Plate, which was plainly indicated by patches of fresh water clearly seen in the salt. Then we ran into the pamperos, and, incidentally, rough weather, which held whilst we made good progress towards Cape Horn.

I have been round this stormy southernmost point of the Americas a good many times, but this was the worst experience of them all. Before describing it, however, I must give an account of what happened when we were preparing to shorten sail before the storm broke. Earlier in the day the nigger had been sent aloft by the bosun to renew some rovings, and whilst there had noticed a faulty grommet, so, finding the work aloft more to his liking than that below, he had returned to the deck, made a new grommet, and went aloft again to seize it to the jackstay. During this time the weather had turned much colder, and, as the nigger admitted to me afterwards, he had seized the grommet to the jackstay, but had not finished the job properly as, his hands being numbed with cold, he had descended in order to sneak to the galley fire for a 'warm up', but had stayed overlong. On returning to the deck he was horrified to see that all hands had been ordered to shorten sail, and that well up, and making for the yardarm on which was the faulty grommet, was the youngest of the Swedes.

It might just as well have been myself, as I was only a few yards behind the young Scandinavian, and, strangely enough, I was admiring him for his agility and ease when he took his weight from one grommet to another. I had hold of the first one, and turned to call him, just in time to see him sway with the fall of the ship. As his full weight was thrown on it, the spun yarn with which it was seized frayed out, and with a strangling cry he fell a full seventy feet, striking the bulwarks before going to his grave. He must have been smashed to a pulp, because after hitting the water he never came up.

We had no time to think much about the Swede's death, but I did notice that the two remaining brothers seemed dazed, and did their work mechanically. I don't think they ever got over it, as from then onwards they became more reserved, and did nothing except work, eat, and sleep, and talked only with each other. However, death or no death, we were in for a hell of a snorter, and we had to work like the devil. All hands were ordered to shorten sail, and everything was taken in except the topsails, mainsail, and jib; then, before the end of

the watch, we were down under the main lower topsail and fore topmast staysail and were hove-to.

I wish I could find the right words to give a proper idea of this storm. A blizzard was raging which turned everything into a sheet of ice, making work both aloft and on deck much harder and more dangerous. The shrieking gale was trying to tear us off the ship, and came mighty near doing it with one or two. The clouds seemed to have lowered and were almost on top of the water, while the light turned a kind of yellow, which, with the driving snow, dimmed our vision to only a few yards. The seas, too, were like mountains ahead of us, and when we were in the trough we almost disappeared; then as we climbed each watery incline the acres-wide crests of foam would smash over the bulwarks on to the deck and do their best to knock the guts out of her. But she was a good British-built ship and stood up to the onslaught of these Cape Horn greybeards with only the creaking and groaning of timbers, the roar and swish of the seas, and the shrieking of the wind in the rigging, to tell of her agony – and ours.

The bulwarks of the *Chelmsford* were about nine feet above the deck, and the port-holes, which allowed the water to escape from the flooded decks, were fixed open, and gratings were lashed across them to prevent those men who were knocked off their feet by the seas from being washed through. Life-lines were run from mast to mast, but during these terrible days all hands were on the poop, and descended to the main deck only when going to and from the fo'c'sle, or for making fast anything washed adrift in the amidships welter of foam.

For three days we lay-to on this tack, and then had to ware ship. For nine weeks, off and on, this manœuvre was kept going before we finally rounded the Horn. These sixty-odd days of extreme hardship, combined with nerve-wracking work, were excuse enough for all on board to swear before the gods they would never go to sea again. Then as soon as a sailor gets ashore he's fool enough to go back, and do all the swearing once again.

With the fo'c'sle awash, clothing always wet, and very little sleep, combined with the absence of any means of warming oneself other than by lighting some spun yarn and breathing the poisonous fumes of burning tar, there can be little wonder that, as in the doldrums, our nerves again played hell, and caused each of us to curse our best friend, to clout, jeer, or kick him. When this had been going on for weeks we all became as jumpy as fleas, and ready to spring at one another for any imaginary insult. So difficult to describe is this sea-tension that when ashore and in one's right senses it is quite clear that it is due entirely to nerves, nerves frayed under the strain. For this reason blame is difficult to apportion; but *at the time* it is surprising how well and truly one can hate.

The joy that came to all on board when finally we ran into good weather was made apparent by the return of an excess of friendliness and a willingness to work, lashing chafing gear for the rigging, preparing and making good all the damage to the ship and its gear when rounding the Horn. What a difference weather conditions make! Here we were with the sun shining, a fair wind, and everybody happy as the Pacific swell rolled beneath us.

Opposite: A fine photograph of an unidentified ship running before a following sea.

It is not entirely true, however, to say that everybody in the *Chelmsford* was happy. There was the nigger and the Swedes. Since their brother's death the two remaining members of this family seemed to have dried up entirely. They worked well, but that is all; they spoke to nobody, and only answered a direct question. One cannot be friendly with a man while such a condition exists, and after all, we thought, a sailor should be man enough to let time heal whatever kind of a blow fate has dealt him. Of course, nobody except myself knew that the nigger was to blame for that grommet breaking loose. They realised what had happened, but were unable to blame anybody in particular, although on more than one occasion I had reason to feel sure that the mate suspected the truth.

The nigger – who, by the way, we called 'Curly', because of his hair – had gone completely to pieces. He seemed to have lost his nerve, and his body had wasted to half its size. His black face, too, had a kind of mottled, grey appearance, as though his blood had turned to water. We never heard a song now, and only rarely did he speak to anybody other than myself.

Just after the Swede's death I was on watch with Curly and noticed that he was not his usual self, but at the time put this down to a touch of funk, as the storm was at its height. On the way to the fo'c'sle, however, he caught hold of my arm and whispered hoarsely: 'The gipsy was right.'

'The gipsy was right?' I repeated. 'What the hell do you mean, and what gipsy?'

'You'se remember the fortune-teller at Cardiff, she say that if I sail my goin' result in de death of three on de outward trip and two on de homeward?' he replied, with the whites of his eyes showing to an extent possible only with those of a nigger in the grip of a superstitious fear.

'Yes,' I replied, endeavouring to be as casual as possible, 'I have a foggy idea of something of that kind, but didn't pay a lot of attention to what she said. Anyhow, where's the connection between what she said and you?'

It was then that he explained how he had caused the Swede's death. Certainly I told him a thing or two, as no sailor can afford to play fast and loose with any part of a ship. The lives of many so often depend on every bit of work being well done. After this confession he begged of me not to say anything, to which I agreed, as there was nothing to be gained; and, moreover, had I repeated what the fortune-teller said I have no doubt the nigger would have been missing one night, and probably myself as well for allowing him to sail. Seamen were very superstitious in those days and he would have been rated a 'Jonah'. Jonah or not, he was 'yellow' to the backbone, and did not possess the guts to even stand up to himself, neither was he man enough to do his work any better. He simply slicked over everything, and many's the time I have seen . . . But these things don't matter, for I took care that no life depended on his work from the time we entered the Pacific.

With a following wind we soon made the Gulf of California, where the weather was all that it should be – calm seas, glorious days, and still more marvellous starlit nights. It was here that we went turtle-fishing, if you can call it that. Launching the small boats, we soon had several floundering aboard. The method of catching them was to row about until one was seen asleep on the surface of the water, then, by getting as near as possible without wakening it, we were often able to grab it by the hind flipper and heave it into the boat.

Returning to the ship the cook was persuaded to dish these turtles up in the form of soup, and those of us not on watch retired to the fo'c'sle and impatiently awaited the signal from the galley that our meal was ready. After being confined to a diet of salt pork one day and salt beef the next, for months on end, anything in the way of a change was welcomed with an avidity almost inconceivable to those who dwell on shore. Our appetites being keen we didn't waste any time when it finally arrived, but went at it for all we were worth. Soup made from freshly killed turtles invariably has a somewhat unusual and pungent odour, but had we taken full warning by the smell of this soup we should have been spared a lot of misery. Having been on beef and pork for months, however, we scoffed this soup before we realised its evil.

Mount Stewart 'could show a clean pair of heels to most others of her day'.

It was rather funny, as before the meal we had been telling stories of various feeds ashore, at this and that place, but in our own minds nothing was, or had been, quite so good as what we now expected the cook would produce. Before the pot was emptied, however, we one by one disappeared to give back to the sea that which we had taken from it.

After making inquiries we discovered that the cook, knowing little of cooking other than how to stew meat and make plum-duff, and never before having been in the tropics, had failed to remove the 'innards' of the turtles. In fact, he had boiled them whole, which no doubt accounted for the poisonous smell and taste. Whether it was a result of this misnamed soup, or the natural order of things, I cannot say, but next morning Curly was down with dysentery – certainly for weeks beforehand he had been looking thoroughly unwell, so it may have been that he was sickening for it. By the morning he was certainly very bad, and as the days followed he grew worse; others of the crew also succumbed to it, among them the two remaining Swedes and the three apprentices.

A day or so later, when returning from watch to the fo'c'sle, I found the nigger delirious, and raving of things past and of things to come, chief of which was: 'Three outward bound and two homeward.' This seemed fixed in his mind, as he repeated it again and again. The poor devil must have had this on his conscience ever since the Swede fell from the rigging. I think, too, he imagined that he was to be the second on the list, and that night when he became normal he told me he was going to die. I thought so too, but somehow or other he turned the corner and got better. By the time we made Santa Rosa, which was six days' sail from where we had caught the turtles, he was well on the way to recovery.

Arriving at this Mexican port we anchored in the open roadstead, unbent all sails, and stowed them away. This was accomplished exactly seven months to the day after leaving Cardiff. We had barely dropped anchor before the elder Swede passed away, and within an hour the other followed. Curiously enough, these two strong seamen seemed to make little fight for their lives, and appeared scarcely to care whether they lived or not.

When we were stowing away the sails the nigger, who was on deck for the first time, and taking things easy, came to me and asked if it was true that both the Swedes were dead. Replying that it was so, he turned away without a word and went towards the fo'c'sle, but before he got there the bosun told him that he was to go ashore in the grub-boat and make arrangements with the native police for the burial of the Swedes. The boat was just leaving, so he climbed down into it, but took no part in the rowing as he was still very weak.

This was fairly early in the morning, and by noon the boat had not returned to the ship. Later, when it did come back, the third mate, who was in charge, reported the nigger was missing. On making inquiries, the mate explained that he had discovered that the nigger had not been to the police about the funeral arrangements, neither could he find anybody who had seen him, so the boat had returned rather than wait any longer.

From then onwards he was never seen. We thought he would turn up the next day, but neither in the town nor on the ship did he make an appearance, and we never heard what happened to him. I have no doubt that he was thoroughly scared, as many a better man would have been who sailed the seas in those days. When I came to weigh up all the facts, of which the other members of the crew were ignorant, the gipsy woman's prophecy was not far out. She had said, 'Three on the outward-bound trip and two on the homeward,' and already three had died, so I firmly believe that this superstitious negro from the Southern States took the first opportunity to clear out before the second part of the voyage began.

Next morning I was detailed with a Norwegian to take the bodies ashore for burial, and it was with this before me that I put my feet on land for the first time in seven months. We were met by two native policemen and half a dozen native convicts, who had prepared the grave overnight. There was no burial service, so it took but a short time before we had performed our duty. There followed weeks and months of unloading and taking in ballast. The unloading was done in surf-boats, and for this we were given a tot of grog daily, as well as a free 'bread-barge'. The taking in of ballast was accomplished by native labour in small dug-out canoes, which carried as little as one hundredweight at a time. After four months of this we were ready to weigh anchor and set sail for Portland, Oregon, where we were to load with wheat for England.

No tears were shed when we left Santa Rosa, as it was a beastly place, and the natives, mostly scarred by smallpox, were none too friendly. It was while weighing the anchor and singing that famous sea-chanty, *We're bound for the Rio Grande*, that the ship rose upon a heavy swell, bringing the capstan back with a jerk, just before reaching the pawl, and we, on the bars, were thrown in all directions, some to the main deck, and myself and another into the sea. It may seem an exaggeration, but is nevertheless true, that I hit the water a good fifty yards from the ship. Although unconscious, I was fortunate enough to be picked up by a boat from another vessel. Curiously enough, she hailed from Liverpool, and there was a sequel to this when, years later, I joined the London Fire Brigade. One of the first men detailed to give me instruction in my new duties recognised me as the man he had helped out of the water years before off Santa Rosa. However, I was better off than my mates who had been thrown down to the main deck, one of whom broke his arm and another injured his spine so badly that in the end he had to be left at Astoria.

About the voyage to Astoria there is little to be told, but when anchored off this port one of the apprentices met with an accident by falling down the fore hold and fracturing his side, which meant his removal to hospital. The authorities there sent word to the Captain that, having had recently a similar case from another ship, when the patient had got out of bed when almost well and again fell and refractured his leg, it was necessary for our Captain to send both a night and a day man to watch the apprentice. For this job I was lucky enough to be sent on night duty. I did my job really well, by sleeping with the youngster, so that, together with a good bed and a decent meal night and morning, the time was all too short, as within five days we sailed, leaving the apprentice behind, and were finally towed up the river by one of those old American sternwheelers to Portland, Oregon.

The homeward voyage from Portland was quite uneventful, but it occurred to me then that, although in the accidents which occurred after leaving Santa Rosa no one had actually lost their life, two had been badly injured, and who could say what the result would have been had our black Jonah remained aboard the *Chelmford*?

16 Churchwarden's Gear

In the Sailors' Home – The full-rigger *Merionethshire* – The first voyage – *That Sunday* –
'Queer fellow' – 'Man overboard!' – Manning the sea-boat – The cry from afar –
Nightfall – A leaking boat – The cost of a life.

W E were all sailing on the following day in the full-rigged ship *Merionethshire* for the Antipodes, and then – only God, the winds, and the freights knew to where in the seven seas, or to when in the calendar of months or years. In those last days of the British sailing ship each voyage was still fraught with many of the uncertainties of high adventure and all the human hardships in the list for those who shipped before the mast.

It was natural, therefore, that the last night ashore, although spent – through sheer necessity – at the Sailors' Home, should somehow become a mixture of sentimentality and jest among the old and the new chums who would all have to live together, somehow, in the confined space of a ship's fo'c'sle, for certainly one and perhaps two or more years.

In the baggage-room at our erstwhile home, Smiler Charlie, who hailed from South Shields, found an old top-hat and a tail-coat, relics of the recent Christmas concert. He tried them on while we were collecting our dunnage ready for the following morning, and Mac and I grinned when, with a florin stuck in his eye, he swaggered about the littered floor.

'Wouldn't it be a lark to sneak this gear,' he exclaimed suddenly, 'and one Sunday, when it's my trick at the wheel, to walk aft dressed up in it?'

'The old man would boot you off the poop,' jeered Mac.

Without another word Charlie tossed the hat to me and, slipping the coat over his arm, led the way to his cubicle.

It was cold but fine when we went aboard soon after dawn and stowed our gear in the half-dark fo'c'sle. We had not been more than half an hour arranging our few possessions before the mate put his head through the doorway and growled:

'Pleased to see some of you men sober. Finish your smoke, change into working gear and lay aft. Get a move on.'

EDITOR'S NOTE
Frank Cousins describes a comedy that turned into a tragedy on board the old *Merionethshire*.

As we walked towards the poop all eyes were turned to where a fashionably dressed woman, a well-set-up man, and a tall, weedy youth, wearing a badge-cap and a brass-bound jacket, were talking together abaft the midship deck house.

We heard the man say: 'Good-bye, old chap. Do your best and don't forget to write. Your mother will be anxious.'

'A first voyager, by the cut of him,' remarked Mac.

Before reaching the break of the poop, I saw the man help the woman across the gangway. Almost as soon as they were clear of the quay the mate shouted:

'Boy, come here! What's your name?'

'Stevens,' answered the youth promptly.

'*Sir!*' added the mate. 'And don't forget next time, son. Now get out of that admiral's gear and into dungarees. Then bring bathbrick and oil and clean the brasswork on the poop. Quick's the word!'

When watches were picked, Charlie and I went to the port watch and Mac to the starboard. Stevens and another apprentice also became members of the port or first mate's watch. Soon we left the river, and the loom of the land faded into the January grey of sea and sky.

We all grew to like Stevens. He was the right type. Quick to learn and always pulled his weight. When Old Bob, the hard case, who came on board with a bag of rags and without oilskins or sea-boots, suddenly blossomed out in new underwear, neatly marked with Stevens' initials, we held an inquiry, and Robert was advised, in a few well-chosen words, to make up the deficiencies in his wardrobe from the slop-chest.

On the seventh day of each week it was the sailor's privilege to wash decks and then to finish work for the day. At least ship's work, for we afterwards washed clothes, bathed, shaved, and finally made merry – all except the man at the wheel, the lookout, and the one we called 'the policeman', whose duty it was to call the watch if required for shifting sails.

That Sunday – the one we shall remember until our time comes for the long watch below – the wind was light and playful, for we had not yet picked up the north-east trades. It came in capfuls, bellied the sails, and then, quickly chasing away across the ruffled surface, left the canvas to flog empty.

In the fo'c'sle a Swede was playing the accordion, our little Cockney a mouth-organ, and someone else had a 'paper and comb'. Charlie, in the top-hat and tail-coat, was conducting the band. Stevens popped in, passed round a tin of cigarettes, and stood for a moment enjoying the fun. Suddenly Charlie shouted: 'It's my next wheel, bullies. What's the betting that I dursn't go aft dressed as I am?'

'A plug o' baccy,' said Palmer, a horny-handed old shell-back, who had mended and made the sails of many a ship.

'Done!' roared Charlie. 'Come, shake hands on it.'

Laughing heartily, Stevens hastened aft to strike the bell, remembering at the same time that apprentices were strictly forbidden to enter the fo'c'sle.

As he mounted the poop ladder the mate cried: 'Hi! Queer fellow, there's a gasket adrift on the main lower tops'l yard. Up aloft and make it up. I'll look after the time-bell.'

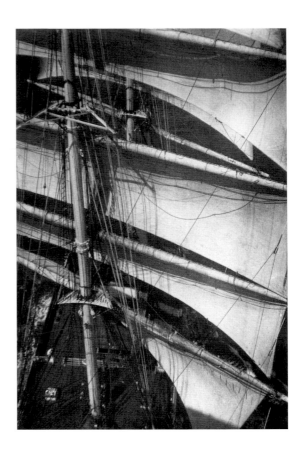

Looking down on the topsail yards on the four-masted barque *Moshulu*, with the deck and sea distant below them.

While Stevens was passing over the main top, Charlie stepped aft to relieve the man at the wheel, followed by roars of laughter. In the fo'c'sle the band was playing *Dixie*, and those who had not gone on deck to see the fun were lustily singing the chorus:

> 'I wish't I was in the land of cotton,
> Cinnamon seed and sandy bottom.'

'Hark!' shouted Moran. 'What's that?'

Through the thick timbers into the silenced fo'c'sle there came the high-pitched cry: 'Man overboard!'

Then we heard the mate's 'All hands!' and scrambled for the deck. After bracing back the head yards we launched the lee boat.

The old man came on deck shouting: 'What the hell's wrong, mister? What's the trouble?'

'Apprentice Stevens overboard from the main lower tops'l yard, sir,' cried the mate.

As we pulled away from the ship the sun dipped below the horizon.

'I can't see anything of him,' the Captain exclaimed anxiously. 'Shake things up, mister; it'll be dark in a few minutes.'

'Did anyone 'eave a lifebuoy over, sir?' asked one of the men.

'I did,' said the mate. 'Would have gone over myself only I can't swim a stroke.'

In the meantime we, in the boat, had been pulling hard. 'A-a-hoy, Stevens!' we shouted together, resting for a moment to see if there was any reply from the almost silent ocean.

From afar there came a faint cry. A sea-bird perhaps, for although we tugged at the oars like mad, and shouted into the twilight, the cry was not repeated.

'Boat's making water fast, sir,' quietly and half-apologetically remarked Old Bob. 'It's pouring through her rotten seams like water from an open sea-cock,' he added a moment later, looking anxiously at the darkening sea and sky.

'Ship your oar and bail,' ordered the mate. 'Now, all together, lads, another hail.'

'A-a-hoy Stevens!' The sound travelled far over the gently breathing sea.

'It'll be ahoy for the blooming lot of us before long,' said the little Cockney; 'we're almost awash.'

'You,' said the mate, addressing the Swede, 'get bailing with that hard-weather cap of yours.'

'It's a pity that the Board o' Trade Orficer and Super wot passed this coffin as seaworthy ain't 'ere now,' grumbled the Cockney. 'They orter be, the pair of 'em. Lashed 'and and foot with a length o' log-line——'

'That'll do, my man,' cut in the mate sharply.

We roared again 'Ahoy, Stevens!' and listened intently for a break in the gentle swish of wind and sea.

From a long way astern a bright light suddenly flared up, casting a glow upon the now dark sea. Then it faded away and night pressed in closer. The Captain was showing us the whereabouts of the ship.

'I reckon the kid's gone, sir,' said Old Bob slowly. 'Likely enough he went straight down into Davy Jones's Locker.'

'We'll return,' said the mate, after a few seconds of oppressive silence, broken only by the splash of the bailers. 'Pull steady and strong.'

With the boat awash, we came alongside the *Merionethshire*, hove the painter aboard, and hooked on the falls.

'Pick him up, mister?' inquired the old man.

'No, sir,' replied the mate; 'and the boat's leaking like a sieve.'

'Leave a couple of hands down there to bail her out before hoisting, and then square the yards,' ordered the Captain.

Next morning the mate walked up to a group of us on the fore deck and said, more particularly to Charlie: 'That ruddy hat and coat of yours cost the boy his life. I figure that he was standing on the foot-rope, half-slewed round to watch you relieve the wheel, when the tops'l flattened and clouted him off the yard. Now go and dump that churchwarden's gear overboard – get a move on!'

17 Posted Lost

Apprentice in the full-rigged ship *Leyland Brothers* – Outward bound for California, April 1906 – On her beam ends – Pampero – Main lower topsail yard carries away – A mental 'black-out' – Man overboard – A Captain's courage – Round the Horn – Heavy seas and bitter cold – Iced-up – A tidal wave off Valparaiso – A ghastly experience – Tuberculosis – Thirst – Auctioning a match-box – A mysterious disease – The American schooner *Mindoro* – The gunboat *Princetown* – A 214 days' voyage, and 'Posted lost'.

THE wind that blew strongly but not viciously across the North Sea and the Dutch lowlands around the mouth of the Scheldt, on 4th April 1906, still retained the keen edge of winter, yet the sun gleamed on the white sails of the full-rigged ship *Leyland Brothers*, in which I was outward bound from Antwerp, round the Horn, to California.

Every detail of this voyage was impressed on my memory at the time by sheer hardship, and by the fact that I had joined the ship as an apprentice only three days before the voyage commenced. Since this fine old square-rigger is no longer cleaving the seas of the world, having been turned into a hulk after being sold to the Portuguese, it may be as well to give here a few particulars of her before telling the story of my experiences during one of her most eventful voyages. She was three-masted and carried double topsails, single t'gallantsails and royals on all masts, with a skysail on the main. Her gross tonnage was 2291 and net 2238 tons. The length over all was 320 feet, with a beam of 40 feet; and from heel to truck she measured 220 feet, making her a 'tall ship'. Although on this occasion no miracles of speed were performed, during a subsequent voyage to Australia this fine full-rigged ship of the last days of sail nearly made a record passage.

Leaving Antwerp we were taken in tow by a powerful tug – which appeared to me ridiculously small for the work it had to perform. Passing rapidly down the Scheldt, we spread our wings to the cold but favourable north-easter and soon left the narrow seas, bound for San Francisco, fourteen days before that great western city was convulsed, and practically destroyed, by one of the worst earthquakes and fires ever known. Curiously enough, we carried in our holds a cargo which was to prove of inestimable value to the stricken town – Portland cement, steel girders, and other building materials. Nor did we

EDITOR'S NOTE
Gerard Fort Buckle, apprentice in the full-rigged ship *Leyland Brothers*, describes his first voyage round the Horn in this fine old ship, which, after many disasters, was 'Posted lost'.

know when we started out on that April morning that we were destined to be several months overdue and 'posted lost'; to show up eventually, however, after having been 214 days at sea without touching port, and over four months without sighting a ship – not even hull down on the horizon.

The first part of the voyage, up to the time when we were off Rio de Janeiro, was almost without event. We were lucky with the trades, picking them up earlier and retaining them much longer than we might normally have expected. Again, when crossing the calms of the Equator our luck held, and in consequence it looked as though we were going to make a very good run to 'Frisco. Trouble lay ahead of us, however, and within a few weeks all chance of doing this had failed.

On a previous voyage the Captain of the *Leyland Brothers* had come through a most terrifying experience, which he related to the mate one evening while I was working on the poop deck. The four-masted barque of which he was then in command was caught in a fierce squall while under full sail. So far over did she heel that her sails were partly submerged and her keel began to appear above water. Captain M—— was so certain that she had gone that he gave orders for the boats to be cut away and 'Every man for himself!' Suddenly, however, the barque righted herself. The crew, without waiting for orders, had let everything go. As she came up her yards were swinging in all directions, and it seemed that something must give way under the terrible strain. Nothing broke, however, and within the space of a few minutes the vessel was away before the wind.

Although this is a digression, at the time when I overheard it being related, as an impressionable boy, I could visualise with almost painful vividness the capsizing of the whole towering mass of masts, sails, spars, and cordage, amid the shrieking wind and foam-capped waves.

When abreast of Rio de Janeiro we spoke to a homeward-bound liner, which passed so close to us that the officer on her bridge was able to shout a few words to our Captain through a megaphone. By a strange coincidence there was on board that liner a friend of mine – a discovery made many years later. This was the last ship sighted by us for over four months. Our luck began to change, and it came with a terrific squall from out of a blue-black wall of cloud when off the River Plate.

In this pampero the goose-neck of our main lower topsail yard carried away, and it seemed that further disaster was threatened. The yard, an iron one and extremely heavy, was hanging in mid-air supported only by the topsail sheets. The ship was rolling and pitching heavily, and every time she did so the yard swung forward and upward, describing in its flight an arc of from fifteen to twenty feet. For an instant it would remain almost motionless at the full stretch of the sheets, and then come crashing back against the mast with a resounding thud that shook the heavy spar and could be heard from end to end of the ship.

Orders were given for the watch to go aloft and secure it – a very difficult and hazardous bit of work. Eventually we succeeded, however, in lashing it to the mast, and there it was allowed to rest, awaiting an improvement in the weather.

Instead of abating, however, the wind increased in force until it was blowing a steady half-gale. Captain M—— decided that the yard must be sent down immediately. In view of the weather conditions he abandoned any idea of getting it on deck and gave orders to swing it out overboard and cut it adrift.

It was during this operation that we witnessed one of the most extraordinary exhibitions of a temporary 'black-out' of a man's mind that I can possibly conceive. As will be readily appreciated, the cutting adrift of the yard was the worst part of the whole business, and required the greatest care. Realising this fact, Mr Bilsborough, the chief mate, had entrusted the job to the most experienced hand on board. Everything was ready and we stood by to 'let her go'. When the order came the man raised his knife and cut the fall *above the hand by which he was holding on.*

Away went the yard and the seaman with it. How he managed to get clear of the tackle and gear attached to the yard as it dropped and dived beneath a wave is a mystery. But succeed he did, and almost before the cry of 'Man overboard!' had sounded along the decks he reappeared on the surface of the sea. Two lines were thrown to him in quick succession, but in each case they failed to reach him. The second mate then ran to the end of the poop and threw a third one. This time the man was able to grasp it just as he was passing astern. He told us afterwards that his mind went completely blank at the moment when he was about to cut the fall.

This famous photograph of men working aloft on the three-masted barque *Garthsnaid* was taken in January 1920 while rounding Cape Horn in atrocious conditions. The log makes mention of the deckhouse being breached by a rogue wave.

With a view to replacing the lost yard the ship was headed for Montevideo. We had not been long on our new course, however, before head winds were encountered. Heaven knows that these are bad enough at any time, but, disabled as we were, the ship could not be sailed close to the wind. We were, in fact, compelled to reduce sail to counteract her tendency to yaw. After beating about for seventeen days and being no nearer our goal, Captain M—— decided to abandon the attempt to enter Montevideo and set a course for the Horn. He had in mind that if driven to it we could make for Port Stanley, in the Falkland Islands. Everyone on board realised that if we were compelled to do this it might mean that our voyage would be prolonged to an alarming degree whilst waiting for the new yard to be fitted. So we stood south again with the galling thought that we had wasted seventeen days of fair wind. When looking back, one cannot help feeling admiration for the man who had the courage to make such a decision and to stick to it so grimly. Captain M—— certainly took a great responsibility. We did not put in to the Falkland Islands, nor did we make any attempt to do so.

It was about ten weeks before we cleared the Horn. During the whole of that time we encountered the worst of weather and scarcely saw the sun. We were driven miles off our course to the south'ard and east'ard by the combination of head winds and currents, eventually finding ourselves within the Antarctic Circle. In these latitudes the ship remained for six weeks, during which time several members of the crew suffered from severe frostbite. Fortunately the weather improved considerably, otherwise we should have fared badly. We had so much ice on board that the ship became completely enveloped. There was not a mast, spar, rope, or inch of the deck visible, and the life-lines were so coated with ice that it was about as much as one could do to get an arm over them. For more than eight days we were at the mercy of the wind. Fortunately it did not change direction during this time; had it done so we should have been powerless. Not a brace or halyard would work, and the sails – frozen stiff – were bellied out as if drawing to a seven-knot breeze.

Some weeks later, just as dawn was breaking, we sighted Cape Horn to leeward, and rounded it on a 'soldier's wind'. It is interesting to note here that when off Valparaiso we encountered a tidal wave of fair proportions. This would have been just about the time that the earthquake occurred there.

We had now left storms and ice well behind us, but not trouble. The crew were beginning to show the ill-effects of the time they had been through. The first to go down was the coloured steward. He was not a young man, had been going to sea for many years, and had been shipwrecked on two or three occasions. Once he had been the sole survivor. When taking his supper to his bunk, one night while he lay ill, he told me the story of his ghastly experience: a story of days in an open boat in the tropics tortured by thirst, of men going mad around him and attacking one another. And he explained to me how he managed to retain his sanity by continually taking off his woollen vest and wetting it in the sea. By this method he was able to keep under control the appalling desire to drink sea-water – and so avoid the terrible results of such an act.

The weather that we had experienced during the past three months caused tuberculosis to flare up, and within a few days we buried him at sea. Just about this time we sighted a 'bosun', that bird of ill-omen, and many were the prophecies made on board of ill-fortune yet to come.

Before we were clear of the tropics we ran short of water in spite of the fact that all reasonable precautions, including rationing, had been taken to protect the supply. Although we were as yet far from being short of food, we had been forced, as a precaution, to ration this also. We still had plenty of salt beef, but no variety in the food we were getting – not that there were a lot of changes under ordinary conditions. We managed, however, to catch and store some rain-water. But it was really almost undrinkable, and there was not much of it; under a quart a day per man for everything, even the lime-juice issue. We all began to know the meaning of *real thirst.*

In order to keep this within bearable limits we took turns in sitting in a barrel into which sea-water was being pumped and allowed to flow out again. We did this in the dog-watch. Every man was allowed three or four minutes in the barrel – minutes of sheer ecstasy. Before the voyage was over we ran short of oil, tobacco, and matches. To save the oil we resorted to sailing without side-lights, keeping them handy, but unlighted. A couple of boxes of matches were kept aft and guarded as if they had been gold. There was only one box among the whole crew, and this was auctioned and fetched a pound. But, as the seller had to receive payment in kind out of the slop-chest, and the purchaser to supply the much-needed matches for the fo'c'sle lamp, I do not think there was much in the deal.

Within a very short time practically every member of the crew was down with scurvy or – worse – beriberi. Mr Bilsborough, the mate, was one of the most seriously affected by this latter disease. I have never seen a man in such a state. He was swollen to dropsical proportions, and his eyes seemed to have disappeared into a couple of cavities. Nor did these two diseases complete the total of our medical problems. We also encountered an eye-trouble the name of which is unknown to me, but it consisted of the eggs of some fly being deposited on the under surface of the eyelid. The suffering endured by the victim can best be imagined. Some of the crew also had symptoms uncomfortably like those of sleeping sickness. These men were never really under medical observation, for the simple reason that when we eventually reached port they disappeared over the side into the boats of the boarding-house masters, as was usually the case with crews in the old-time sailing ships. Officially, therefore, the disease could not have been recognised.

The two great difficulties with which Captain M—— had to contend were to keep the crew sufficiently fit to work the ship, and to keep their spirits up. Of the two, the latter was certainly the harder. During this time I witnessed several fights that started for no other reason than that a man took a dislike to another's face. Fortunately they were feeling far from well, and the fights ended before they had really got going. The strain that Captain M—— went through can best be judged by the fact that his hair, which was jet-black when I joined the ship at Antwerp, turned almost white during the seven months at sea.

We were now, at long last, getting within sight of the end of the voyage, and were beginning to congratulate ourselves on this fact, when we were again faced with dis-appointment. Within three days' sailing of 'Frisco we struck head winds and spent the next *eight weeks* running towards and away from that port. During this time we spoke to the

Hong Kong Maru. She put a boat off with a doctor in it, but he was unable to render much assistance, as no one would come aboard for reasons of quarantine.

A few days later we sighted the American schooner *Mindoro*. Her Captain turned out to be a good fellow. We signalled him asking for help. He hove-to and, this time, *we* dropped a boat and rowed across to the schooner. About half an hour later the boat returned laden to its gun'les with potatoes, onions, and other stores. Nor would the Captain of the *Mindoro* take any payment. This food, kept for the sole use of the men who were most in need of it, had amazing results. The change in their condition was marked. There can be no doubt that many of the crew had to thank the Captain of the *Mindoro* for saving their lives. Certainly Mr Bilsborough would never have lived to reach port had it not been for the vegetables. I soaked onions in vinegar and gave him well over a pound a day to eat.

On 4th November we reached the Golden Gate, and here encountered the gunboat *Princetown*, which had been sent out by the United States Government to search for us. However, we made 'Frisco under our own sail.

At the same time as the port doctor arrived, a water-boat also came alongside to fill our tanks. Believe it or not, we all sat round buckets drinking fresh water!

So ended the 214 days' voyage from Antwerp to San Francisco of the *Leyland Brothers*. In fairness to her Captain, officers, and crew – and there may be some old shipmates who will read this – it should be noted here that very shortly after this terrible voyage she all but made a record passage to Australia, missing doing so by a mere two or three days, despite being becalmed on the Line for well over a fortnight.

The Golden Gate, San Francisco.

18 When the Sea Calls

Biscay seas – The three-masted barque *Curlew* – Occupants of the half-deck – Fear aloft
– Greasing the fore topmast – Sailmaker's advice – In the grip of a curious dread – The
mental struggle of an apprentice – The call of the sea – The mate's reason – Running her
easting down – The hurricane – Pooped – A human life goes overboard in the white
smother – Sea breed.

GREY-GREEN Biscay seas, beneath the fast-flying cloud-banks of a gale that had
veered suddenly to the nor'-west, swept towards an invisible rockbound shore from
out of the wintry dawn of a February morning in that vast watery solitude of
31,000,000 square miles, the Atlantic. They came in long, foam-capped ridges and passed
beneath the barque *Curlew*, outward bound for the Antipodes.

From her wet and shining deck the whole world of sea and sky appeared to be flying past
the mere thousand tons of wood and canvas which formed the only thing to retain its shape
and relative position in the midst of a reeling and roaring universe. After days of weary
beating to the westward from the chops of the Channel in the teeth of a strong sou'-
westerly, the wind had changed direction and increased to gale force, but ample sea-room
had been obtained, and the *Curlew*, with far more canvas aloft than would have been carried
by most captains, had squared away to the south'ard and was running with the wind well
on her quarter.

The long uprearing seas, with patches of light-filled emerald below their feathery lines of
blown foam, had not yet come into perfect alignment with the wind, and often the barque
rolled down the mottled back of one great sea to scoop aboard the crest of its successor.
Tons of green water and hissing foam swirled around the half-deck, in which the three
apprentices of the starboard watch were lying wedged in their bunks, smoking and talking.

They knew well that the four hours in comparative warmth, sheltered from the bitter
wind and stinging spray, would pass quickly, even if the call did not come, as they expected
it would, for all hands to shorten sail. Tom Barlow was completing his last few months' sea-
time before sitting for his second mate's certificate, and already possessed the broad frame

EDITOR'S NOTE
Captain Archer Wayth gives a vivid picture of the half-deck and life at sea in the middle of the nineteenth
century in a story of 'When the Sea Calls'.

and muscular limbs of the young sailor. As a complete contrast, Jack Summers had the pink-and-white complexion and round face of the healthy schoolboy, which in fact he had been less than two months before. The third occupant of a bunk in the clean-painted but ill-lit half-deck, which every now and then resounded to the thud of heavy water coming over the bulwarks and hitting the two-inch-thick teak planks of which this little six-bunked house on the main deck was formed, would have seemed a complete misfit to anyone with a nautical eye. Ted Meadows was pale-faced and thin, but nevertheless had a half-humorous twist to his blue lips.

'Lucky for you, Jack, the mate was in a good temper to-night,' and a puff of cigarette smoke obscured the half-closed eyes and good-natured but somewhat broad and sea-tanned face of Barlow, whose right it was to open or close any conversation in the half-deck.

Jack Summers said nothing, but there was a pained look and more than the usual colour in his face, as he stared with unseeing eyes at the swinging lamp, which still burned,

'Aloft and furl it!'

although a few stray gleams of light penetrated the thick glass of the tightly screwed-down port.

'All things considered, including us misguided, half-fed "cadets in sail" – as we are politely called in the shipping offices ashore – Shell-back Henderson is not so bad as first mates go; and he wouldn't have lashed out if you'd told him that you didn't understand the order,' said Barlow, with a questioning look across the six feet of space which divided his bunk from the one in which lay the object of the mate's wrath. 'Besides, you're only a first-voyager, and it's willingness to learn and no ruddy nonsense they want, that's all.'

Still no answer came from the wide-awake boy opposite. The roar and thud of a boarding sea, which hissed and gurgled round the half-deck, prevented the silence from becoming strained.

'Well, if that's how you feel about it, I suppose it's no business of mine, but look out for squalls from the poop next time.' Barlow turned on his side and was asleep long before Summers' puzzled brain had ceased to torment him.

'Aloft and furl it!' These words, jumbled with a horrible sensation of alternately swinging and falling through space from the t'gallantyard into monstrous seas, which reached up tenuous arms of livid white to clutch him, recurred again and again during the sleep of exhaustion that followed. Nothing of the roaring gale and the ever-increasing violence of the seas which swamped aboard and beat against the deck house penetrated to Summers' brain, whatever may have been the epigastric effect of the wild downward swoops of the labouring barque. In the blackness of the night, after one of the watch on deck had, by orders, turned out the dangerously swinging lamp, he awoke, shivering, and paralysed with fear. It seemed that at last he had let go the jackstay during a gyration through space, and had dropped, with terror gripping his very soul, into the ice-cold seas. . . . He gasped . . . God! he was choking, fighting to lift the weight of water that smothered and crushed him. . . .

'Shut that blasted door, Robins! You've let half the North Atlantic come in, and there's Summers on the floor tangled up in his sopping blankets, in a delicate state of health too. Why didn't you use the lee door?' With a splash, Barlow jumped down from his bunk to rescue his dripping oilskins, muffler, and sea-boots, washing about in the water that lapped well over the lower bunks with each heavy roll of the ship.

'You pampered pets of the starboard watch needn't grumble, having *had* most of your watch below; besides, I did come in by the lee door, only the old hooker rolled at the wrong moment, and I preferred being washed inside to over the side. Henderson sent me to call you chaps. Hey! Hey! Hey! Rise and shine! Edward the Confessor, show a leg!' he yelled, shaking the recumbent form in the top bunk, who alone had remained dry and oblivious of the sea that had washed in and was swirling some two feet deep round the cabin.

Awakened by the cold water, and the wet blankets that clung to him, Summers struggled to his feet, realising that yet another nightmare was in store, although intensely relieved that the ship and its life was still around him. Wet to the skin, there was only time to slip on, over the clothes in which he had turned in some two hours previously, a dripping oilskin and muffler, before tying the 'soul and body' lashing round his waist to keep out the icy wind. He resolved to struggle aloft when the order came to shorten sail, even if it meant . . . and he avoided completing the thought.

'Come on, you sons of sorrow! More wind, more knots, and the sooner we'll be down among the flying-fish with the balmy trades,' Barlow called, as he cautiously opened the door.

'The only balmy things we're likely to see are ourselves, for ever thinking there is any real fun to be had at sea. . . . Ugh!' exclaimed Meadows, as he shivered outside the deck house.

The little group waited in the shelter of the half-deck, with the bitter wind whistling overhead, to peer forward into the thick blackness – thick with flying spume and rain – before grasping the life-lines that had been stretched along the deck.

For two hours men fought, with every ounce of strength and nerve they possessed, to take in canvas that already had been carried too long. With numbed hands, and often up to their waists in the seas washing from side to side, they heaved on wet-cold bunt-lines and downhauls. Bleeding fingers clung with the frenzy of self-preservation to bucking yards, and tried to obtain a hold on wind-filled canvas, which continuously wrenched itself free, tearing off finger-nails and straining muscles to breaking-point. The effort to keep upright on the swaying, jerking foot-ropes stretched below the sixty to ninety feet long yards made the task, performed in the darkness and high up between sea and sky, a long and dangerous one.

Those on deck fared little better. Above the howling of the gale there came, every ten or fifteen minutes, the bellowed order, 'Hold on for your lives!' Each man jumped wildly for the rigging, and a second later the barque reeled under the mighty blow of a thirty-foot sea full on the quarter. The air was filled with a rushing, roaring sound. Grip was tightened on whatever had been grasped that was close to hand, and everyone awaited the awful smothering plunge beneath ice-cold water, hoping, and yet wondering whether or not, in the darkness, they had clutched something strong enough to resist the drag of the sea as it crossed and recrossed the deck.

Those lucky enough to have reached the sheer-poles of the rigging, and so raised themselves above the wash of green water, were lashed furiously by clouds of heavy spray, which cut and stung like a wire flail, and they sought only to retain their hold and turn the least raw sides of their faces to the sea-whip.

The ten-foot freeboard of the laden barque raised the deck so little above the water that when a wave, steeper and more menacing than its neighbours, rushed out of the gloom, a livid mass of slightly phosphorescent green and white, it appeared that the hissing, foaming crest, as high as the lower topsailyard, must surely overwhelm the ship.

With beads of perspiration on his forehead, despite the bitter wind, Summers knew that he had not kept faith with himself. He realised that he was a coward, and, with the pressure of the wind behind him, clung to the shrouds half-way up the foremast, paralysed by a fear that he could not define. That his messmates of the half-deck were aloft, with the second mate and many of the hardened seamen from the forecastle, on the wildly swaying and jerking yards that he could see dimly outlined above, amid the thunder-claps of the canvas, cut him so deeply that every now and then he had struggled a few feet higher above the deck. In the darkness and storm-wrack his absence from aloft might pass unnoticed if he lied sufficiently well afterwards. Such reasoning, however, left unsolved the great problem that had worried him since he stepped aboard the *Curlew*, proud of his bright buttons and gold-braid-encircled, flag-badged cap. Would he ever be able to swing by one hand, like the others, in that maze of swaying, wrenching rigging that seemed to reach up into the skies?

With each staggering roll of the ship he hugged the ratlines, quite oblivious of the danger of trusting to these thin lines stretching from shroud to shroud. His thoughts became concentrated on the immediate difficulty of maintaining a hold, when the rigging seemed to carry him giddily through space and then endeavour to shake him into the boiling horror below. He sweated with the agony of fear and indecision. That the heavy work of shortening sail in a rising gale needed the unselfish support of everyone aboard he knew quite well, but he did not realise when this work had been accomplished, and the *Curlew* kept a point or two more away from the wind.

Shortly after the pressure of the gale against the weather rigging had eased and the rolling changed to a vicious pitch, which had all but torn his numbed fingers from their grip on the ice-cold wire, he felt a sea-boot rest tentatively on his shoulder, and the sudden realisation of its weight and meaning caused him to start hastily to descend. It was not until the deck was firm under his feet, however, that he understood fully all that the hour of terror in the rigging implied.

'Nearly trod on you as I came down,' laughed Barlow grimly. 'Like hell's belfry aloft, wasn't it?'

The harsh voice of the mate boomed out of the darkness: 'What are you doing here, Summers?' Then, more kindly: 'Been aloft, have you? Well, this is nothing to what we'll *enjoy* when running our easting down, so you might as well get used to it – but don't go aloft again until I tell you. Understand? Now go to the poop and strike the bell.' A moment later he roared into the night: 'That'll do, the watch!'

'Glad you've made it right with the mate,' said Barlow, as he threw himself into his bunk a few minutes later, and appeared to drop off to sleep immediately.

All around were the sparkling sapphire waves, topped by the little white manes, of the South Atlantic. The *Curlew*, with never a yard moved nor a halyard, bunt- or clew-line touched for days, was bowling along before the steady north-east trade wind, that was carrying her swiftly towards the Equator. With the start of the fine weather there commenced also the nautical education of the first voyagers in the half-deck. The vessel's storm-canvas was replaced by an old suit of patched sails, which were hauled out from below decks, examined, renovated, and sent aloft to be bent on to the yards. The stronger and newer canvas would be required again when the ship traversed the stormy seas of the great Southern Ocean, between the Cape of Good Hope and Australia.

The hot sun and tepid breeze dried everything below, and the musty damp smell in the half-deck disappeared mysteriously. Life for all on board, although a busy one, repairing the ravages of storm and stress – now almost forgotten – was, nevertheless, an easy and light-

Right to the truck of the mast on the
barque *Queen Margaret.*

hearted affair compared with what had gone before. There came a day when Summers could
no longer hide what had become a continuous agony of dread. So far he had managed to
avoid being sent aloft by the simple expedient of attaching himself to the sailmaker, and
working hard during his watches on deck at that which was cunningly avoided by the other
apprentices.

The end came suddenly, and Summers never quite knew whether the mate suspected his
secret or not. 'It's about time m'son, that you gained more experience aloft. Every man, and
boy as well, will be needed up there soon.' The deck seemed suddenly to drop away from
under Summers' feet, but he managed to stammer something which sounded in his ears like
an echo. With an effort he discarded the leather palm and big needle he had been using,
under the critical eye of the sailmaker, to fashion a spare cabin-skylight cover.

'Get a pot o' grease from the bosun and give the fore topmast a coating.' Then, stopping
for a moment as he was about to walk away, the mate added impressively: 'Remember to
begin at the mast-head and work downwards, hold on to the shrouds, never to the ratlines,

and always keep one hand for yourself and one for the ship.' Without waiting for a reply he moved towards a group of men splicing wire near the foremast.

When the dirty yellow grease had been obtained, and Summers was walking along the deck trying hard to obtain mastery over the peculiar dread of climbing to any height, quite regardless of such considerations as the movement of the ship or whether there was a real danger or not, he heard the voice of the old sail-maker, who had left his pile of canvas and was standing by the shrouds of the foremast:

'Never ye looks down, sonny. Keep yer eyes glued first to the futtocks, and when ye've clambered over 'em wait a few minutes a-stirring of the grease and gitting accustomed like, then hup aloft ye goes with never a glimpse at deck or sea. Bend yer eyes and yer thoughts to yer job, m'lad, and ye'll soon be as lively among the sticks and the yarn as ye are a'ready with the wheel, aye and the sail-needle too.' So quietly was this practical advice given that no one overheard, and it acted as the old sailor had foreseen.

The terrible dread seemed for a moment to release its grip as Summers reasoned that if he never glanced downwards, and kept control of his thoughts, all would be well. Swinging himself quickly on to the bulwarks and up to the sheer-pole, he stopped and met the confident gaze of two grey old eyes beset with wrinkles. 'Thanks, "Sails,"' and there was a note of determination in his voice as he started again to climb with eyes searching for the dreaded projection in the mass of rigging converging above him.

Progress was slow, as each swinging ratline seemed a few inches too high. The rigging narrowed, then with eyes half-closed he grasped the futtock shrouds and climbed out, clinging like a fly to a ceiling, with his heart beating violently. Once he nearly lost consciousness and let go. With an arm over the top it became impossible to maintain both a foot-hold on the ratlines and a hand-hold over the iron edge above.

A laughing face looked down and a friendly hand came out and gripped him firmly. 'Hang on with your eyelashes, now pull yourself over – let your legs swing!'

Exactly how it was all accomplished Summers never knew, but with fear gripping his heart he looked into the grinning face of Tom Barlow.

'Phew! It gave me a proper fright when your face went as white as a new sail and your eyes closed. I thought you were going to let go. Henderson sent me up by the lee rigging to give you a hand over the futtock shrouds, and you nearly unhooked my perishing and painful arm. What's the matter, lost your nerve?'

For a minute or two there was no answer. Summers was breathing heavily and his limbs were trembling. At last he spoke: 'Tom, I've never been up here before. The mate must have known that when he sent you to give me a hand. God! what a coward and a liar he must think me, after letting him – and you all – believe that I helped to take in sail that night away back in the Bay.' The words came slowly and quietly, while Summers' unseeing eyes looked far out to where a shoal of silver-winged flying-fish ruffled the satin-like sheen of the tropical sea. 'I'll never make a sailor,' he murmured brokenly. 'It's no good, there's something – call it funk if you like – that – will——'

'Rot! Sheer rot! We all feel a bit squeamish at first, but it passes off after an hour or two,' Barlow interjected hastily. 'But you were a fool to let Henderson believe you'd been on the upper tops'lyard that night – perhaps he didn't think so – I wondered why he told me to see that you neither fell nor funked it.'

These words stung Summers, despite the relief he was now feeling, and he searched inwardly for something that would enable him to retain at least a shred of self-respect. He found it in the thought that when great seas had thundered aboard, washing from their grip case-hardened seamen and nearly carrying them to certain death over the lee bulwarks, he had not felt the same cowardice or terror which weakened his limbs and numbed his brain when aloft.

'And yet I like the sea,' he exclaimed aloud.

Because it seemed that Summers was struggling inwardly with himself, Barlow waited and said nothing. At that moment, however, there came a hail from below: 'Hey! No skylarking up there! Get on with yer job, or I'll show ye both the only rope in the ship!'

It was the mate shouting through cupped hands, and Summers looked down involuntarily at the narrow plank-like deck, the small figures, and the moving, white-topped waves. Immediately there came over him the old nausea when gazing down from a height. The reason why, when the chance came for him to go to sea, he had begged a reluctant parent to agree, he did not quite know. There was something in him which responded fiercely to the call, but cruelly left him without one of the qualifications for the life of a sailor. His whole being revolted also at the thought of descending to admit fear before the withering scorn of the mate and the derisive laughter of everyone aboard.

'Come on, up we've got to go and smear that ruddy grease on the old pole. As it is, he'll make it hot for both of us when we do come down – why, we've been here over a quarter of an hour! Barlow exclaimed, as the sound of the ship's bell came from below.

Wresting his eyes away from the deck, Summers looked up towards the almost bare pole above the topmast shrouds. He felt that to scale it would be impossible, even if he never glanced down. In a second, however, there came the realisation that the fear of being *thought afraid* was greater by far than the short agony of climbing and——

With decision came also a sense of relief, though his limbs trembled when he reached the highest point of the rigging on the topmast. So calm had the ocean appeared from the deck that he had scarcely noticed the swelling of its bosom with each slumbrous breath. Now, however, he watched the mast-head describe a circle round a little puff-ball of cloud.

'Up you go, "blue nose". Hang on with one arm and wind your legs round it, then slap on the grease with the other. If you feel like slipping, close your baby eyes, and slide down the ruddy pole – don't let go, that's all, because there are sharks who haven't had their breakfast gazing up longingly at you.'

Sharks! Why yes, of course; he had seen their black fins cleaving the water astern; and how they had fought for the rubbish from the galley! Somehow the thought failed to arouse in Summers' brain the terror it might well have created, and he found himself gripping the mast-head and smearing the pole with grease. Every handful taken by the little cracks in the wood brought him nearer to the secure foot-hold below. Once he felt himself slip, and swinging both arms and legs round the mast he gripped it tightly. Even when his feet touched the rigging he dare not glance down, and wondered for a moment how he could release his hold on the topmast in order to get a grip on the narrow shrouds.

'A thoroughly humane piece of work, prolonging the life of something that is more beautiful than useful,' Barlow exclaimed sententiously, and not altogether without a note of relief in his voice. 'Now hurry down and report while the mate is on the poop.'

A few minutes later Summers was standing on the raised after deck with the mate looking quizzically at him.

'Oh, you've done it, m'son, have you? Well, that's the first time I've ever sent an apprentice to the mast-head when *he's never been aloft before.*' Not waiting for a reply, however, he added more kindly: 'I think ye'll shape sailorwise after all. Anyhow, I'm as glad to see ye down on deck, without that scared look, as ye are to be here.' Then, after a short pause, he continued more thoughtfully: 'Mind ye, we're too short-handed to carry a passenger. Better get used to swinging about up there before it sets in dirty when we turn to the east'ard.'

In the glassy swell of the doldrums the *Curlew* rolled, creaked, and sweated for what seemed endless days. A few ripples would momentarily disturb the mirror-bright surface that extended around the lonely ship to the clear-cut horizon. Each time a puff of wind came the yards were trimmed laboriously in the great heat to take full advantage of it. More often than not, however, these light airs came no nearer to the aligned canvas than a mile or two. The tar in the seams bubbled and spread itself around the decks, as well as on to the bare and blistered feet that trod them. The sails hung limp from the tracery of masts, yards, and rigging, which were dark-etched against the lofty gold-blue sky. The ship, with all its symmetrical detail, was reproduced by Nature's own hand on the oily green surface of the lifeless ocean.

In contrast to the peace of the sea, irritability and discontent made their appearance among the mixed British, Swedish, and Dutch hands in the forecastle. More than once open defiance of discipline was threatened, and fist fights occurred for the first time during the voyage. On the poop, the keen eyes of Captain Rattry, or those of the mate, were for ever searching the watery plain to determine the direction taken by the streaky little ripples, mere cat's-paws, that ruffled the surface. Curious air currents came from out of the sudden accumulations of blue-black storm-clouds. In the tropical deluges that followed clothes were torn off and overheated bodies cooled in the tepid rain. The whole ship steamed; and for a brief half-hour the sea around was beaten until it danced with watery beads to the staccato drumming of the downpour. The smell of brine filled the air. Above and below decks nothing remained dry. The atmosphere was hot and heavy with moisture. Then a copper-coloured light streamed through a rift in the indigo clouds, hurting the eyes with its brilliance, and back came the scorching, pitiless sun.

During the hours of darkness, while great stars shone down from luminous space, a soft blue light enveloped the ship. From the lofty yards the apprentices looked down on to the star-powdered sea. Time and again Jack Summers would go aloft with others from the half-deck, but never could he gaze with impunity at the pictures which the heavens painted on the stilled ocean. Out on the jib-boom in the sunlight, however, with the dark shadows of bonitas and dolphins gliding with effortless ease through the opaque waters so close below, he felt no sign of failing nerve, and knowing nothing of cause and effect he became puzzled and depressed.

For nearly twelve hours an arch of dark cloud had obscured the southern horizon. No longer was the ship becalmed in the windless seas of the Equator. With a bone in her teeth she had bowled along for many days with all sails set, doing a steady eight knots. The wind had gradually lost its soft caress, and now had the keen edge of proximity to the Antarctic ice.

It came one day in the morning watch. At first a flat and ominous calm, with the light shining through a thin film of cloud. The sails were trimmed and the ship's head turned towards the rising sun. Then a series of squalls struck downwards from out of an almost clear sky, followed within an hour by the piping of the great west wind. The *Curlew* had passed well to the southward of the fortieth parallel of latitude, where the ocean girdles the world. For a whole day the bitter wind moaned dismally through the rigging; and the icy down-draught from the sails once again became noticeable on the deck.

A sea coming aboard the four-masted barque *Penang*.

The sea around had lost the blue-and-silver sheen that it had retained while the ship sailed through that happy realm of seamen which is ruled by the south-east trades. Life aboard had also changed, from what the boatswain called 'a peaceful Sunday afternoon to a rowdy Saturday night'. Heavy storm-canvas replaced the lighter and older fair-weather sails on the yards. While this work was in progress the apprentices of the starboard watch took their turn at overhauling the rigging of the foremast. With the increasing roll of the ship it became a time of severe trial for Jack Summers.

A sudden shift of the wind against the sun, from west to south-west, not only lowered the temperature to freezing-point, but also changed the aspect of the sea from a cold aquamarine waste to a threatening expanse of grey-green uprising seas, moving in an easterly procession beneath fast-driven, snow-filled cloud-banks.

'Here it comes at last!' exclaimed Captain Rattry, whose rugged, weather-worn features, keen blue eyes, black beard trimmed to a point, and heavily braided cap made him the beau-ideal of deep-water sailormen in the early 'nineties.

'Call all hands, Summers.' From him, only the mates received the prefix of 'Mister'.

The watch below turned out quickly, for most of the older men had been expecting the order, and sail was shortened until the *Curlew* was scudding before a rising gale under lower and upper topsails and staysail only. Throughout that day and the succeeding night the wind steadily increased in violence. The hurricane squalls were often accompanied by a haze of blinding snowflakes. With ever-increasing frequency a foam-crested mountain of water would lift the barque by the stern and carry her forward in a welter of flying spume.

Towards evening a narrow but vivid streak of orange light broke from between the leaden clouds along the western horizon. For a few minutes the vast expanse of tumbling sea was tinged with flame. Each time the creaking, labouring ship dived into a watery valley the pressure of the wind was suddenly released from the deck, and while rising on the swell of a gargantuan sea the lower main topsail would suddenly catch the full blast of the gale, and with thunderous claps threaten to tear itself from the bolt-ropes. The spuming crests were blown with such force across the decks that it was impossible to look to windward.

Life-lines had been stretched the whole length of the ship, but in order to reach the poop ladder, when the starboard watch turned out at one bell, Summers had to wait for a favourable opportunity, as the waist of the ship was being swept by hundreds of tons of seething water, moving and burying deep bulwarks and rails with every leeward roll. A tarpaulin had been lashed in the weather rigging of the mizzen-mast, and within its meagre shelter he saw the indistinct outlines of the Captain and mate. After a tussle with the wind, which seemed determined to blow his legs from under him, he approached the oilskinned forms. Discovering that the information regarding the compass course, the direction, and force of the wind, usual before one or other of the officers departed below, was not being given, and that only with a great effort could he maintain an upright position without grasping the ice-cold rail, Summers crouched in the shelter afforded by the cabin hatch, ready to strike off the lagging half-hours on the ship's bell. Once during a slight lull, when it became possible to see through the streaming darkness, he gazed out over the stern while the ship was in a watery hollow. The sight was so appalling that he almost ran forward on the deck to escape what looked like certain death. A livid white-and-green monster came hissing and roaring out of the blackness towering high above the poop, and seemingly so close and so steep that nothing could prevent it falling on to the deck and burying the whole after part of the ship.

Although the stern of the *Curlew* was flung high in the air, and she trembled as the acre or two of foam passed under the keel, very little heavy water came aboard. The two men lashed to the wheel seemed quite oblivious of the danger which repeatedly threatened them from behind; and, beyond steadying themselves with legs well apart, neither the Captain nor the mate appeared to notice either the lofty, curling seas or the upflinging of the stern as they passed.

Just before midnight the moon broke through a rift in the scurrying clouds and flooded the

The four-masted barque *Pamir* photographed in a full gale on her 1947 round-the world voyage, the last by a commercial square-rigged ship.

raging sea with a silver light. Captain Rattry moved uneasily towards the two men at the wheel, looking up at the straining sails and then at the sky ahead, while the mate stepped towards the poop ladder. Something in the scene around, which gave the impression of a moving range of snow-capped mountain peaks, stirred a responsive chord, and Summers was no longer awed by the fierce anger of it all. He revelled in the wildness of the night, and longed to fight the storm, though in exactly what manner he could do so never occurred to him.

Suddenly there came a distinct lull. From a shrieking crescendo the noise of the wind died away to a low moan. That something more was threatened than the ever-present danger of sailing across the widest and most stormy expanse of ocean in the world there could be no doubt.

When the call 'All hands!' was passed from the poop to the half-deck and forecastle, Summers, whose duty it was to arouse the apprentices of the port watch, overheard the remarks of the men as they came on deck, still tying the wrist-lashings of their oilskins.

'De vind, it change, and ve are scudding in dis sea, mein Gott.'

'Blimey, the Cap'n has 'ung on too long. We're a-going to lose the number o' our mess this night, Dutchy, if the ole man wears ship to 'eave 'er to.'

Just then came a loud shout from aft: 'Hold on, all hands!' With the rapid falling of the wind the seas had increased their height, and for the same reason the way of the ship through the water had decreased. The next minute, with a terrifying roar, an avalanche of water fell on the poop deck. The ship seemed to settle down to the level of the boiling sea under the tremendous weight. Not only did the wave break over the stern, but it also poured in amidships, filling the main deck level with the bulwarks.

As the warning shout of the mate came from the mizzen rigging, Ted Meadows stepped out of the half-deck. Perhaps he never heard, or could not reach a place of safety in time, but, from the sheer-pole of the main rigging, Summers saw him caught by the wash of the sea, which poured off the poop deck as well as from over the bulwarks on both sides. For a moment a yellow oilskin appeared in the swirling waters that filled the main deck. Then the *Curlew* rolled almost on to her beam ends and spilled the three or four hundred tons of angry sea, with a human life somewhere in its white smother, through the wide breach it made for itself in the lee bulwark.

Of the wheel only a few spokes remained, and the barque swung round broadside-on to the mountainous greybeards which had the whole Southern Hemisphere in which to obtain height and force. Nearly half an hour went by, and nothing could be done. Sea followed sea, and each sent its blinding spray into the rigging and its roaring flood across the decks. Little of the ship was visible from twenty feet up on the ratlines of the main rigging, to which point of doubtful safety Barlow and Summers had climbed, together with three of the forecastle hands.

With a long moaning sigh the wind returned, but it was from the south-east, and although the *Curlew* was nearly taken aback, the fore topmast staysail caught the wind, and her head came slowly round into the seas. Captain Rattry, from high up in the mizzen rigging, roared into the wind: 'Aloft, and put your knives into it——' Whatever else he might have said was cut off by a loud shriek of the gale.

How many of the crew were left to carry out this order, on which those huddled in the rigging knew only too well depended their one chance of life, nobody knew, but after a desperate struggle out to the upper topsailyard there was a sharp report as more than one knife cut adrift the iron-hard sail. The wind roared and shrieked in demoniacal fury, and with it came gusts of hail, driven into the faces of the men unable to move from the yard. A heavy cross-sea, produced by the change of the wind, caught the ship on the port beam and, with little canvas to steady her, the terrific force of both wind and wave threw her suddenly over to an angle of about forty degrees.

The upper topsailyard to which the men were clinging gyrated through space with the action of a gigantic catapult. Summers heard an agonised cry, which sounded above the gale, and a body with outstretched arms was, for a brief second, silhouetted against the rocketing clouds. At that moment there came into his faltering soul an irresistible command to hold on in spite of cracking limbs and reeling brain. His sea-booted feet slipped from the rope below the now almost vertical yard; and, in the agony of a dread known for as many years as his young memory served, he would certainly have let go his hand-hold on the jackstay but for the invincible command which seemed at this moment of extreme need to take entire possession of his innermost being, stilling and strengthening so that he held fast.

The *Curlew* was in a sorry state when at last the men were able to come down from aloft, but she was riding well the long and mountainous seas in the half-light of the stormy dawn. The fore topmast had gone overboard. Eight of the crew, including Ted Meadows and the two men at the wheel, had been either washed over the side or flung from the yards, and the wreckage included long sections of the bulwarks on both sides. The tops of the hurtling seas now washed across the exposed deck, giving her the appearance of a half-tide rock.

The wind eased with the coming of full daylight, and as the exhausted men crawled up the poop ladder, for both deck houses had been wrenched from their fastenings and carried overboard, there came to Jack Summers the sure knowledge that he could now answer the call of the sea.

It was some time later when the mate, reviewing the events of the past forty hours, remarked to Captain Rattry: 'He's not a bad sort of lad, Jack Summers, but God knows why it wasn't him instead of Dutch Hans that was shaken off the topsailyard when that cross-sea struck us. He was always scared of going aloft.'

'Yes – I know.' The Captain's words came slowly and thoughtfully. 'His father was blown off the fore t'gallant yardarm when I was an apprentice in the *Invershay* – Jack was born soon afterwards.'

19 Burned Out

October 1874 – The full-rigged ship *May Queen* – Coal – Off the Cape of Good Hope –
Slow sailing – Cargo on fire – Shovelling in gas-filled hold – No hope of saving the ship
– Launching the boats – A last sumptuous meal on board – Abandon ship – Releasing
the fowls – A dear friend – In the lifeboats – A big sea – The vastness of the ocean –
Terrible privations – A ship that passed – Half unconscious – The Arab ship *Iskender
Shah* – Saved.

ONE grey October morning in the year 1874 I left the Tyne, outward bound for
Rangoon, aboard the full-rigged ship *May Queen*. We were deeply laden with an
unromantic but somewhat dangerous cargo of coal, and carried a crew of twenty-
five, many of whom hailed from Leith, where the vessel was owned.

During the first three months of the voyage we made but slow progress, owing to adverse
winds and calms. It was not until Christmas that the Cape latitudes were reached, and then
by good luck there came a favourable breeze which carried us, square yards, round the
southernmost point of Africa into the Indian Ocean.

Beyond the usual everyday incidents of life in a sailing ship nothing occurred during our
slow crawl north until we had crossed the Equator; then, late one afternoon, a hand came
aft to report that a faint appearance of steam could be seen issuing from the fore hatch. The
Captain, with several of the crew, quickly disappeared below, and after careful investigation
returned to the deck with the expressed opinion that it was just a little steam being
generated by the cargo of coal, owing to the protracted voyage.

One could see, however, by the Captain's manner that he was far from feeling easy; and
orders were given to close all ventilators and to put on the hatch covers with the object of
choking out the fire if the cargo had become ignited. Just then eight bells were struck, and
the wheel and the lookout were relieved, while the watch coming on duty was given strict
orders to report at once any developments. At daylight next morning the hatches were
removed, and steam mixed with gas fumes and smoke came rolling up in dense clouds.

Things now looked so serious that all hands were assembled on deck and formed into
two working parties. One, obtaining shovels from the forepeak, was sent below to trim the

---

EDITOR'S NOTE
Edward Gordon, an apprentice in the fuil-rigged ship *May Queen*, describes the burning of this ship while
crossing the Indian Ocean.

coal, while the other was set to work the pumps in order to flood the main deck. With the scupper vents plugged, the water poured into the burning cargo below through holes hastily bored by the carpenter in the main-deck planking.

In the great heat of the tropics this proved gruelling work for the men shovelling below, amid the burning coal and in a stifling and poisonous atmosphere. After a short spell they staggered on to the deck, carrying one of their number badly gassed. Up on the fo'c'sle head they collapsed, half-insensible and vomiting, remaining unfit for duty until the following day.

There could be no doubt now that the cargo was on fire; and the pumps were kept hard at work. Early on the following morning an explosion of gas blew off the after-hatch covers on which some of the tired men were sleeping. Luckily they were thrown on to the deck and no lives were lost. Later in the day it became apparent that all our efforts to subdue the fire were unavailing, and that the doomed ship would have to be abandoned.

The boats, quickly unlashed from the skids, were launched and towed alongside. Then followed the stowing of biscuits, water-casks, and other necessities. Meanwhile the heat on

The full-rigged clipper ship *May Queen*, built by Alexander Hall & Sons, Aberdeen, the firm which is best remembered for its development of the Aberdeen or clipper bow in 1839.

the main deck was becoming so unbearable that the men could not approach the hatch. At midday all hands were told to stop work and get dinner. This proved to be the best and last meal we had aboard the *May Queen*. The cook rose to the occasion nobly, providing a sumptuous spread, obtained from the stores intended for the Captain's cabin. Although sixty eventful years have passed, I can still remember that it was composed of haricot beans, fowls, butter, and jam.

Think of it, ye old-time windjammer seamen! It is you *only* who can appreciate fully the contrast of this menu to the weevily and hard biscuits, old salt-horse, and the bad-smelling pork and pea-soup feeds you were accustomed to; and apprentices fared little better in those hard old days.

Sailors have a big sense of humour, and are quick to apply it. The present opportunity, therefore, was not to be lost. One of the men, after due consideration of the spread in front of him, remarked sarcastically: 'It's an ill wind that blaws naebody guid.'

Despite the peril, the feeding and rough banter assumed the aspect of a joyous feast – such was the spirit of the old carefree school of sailormen. In the meantime, however, the fire had not been idle. Suddenly, with a terrifying crash, the foremast went by the board, and lay at an angle over the port rail with some of its upper yards and tophamper dragging through the water.

The Captain now ordered the men to leave the ship, as the flames were bursting through the fore hatch. Each with his small canvas bag containing a few necessaries clawed his way from the fo'c'sle along the main-deck rail into the boats being towed alongside. Here an incident happened aptly showing the coolness and nerve of these men in danger, and the kindly feelings with which they regarded their dumb animal shipmates.

We were about to cast off when someone remembered that the fowls were still securely fastened in the deck coops. At that moment two of the crew of our boat appeared on the rail, and on hearing this threw their bags down and disappeared through the smoke to liberate the fowls to a more merciful death than roasting alive. To us in the boat, placed in such a critical position, the rescuers seemed to take an inexplicably long time. With the painter in hand ready to cast off, we shouted for them to hurry up. Their answer came to us in a very unexpected manner. From the vicinity of the smoke-hidden coops there arose the muffled refrain of an old and peculiarly appropriate chanty: 'I thought I heard our old man say, "Leave her, Johnnie, leave her. It's time for us to leave her."'

A few seconds later the two perspiring and smoke-begrimed men appeared, and tumbled over the side into the boat, breathless, and unable for a time to tell us the reason for the unaccountable delay. The fowl-coop doors had become blocked, it appeared, by the foreyard from the fallen mast lying across the deck. This heavy spar proved too much for their united efforts, and, unable to obtain an axe with which to break open the coops, they could find no way of releasing the fowls. Regardless of the danger from further explosions of gas, and of the flames now so close, the idea suddenly occurred to them of bending the staysail halyards on to the obstructing yard. After a severe tussle, and the usual accompaniment of a chanty to give vigour to their pull, they succeeded in moving the spar and releasing the frantic occupants of the coops. Our boat sheered off just in time to escape being crushed by the mainmast, as it fell over the side into the space of water we had vacated.

On dropping astern, I looked at the old *May Queen* and the sight struck home. This new sensation came over me unexpectedly. A lump rose in my throat and it seemed that I was losing a dear friend. It was my first voyage in the doomed ship, and it occurred to me then that the time aboard her had been too short for such an attachment to be genuine. One is inclined to ascribe the cause to the surroundings and isolated life led aboard a sailing ship, cut off for months and even years from all outside influence. Doubtless the fact that the now forlorn and dying thing that had once been a home, an object of beauty to our eyes, a ship which had carried us faithfully over leagues of trackless waters in shine and storm, was passing for ever from view in the vast loneliness which is the sea, helped to bring so suddenly to the surface this feeling of keen attachment. It had been born unconsciously in the past and needed only this last tragedy to bring it to the fore in the hearts of all of us.

The three boats, one being in the charge of the Captain and first mate and the other two under the care of the second mate and bosun, were connected together by a rope, in order that we might keep in touch with each other in the darkness of the night. Our plan was to stand at a safe distance from the blazing ship until she went under, so that, within a wide radius, the glare of the burning derelict would in all probability attract the attention of a passing ship. Failing this, however, there was the dread alternative of sailing to the nearest land, the island of Ceylon.

Towards the end of the day the sky turned a sickly green shade, and dull indigo clouds rolled up from the horizon. This combined with an oily sluggish sea, seemed a likely precursor of dirty weather. About sunset the heavens cleared low down in the distance, and the sun, with a faint halo encircling it, disappeared in a blaze of crimson light. Fanned by a slight breeze, the fire aboard the derelict had made such rapid headway that when darkness came, as it does so quickly in the tropics, all that was left of the ship became a shapeless mass of glowing fire, the flames by this time having spent themselves. Seen from the boats, the crimson hull, with its lines foreshortened and the stump of the solitary mizzen-mast standing grimly up as if left to con the vessel, became lost in the pathway of red reflections caught on the waves below. Effectively placed against the dark background of the sky, the scene was both awe-inspiring and grand.

Later in the night it began to blow hard, and our thoughts for the time being were centred on the management of the boats, until attention was again drawn towards the derelict by a sudden flare, followed by a dull report, and a great hissing noise from the surrounding sea. The glowing hull just slid from view. It was the last of the old ship. An immense cloud of steam rose up from the waters, hovered awhile, and formed a fitting pall to the tragic burial before it became lost in the darkness.

So dramatic was the finish that it made a deep impression on us all. The night-enshrouded waters seemed suddenly to press in close around and emphasise the vastness and solitude of the sea. By midnight the wind was blowing a gale, with vivid lightning flashes, and, with the high sea that was running, all our attention was occupied in keeping our own boat scudding before it. With hissing white crests, the huge waves formed a wall on each side of us, which shot up and became lost in the blackness around. The rope connecting the boats had to be released, and in the darkness and driving spray it was impossible to keep any lookout.

To prevent the swamping of the boat we had to bail out the water unceasingly and keep tugging at the oars. Occasionally a heavy sea would roll up from astern, pass over the boat and then sweep out at the bows, carrying with it some of the vital stores of food and drinking water. In the turmoil of the sea and the pall-like blackness it was impossible to see exactly what happened when a wave engulfed us.

Our next shift was to make a sea anchor, by lashing a few oars to the boat's painter; and by throwing this overboard we managed to turn and ride head to sea throughout the remainder of the night. Soon after the coming of the first pale light of day the wind abated, and when the sun rose above the horizon, dispelling the clouds, its rays revealed a wild and empty sea. Each time the boat soared upwards on the crest of a wave the whole watery expanse was scanned with the hope of sighting a sail. Of the other two boats, from which the tow-rope had been released during the gale, there was no sign. More than ever did we feel alone on this first morning adrift amid the seemingly limitless and unbroken reach of sea and sky.

On examining our resources it was found that everything movable, including the water-keg and supply of biscuits, had been washed out of the boat in the darkness and heavy sea. The necessary arrangement was made to keep a lookout day and night, relieving each other at intervals. No risks were taken and nothing left to chance in our endeavours to ensure that no ship should pass us unseen. The reaction of the physical and mental strain borne throughout the preceding night gradually made itself felt as the seas decreased in height and force. One by one the men sank into heavy sleep, without troubling even to change their attitudes or positions.

Taking the first watch I kept a lonely vigil, in a silence which but for the wash of the sea would have been as profound as that of the grave. In this solitude and aloofness from the living world a strange feeling of awe stole through my whole being. Never before had I felt my own self-importance shrink to an almost abject humbleness. The nearness of the Almighty came to me with overwhelming suddenness. At the end of an uneventful day, and refreshed by their long slumber, the men turned out their pockets in eager search for tobacco. The supply was meagre, but if carefully used it would last for a day or two. My own contribution to the pathetic little store was two boxes of sodden matches, which were carefully laid out to dry.

Somewhat timorously one of the men, who had been a garden-boy in his young days, suggested that to make the tobacco last as long as possible it should be damped again previous to being smoked. His experience was, that when used to kill insects in glass-houses the tobacco was always well damped to bring out its full strength, and that it took a much longer time to consume than when used in a dry state. The sun-drying of the sodden weed ceased almost at once, and careful rationing commenced. This was the end of our first day in the open boats exposed to a blistering sun, from which the night gave us welcome relief.

Next morning at daybreak the unbroken line of the sea caused a depression of spirits as we contemplated and realised our dangerous position. How small indeed was the chance that in this vast Indian Ocean any vessel would pass sufficiently close to see us was made apparent by the knowledge that within the last two months we had sighted only two ships. Although unrealised by many people in these days, this was by no means an unusual experience in the more spacious times of individual sailing-ship navigation. Turning, then, to our means of subsistence, and of reaching Ceylon, 1000 miles away, the outlook was no brighter. All we could do was to let the boat drift and keep a sharp lookout, with the faint hope that an Australian trader, making the voyage to or from Ceylon, might sight us in daylight. Even this chance was slight, as we were far to the westward of their usual track.

Unsatisfied hunger and the craving for water – which no imagination can picture – were already beginning to tell on some of the men, who, with swollen tongues, and in spite of being warned of the dire consequences, drank sea-water. How thankful we were when night graciously obscured the scorching, glittering sun, and softened the long spell of terrible loneliness during our second day adrift.

Next morning this feeling of depression and of isolation from the living world became intensified to a distressing degree as daylight broke, revealing to our partially refreshed senses the immensity of the elements that encircled us. We seldom broke the stillness of our lone condition by conversation, and, curiously, when we did speak to one another it was in subdued tones in keeping with our surroundings. To-day, with moisture visible in their eyes, some of these strong, rough, and seasoned men became as tender-hearted as small boys

Coal was the commodity that, along with wheat and nitrates, prolonged the life of the sailing square-rigged ship into the era of the motor ship. Here vessels lie in Newcastle, New South Wales, from where coal was exported to the west coast of America and around the Pacific.

Loading wheat at Port Pirie, at the head of Spencer Gulf. The port owed its growth to the boom in the wheat trade in the second half of the nineteenth century; and wheat continued to be carried by sail until the Second World War.

when they talked of home and loved ones, which invariably was their theme, although sometimes the chance of being rescued was added.

Our pessimistic old carpenter, who had become somewhat light-headed, started to tell yarns heard in many a fo'c'sle, describing the experiences of other ships' crews placed in a similar plight, and enlivening his stories with vivid details of the lingering agony of thirst and hunger. About this time two of the men who had succumbed to the strong driving power of thirst, and had drunk sea-water, lay in the bottom of the boat in a torpid stupor. One passed away in his sleep before sunset, and with a single prayer we disposed of his body over the side.

At daybreak our dulled senses were roused by the lookout shouting hoarsely: 'Ship ahoy!' Instantly the men, in attitudes of eager expectation, were gazing in the direction to which the lookout was pointing, and, sure enough, looming out of the misty half-light of the tropical morning, we could dimly see the shadowy form of a barque, passing us on our starboard quarter at a fair speed but apparently within hail. Hope sprang afresh in our hearts as we waved and shouted to attract the attention of the watch on deck.

Would they hear us? During the next few minutes the suspense was almost unbearable.

We shouted as only men in our condition could do, and crushing beyond all imagination was our disappointment and despair when we saw that our hail was unheard. Slowly the vessel receded into the mist and then gradually disappeared from view. It was a cruel position, and one could see the suffering depicted in the lines and ashen colour of the haggard, hopeless faces in the boat. This was our fourth day adrift, without other sustenance than the precious tobacco we had used so carefully. The other victim of sea-water drinking had died in the night and had been put over the side, which reduced the number of survivors to eight, all of whom were in a more or less exhausted condition.

With an expectancy dulled by daily disappointment, we now looked on all sides for an object to break the monotony of sea and sky. Exposed for every minute of the long daylight hours to the scorching glare of the sun, with its rays not only beating down unmercifully but also reflected upwards from the oily surface, we suffered physical agonies, while in the solitude and desolation our thoughts were full of gloomy foreboding, for we felt now that our position was hopeless.

It is difficult to convey any idea of my own feelings during this part of the ordeal. They can only be described as a series of indistinct dreams, baffling in their complexity. They still remain haunting memories which confirm the faith that in times of extremity the mind becomes numbed to meet the condition. To-day a Swede gave a delirious cry as he jumped overboard and sank immediately. At this point in my roughly kept log the dates and happenings are so mixed up that they must have been the outpourings of an unbalanced brain. Our feet and hands were terribly swollen and had broken out into open sores in many places; while to alleviate the sufferings from thirst, and exposure to the sun, we soaked our clothes in sea-water before swathing them round our bodies. By this time the boat had become a derelict, entirely at the mercy of the elements, with only myself and two other men capable of any movement – the remainder lay in a stupor between the thwarts.

Another day of suffering and despair passed slowly by, and the night which followed was the first occasion on which no lookout was kept. In a half-conscious state I was lying back looking up into the mysterious depths of the starlit heavens when the silence was broken by a faint sound, different from the monotonous, low, and soft wash of the waters against the boat, to which I had become accustomed. Although slight, it was nevertheless a noise which penetrated deep into the senses. Was I dreaming, or was it the results of approaching delirium? I held my breath and listened, while my dazed wits and feeble body slowly gathered energy enough to raise myself up and gaze in the direction from which the sound had come.

Once more the thrill of hope arose within me. The dark mass of a full-rigged ship, with no lights showing, could be dimly seen in the gloom gliding silently across our bows. How my weak frame shook at the sight of her, moving at what I calculated was little more than a ship's length from me! Instantly I shouted, but my cry was startlingly feeble, and no answer came across the dark water. Two of the men, aroused by my hail, shouted in unison, but with no better result. It looked as though it was going to be a repetition of the terrible disappointment of two nights before, as the ship still held to her course.

Time was precious, and what we inwardly knew to be our last hope of rescue had almost gone. Then, like an inspiration, came the thought of the remaining matches in the dried boxes. It was now or never, and with weak, trembling hands, and a heart nearly bursting with anxious excitement, I set fire to a box, which flickered and then burst into a small flare. With death waiting on the heels of chance it seemed that my whole being was gathered into this one fateful moment of unbearable suspense. By this time the ship was showing her quarter and stern to us. Had our relatively insignificant little flame been seen? Minutes of strained gazing through the gloom seemed an age, and the ship had almost disappeared into the night.

Suddenly a light was shown over the stern rail, and was followed by a loud hail. So sharp were the feelings of revulsion that came over us that we could do no more than gaze, helpless and tongue-tied, at the yellow glare in the indigo void. Then we heard the creaking of ropes, blocks, and yards, and with a joy which brought tears to our eyes we knew that we were saved. The way of the ship was being stopped.

There is little more to add. With careful nursing and suitable nourishment, given by the Captain's wife, we slowly regained strength enough to tell the story of the tragic fate of the *May Queen* and of our own sufferings in the boat. We were aboard the Arab ship *Iskender Shah*, owned by Tipoo Tib, an African potentate. She was what, in sea-terms, is called a 'country ship', being officered by Europeans and manned by Lascars and Arabs.

The *Iskender Shah* traded between the island of Mauritius and Calcutta, with coolie passengers and general cargo. She was making for the latter port when she picked us up. The Captain told us of the narrow escape we had of being passed unnoticed in the darkness. On the main deck, with its high bulwarks, it was impossible to see anything close in towards the ship; and the coloured passengers and crew were absorbed in a native concert with drums, which providentially awakened me from the comatose state in which I lay across the stern of the boat. Both 'lookout' and 'wheel' had failed to notice anything beyond the immediate vicinity of the deck.

The Captain was mounting the poop ladder, preparatory to going below, when our little flare caught his eye for a second through the stern rail. By the time the top step was reached the light had flickered and gone out. He had just time, however, to obtain a fleeting glimpse of our boat in the circle of light. After flashing a lantern in answer to our signal, the ship's way was stopped, and a boat launched. It returned out of the night with the derelict and its crew. We heard afterwards that those cast adrift in the other boats had also been picked up.